HISTORY OF LINCOLNSHIRE

Volume IX

CHURCHES, CHAPELS, AND THE PARISH COMMUNITIES OF LINCOLNSHIRE 1660–1900

R. W. AMBLER

Churches, Chapels and the Parish Communities of Lincolnshire 1660–1900

R. W. AMBLER

Lincoln
HISTORY OF LINCOLNSHIRE COMMITTEE
for the Society for Lincolnshire History and Archaeology
2000

Published 2000 by
The History of Lincolnshire Committee, Jews' Court, Steep Hill, Lincoln

© 2000 by The History of Lincolnshire Committee and R. W. Ambler

ISBN   hard back   0 902668 17 X
ISBN   paperback   0 902668 18 8

Cover illustration: High Street, Ruskington. This photograph was taken between 1861, when the nave of All Saints' church was restored and 1873, when the chancel was enlarged. The photograph shows the parish church dominating the village. The top-hatted figure of a person, who is probably the incumbent or his curate, occupies a central position, the church has been restored and, to the right of the picture, there is the wall of the newly built National school. In reality the position of the Church in this large village was less secure. The behaviour of its inhabitants was far from deferential and the Wesleyan and Reform Methodist chapels were well supported. Later, a Congregational church was promoted by some of the leading figures in the local community. *Courtesy of anonymous source.*

Cover design by Max Marschner, Ampersand Designs, Lincoln LN5 8PN

Typeset and produced for the publisher by Yard Publishing Services, Sudbury CO10 2AG

Printed by Interprint, Malta

British Cataloguing-in-Publication Data
  A catalogue record for this book is obtainable from the
  British Library

This book is dedicated to

Margaret, Rebecca, Frances, and John

CONTENTS

ILLUSTRATIONS

Table:

county was strengthened by changes to the boundaries of the diocese of Lincoln from 1836 when it lost its ancient interests in Bedfordshire, Buckinghamshire, Hertfordshire, Huntingdonshire, and Leicestershire. Yet, despite the reduction in the size of the diocese by more than half, the association between it and the county was still not exclusive. Nottinghamshire was added to the diocese, and remained a part of it for forty-eight years until the creation of a separate diocese of Southwell left the diocese and county of Lincoln as coterminous areas.[2]

Beneath the boundaries that defined the responsibilities and the limits of civil and ecclesiastical administration, the varied natural regions of Lincolnshire contributed a further dimension to the wider framework within which the parishes of the county functioned. In simple terms Lincolnshire's agrarian base was divided between uplands and lowlands, but there was variety within this basic division. The uplands encompassed both chalk Wolds and limestone Cliff and Heath, while in the lowlands there was the clay and salt marsh of the coastal Marshes, the peat and silt fens, the Isle of Axholme, as well as the clays and miscellaneous soils of the Vale of Ancholme, the Trent valley, and the fen edge. These were not merely descriptive categories, but also denoted a set of different farming systems, land use, and social structures. They are also open to further refinement. A 'well-defined set of eight regions which had their own economic, social, and sometimes religious character' has been identified in south Lindsey alone. These different and changing material circumstances influenced the social as well as the economic development of the parishes that lay within them and provided still another dimension to the framework within which the parishes of the county functioned. The patterns of authority, both formal and informal, that characterized each region were conditioned by relationships based on the ownership of property and its tenure, as well as less easily definable ties that stemmed from kinship, service, and obligation.[3]

The values, sentiments, and attitudes that were developed as parishes responded to external change, and which informed the conduct of their affairs, were part of the process through which they became communities rather than just administrative units. Community is a term that has often been deployed in historical writing to describe an idealized set of relationships existing within the context of a particular area or place. In his study of the history of Lincolnshire in the 17th century Clive Holmes pointed to what he perceived to be the the erosion of 'the emotional awareness of group identity' in the villages of the county. This sense of identity was seen as the product of 'the closed corporate peasant community', part of a world of village communities that was 'lost' as a new order developed that embraced religious as well as secular life. Similarly, James Obelkevich in his seminal study of religion in the rural society of the south Lindsey area of Lincolnshire in the 19th century approached the religious development of the area in terms of a 'traditional village society' that was supplanted by a 'capitalist class society', part of the social and economic development of the area covered by his study.[4]

It is hoped that this book will add to the insights provided by this earlier work on the county by approaching parish communites, not simply as part of a disappearing world that was being supplanted by values and attitudes that were less desirable than what had gone before, but as active participants in the processes of change, responsive to the demands that were imposed upon them by the central authorities in church and state and capable of developing distinctive reactions to them. It will not necessarily provide the basis for any overarching theory or general argument, but is offered as an attempt to explain and understand the development of religious life in the period through an exploration of its place in the lives of the local communities of the county.

Notes to Chapter I

1   D. M. Owen, *Church and Society in Medieval Lincolnshire*, Lincoln, 1971, p. 2; S. and B. Webb, *The Parish and the County*, London, repr. 1963, pp. 4–5.
2   N. Bennett, 'Ecclesiastical Boundaries' in *Atlas*, pp. 50–51.
3   J. Thirsk, *English Peasant Farming: the agrarian history of Lincolnshire from Tudor to recent times*, London, 1957, pp. 2, 50.
4   *Rel. & Rur. Soc.*, p. 6; *Societies, Cultures and Kinship, 1580–1850: cultural provinces and English local history*, ed. C Phythian-Adams, London, 1993, pp. xiii, xiv, xv, 4.

CHAPTER II

RESTORATION AND DISSENT

The Church Restored

CONTINUITY AND CONFORMITY

The consecration of Dr Robert Sanderson as forty-fifth Bishop of Lincoln on Wednesday 28 October 1660 marked the formal beginning of the process by which the Restoration settlement was enforced in the diocese and county. Sanderson was absent from his enthronement in Lincoln cathedral just under three weeks later, but he was well acquainted with Lincolnshire, having been Rector of Boothby Pagnell for over forty years. During this time he had experienced at first hand what his Preface to the 1662 Book of Common Prayer described as 'the late unhappy confusions' of the Civil Wars and Commonwealth but had contrived to maintain a measure of continuity in parish life and worship. As had also been the case in other parishes of the county, the varying degrees of commitment that his parishioners had demonstrated towards the rites and ministrations of the Church of England provided a local basis for the settlement of the church at the Restoration. Like Sanderson, the majority of parish clergymen had continued to serve their cures during the Civil Wars and Commonwealth. Like him they had put the local unity and peace of the church above individual conscience, especially in matters of relative indifference such as the ordering of its ceremonies. It was on this basis that, as bishop, he looked for and obtained their conformity in 1660.[1]

Although the final shape of the Restoration of the Church of England at parish level was not defined until 1662, Sanderson was quick to take control of his diocese in whatever ways were available to him. Within a week of his consecration he had admitted John Green to the rectory of Cumberworth and begun the 129 ordinations involving 418 individual clergymen that marked his twenty-eight month episcopate. It is not clear what difference this made at parish level. The fulminations of John Cock of Doddington against the permission that had been given during the Commonwealth to 'cobblers, tailors and such like mechanics to usurp the pulpit ... as though they had been inspired with as miraculous a donation of the spirit of God as the prophets and apostles of old' are testimony to the authority episcopal ordination still carried. Ultimately the authority of ministers in their parishes depended on the relationships that they had developed with the communities they served. Sanderson's death in January 1663 gave him little opportunity to put into full practice the mild measures by which he was reputed to have sought to win obedience, so that at local level the period of nearly two years that elapsed between his consecration and first visitation of the diocese were in many ways a continuation of the situation that had been maintained through the Civil Wars and Commonwealth.[2]

The Act for the Settling of Ministers passed in late 1660 had confirmed all incumbents appointed since January 1643 in their livings, although it also restored those still alive who had lost their benefices because of their loyalty to the old order. The potential disturbance that these restorations might have brought had been minimized by the passage of time, while not all the men who had lived long enough to take advantage of the Act's provisions were successful in having their livings restored. Of the eighty Lincolnshire clergymen who lost their livings through sequestration for political or theological reasons, twenty-two returned to twenty-four benefices, displacing nineteen others in the process. Potential disputes over sequestrated livings were also defused by the preferment of claimants to other places, while non residence meant that the return of others had little effect on the day to day lives of their parishioners. Only a few Lincolnshire clergy suffered under the provisions of the Act for Settling Ministers to deprive ministers who denied the validity of infant baptism, had petitioned for regicide, or opposed the Restoration. These included Moses Mell of Kirton in Lindsey, who was a Baptist. After allowance is made for the normal cycle of death and removal from 1642 to 1660, the number and extent of these restorations and displacements have to be set against the continuity provided by the 169 clergymen who are known to have remained in their parishes for most or all of the period.[3]

WORSHIP AND ITS CONTEXTS

It was not until the Act of Uniformity, with the Book of Common Prayer attached, had received Royal Assent in 1662 that the new responsibilities of the clergy and officers of parishes for church worship and discipline were fully defined. Sanderson and his officials were successful in imposing not only order, but uniformity, on the parishes of Lincolnshire because they were able to build on the elements of continuity that had been preserved during the vicissitudes of the Civil Wars and Commonwealth, although the relative ease with which this was effected may also have been a sign of indifference at parish level to what actually happened in church. Sanderson's articles for his primary visitation of the diocese in 1662 were virtually identical to those for six other dioceses and continued to be used, with some adaptations, until the 1670s. The enquiries on church buildings, their furniture, and ornaments asserted the importance of the proper furnishing of churches – a visual statement of the new order in church and state – and their enforcement caused few overt problems. There was to be a stone font in a 'convenient' place towards the lower part of churches, a communion table standing, according to the Prayer Book rubric, in either the body of the church or in the chancel. A pew and pulpit were to be provided for the minister.[4]

The need to provide printed material for use in the conduct of services and in support of church discipline was less easily fulfilled, while in the eighty-nine parishes of the archdeaconry of Stow the most common presentment was for lack of the tables of the prohibited degrees of marriage and of the Book of Homilies. There were forty-four cases of each. A further forty churches did not possess a copy of the canons, or law of the church. The lack of a Book of Common Prayer in twenty-four churches can be explained by difficulties in obtaining copies. It was not distributed until after 1 August 1662 and was difficult to obtain then, but in other respects the main requirements of the visitation were met. The chapel at North Hykeham, in Lincoln archdeaconry, was exceptional for the lack of a book of homilies and a table of marriages as late as 1664. Surplices were missing in thirty-one parishes in Stow, but although their use had been a matter of more principled dispute since the 16th century the reports of their absence at the 1662 visitation related to neglect during the Commonwealth.[5]

The faculties for church work that survive from the episcopate of Sanderson's successor, Benjamin Laney, are evidence of the extent to which the 1662 settlement found expression in work undertaken by parish communities on the fabric of their churches. In 1664 Washingborough church had 'seates, formes and deskes' that were 'very much disordered and preposterously placed'. The faculty to reorder it was said to have been initiated by the minister, churchwardens, and other inhabitants with the support of 'all or the greatest part of the parishioners'. In an arrangement favoured by conservative high churchmen, the nave, where the regular dominical services were held, was separated from the chancel where Holy Communion was celebrated. The seats of the nave were divided between males and females. With Leon Hollingworth, gentleman, sitting at their head in 'his accustomed place' the internal arrangements of the church at Washingborough embodied the ideal of the hierarchically conceived and sexually differentiated, but settled parish community, with its inter-dependent religious and secular values, that lay at the heart of the Restoration settlement in church and state.[6]

The churches of Pinchbeck and Surfleet were reordered in a similar way in 1663. Sir Henry Heron's great pew stood at the front of the church at Surfleet and the seating stretched down to the lowest pillar in the middle aisle. The nine occupants of the seat here included two widows and the 'woman in Sweetland's house'; but the order that was achieved in the church did not match the reality of life in two parishes where discordant behaviour was almost a routine part of the transactions of the community. Both parishes had a recent history of riot and affrays arising out of fenland drainage disputes. In January 1699 Pinchbeck people were among the 1,100 rioters who assembled 'under colour and pretence of Foot Ball Playing' to demolish the drainage works in the Deeping Level.[7]

The parish officers of Pinchbeck and Surfleet were able to carry through the refurbishment of their churches despite the divisions that existed in their parishes. Their counterparts in other places were less able to command even this level of support. The arrangements that were involved in the twenty petitions for faculties for church repair in the thirty years from 1663 where church work was financed by depleting existing resources are evidence of the failure of local officers to carry the support of their parish communities for this type of work. There were only some thirty inhabitants at Hawerby cum Beesby and the 'great bell' from Hawerby was sold for £14 18s 8d in 1666, as part of the arrangements whereby Beesby church and the steeple at Hawerby were demolished and Hawerby church repaired and rebuilt. The resources of the much larger community of Waltham were greater, but the church's biggest bell was sold off with other material in 1680, and the remaining two bells recast into three, in order to rebuild the 'steeple', although on a scale 'somewhat lesse than formerly'. Limited amounts of work of this kind, with minimal levels of repair and maintenance, enabled churchwardens to make presentments that they hoped would keep them clear of the church's authorities. Nonetheless a letter that accompanied the metropolitan visitation articles of 1686 referred to reports of the 'very decaying, if not ruinous Condition' of 'many of the Churches, Chancels, and Chapels' in the diocese of Lincoln.[8]

For Bishop Gardiner, working in a climate of official toleration for Protestant dissent in 1697, church buildings were important as the settings for a distinctively Anglican sacramental worship. He drew attention to chancels that lay wholly disused 'in more nastie manner than any Cottager of the Parish would keep his own House', and others used for schools, with broken seats, pavements and windows, 'not to mention other rudeness and indecencies which are not fit to be permitted in a place set apart for God's Worship'. The 'pious and learned' layman Thomas Place of Winterton worked voluntarily to remedy deficiencies in the church buildings and to provide a seemly context for worship in parishes in north-west Lincolnshire, 'building, repairing, and beautifying' Winterton church in the 1690s. He also planned to promote Sunday lectures by Anglican divines at Brigg in preparation for building a chapel there. Place's Brigg initiative was intended to 'quell' the 'sectarys' and 'such like cattel'. It was

the enquiries of bishops or archdeacons became increasingly confined to matters relating to the state of the church fabric. It was a change that came less quickly in some parishes, where officers remained more conformable to ecclesiastical discipline and continued to present a range of offences into the 1690s. Although the number of these places diminished even before Toleration the churchwardens at Normanby le Wold continued to report parishioners who did not attend church in 1690. The use of the return of 'omnia bene' at visitations became prevalent less as an objective response to the enquiries of bishops and archdeacons or, as it is sometimes interpreted, a reflection of the indolence of parish officers, more as a statement that attempted to protect parish communities from outside interference as they shaped their own priorities independently of the church authorities.[16]

Dissenters and civil authority

It was less easy for dissenters to come to terms with the civil authorities whose concerns extended beyond as well as into areas that were matters for compromise at parish level and for whom religious allegiance could be important as a matter of state. Although there were 2,586 prosecutions for failure to attend church at the Kesteven Quarter Sessions between 1674 and 1687, there were relatively few presentments for the offence in the church courts. Only 423 individuals from the division were cited in the archdeacon's court for religious nonconformity between 1674 and 1679. Another 176 cases were brought before both the Quarter Sessions and the archdeacon. Leasingham was one of the parishes from which there were frequent presentments to the ecclesiastical authorities for non-attendance at church from the 1660s, but they became less common in the early 1680s when dissenters began to be a matter for the Quarter Sessions. The first of these indictments in 1683 coincided with a peak of 291 in the annual total of prosecutions in Kesteven relating to church attendance. It was the year of the Rye House Plot in which a group of dissenters plotted to murder the King and his brother, while the death of the county M.P., Sir Robert Carre, provided Robert Bertie, Earl of Lindsey and lord lieutenant of the county, with both the pretext and the opportunity to attack his political opponents. Single justices also took unrecorded action against people who were occasionally absent from church, while there were eleven separate prosecutions under the Conventicle Acts in Kesteven from 1674. Most of the prosecutions for dissent recorded in the division were concentrated in 1675 and 1676, and again in 1681 and 1682. In 1676 the bishops had advised the King that it was generally the Baptists and Quakers who were the most politically dangerous. The Kesteven justices of the peace had largely confined their actions against conventicles to those belonging to Quakers, but Baptists, such as John Ward of Carlton le Moorland, were among those brought before the Quarter Sessions in 1677, 1680 and again in 1681 for not attending church. There were Baptist complaints at the severity of the measures taken against them in 1686 when at least a thousand were reported as being indicted at the Lincolnshire assizes. Even Presbyterian ministers were unable to escape imprisonment in 1685 during the period of alarm occasioned by Monmouth's rebellion .[17]

For all the attention afforded to them, Protestant dissenters from the Church of England were only a small minority of the population of Lincolnshire. Since they were not uniformly distributed throughout the county, the effect of their presence varied from place to place. There were 2,595 dissenters in Lincolnshire in 1676 compared with just under 85,000 adults who were described as Anglican conformists or, more accurately, people who manifested no overt allegiance to dissent. The situation was complicated by the number of people who were described by Bishop Fuller as 'half conformists', such as the Presbyterians from Billingborough and Horbling who accommodated themselves sufficiently to the Church of England to not be returned as dissenters. Overall there was one dissenter to every 33 or 34 conformists. This was three per cent of the adult population of the county. The Earl of Lindsey's opinion that in the 1660s the greatest number of 'Quakers, Anabaptists and other sectaries' were from the Isle of Axholme and the Marsh takes account of the tendency of religious dissenters to cluster in certain areas of the county, but he did not discern the whole picture. The Fens of south Lincolnshire, like the Isle and the Lincolnshire Marsh, places with looser forms of social organization and a tendency for landownership to be fragmented, had concentrations of dissenters, but they were also present in the very different milieus of the southern Wolds, in some of the parishes on their northern fringe, as well as to the west and south of Lincoln. A group of parishes in north-west and south Kesteven, including the towns of Bourne and Stamford, had a less high, but still noteworthy dissenting presence. Brigg was one of the market towns with a significant cluster of dissenters, although the main strength of the Baptists, who were the largest body of dissenters in Lincolnshire, lay in villages (Fig. 1).[18]

The Development Of Dissent

SECESSION FROM THE CHURCH

The new Book of Common Prayer, a revision of the Elizabethan Prayer Book and Ordinal, received Royal Assent with the Act of Uniformity in May 1662. Every beneficed clergyman had to read morning and evening prayer from the new prayer book and 'declare his unfeigned assent and consent' to it by the Sunday before St Bartholomew's Day, 24 August.

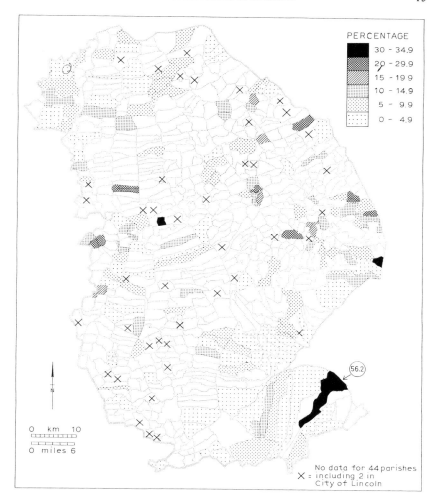

PERCENTAGE

30 - 34.9
20 - 29.9
15 - 19.9
10 - 14.9
5 - 9.9
0 - 4.9

56.2

0   km   10

0   miles   6

No data for 44 parishes
X = including 2 in
City of Lincoln

Fig. 1   Protestant Nonconformity in 1676, showing the number of people, other than Roman Catholics, who absented themselves from communion in the Church of England. Protestant Nonconformists are shown as a percentage of those who conformed as returned by parish in the 'Compton Census' of 1676. While Protestant dissenters were clustered in certain areas of the county such as the Fens and Isle of Axholme, there were also high concentrations in the parishes of the Marsh. The looser social structures of these areas gave greater freedom to religious nonconformists, but they were also to be found in other places in the county, notably the Trent valley, especially to the south-west of Lincoln, and in southern Kesteven. These areas were less generally favourable to the development of religious dissent and its presence here has to be explained in terms of the situation within individual parishes.
Source: Compt. Cen.

These requirements brought practical problems but, however late, the majority of Lincolnshire clergymen accepted the Act of Uniformity and Prayer Book. It was not until 2 November 1662 that the paper signifying the 'assent and consent to the lyturgie of the Church of England' of Edward Smyth, Rector of Beelsby was signed by the parish churchwardens. A general impression prevailed that the whole matter had proceeded smoothly. The report that only six clergymen in the county had left their livings was an indication of a general sense of continuity at parish level. In fact the number was greater – thirty-two – but these included four who later conformed, two the date of whose departure from their livings was uncertain, and the Master of Grantham Grammar School. The extent of the disruption in Lincolnshire parishes can be gauged by the fact that nationally 1,065 clergymen left their livings in 1662.[19]

Many of the ministers who left the Church of England were only very narrowly separated from it. William Laughton, who had become Rector of Somerby by 1668, quitted his living at Doddington with Westborough in 1662, but later conformed. He was one of four Lincolnshire clergymen to do this. When John Richardson, who had been Rector of St John's Stamford went to live at Kirton in Holland in the 1680s he attended the parish church regularly, joined in the services there and attended Holy Communion, although the parish clergyman would not accede to Richardson's conscience and allow him to receive the elements sitting. Twenty-eight other ministers made a clear break with the Church of England, of whom eleven remained in the county as nonconformists. Nine were Presbyterians and two Independents or Congregationalists. Many of them had some land in Lincolnshire or enough worldly possessions to cushion the loss of their livings. At least sixteen Lincolnshire ministers who left the church quitted the county, but there were others who moved into it. John Wright had been Rector of Edmonthorpe in Leicestershire, but was a Louth man by birth. He went to Leasingham, and although he later became a Presbyterian minister under the patronage of Lady Bury at Linwood in Blankney, it was probably the property that he had in Leasingham which took him to the village. On the other hand Michael Drake, the former Rector of Pickworth, lived in some poverty at Fulbeck. Even after he began to preach to a dissenting congregation at Lincoln his income did not exceed fifteen pounds a year. When he died in the city in 1696 he had goods totalling £38 although his library, valued at £10, showed his priorities.[20]

Some ministers survived outside the established church by keeping schools. Theophilus Brittain, the former Rector of Brattleby, lived at Roxholme, where he also farmed. Twenty-two years later he was preaching in Sleaford for which he received 5s each Sunday and a grant of £6 a year from the Common Fund instituted by Congregationalists and

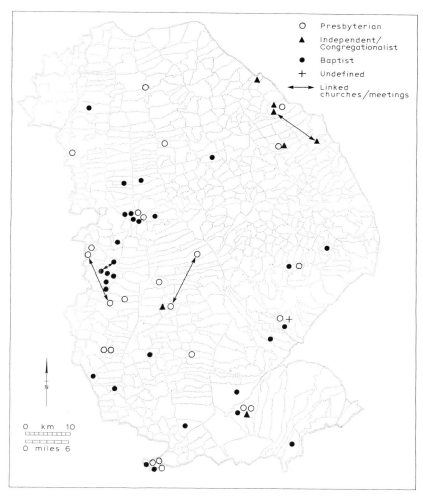

Fig. 2 *Nonconformity under Indulgence showing places where churches and ministers were licensed under the Declaration of Indulgence of 1672. Since Quakers did not apply for licences this material is more useful for Presbyterians, Independents, Congregationalists, and Baptists, although Baptists are also under-represented. Important churches, such as those at Coningsby and at Asterby and Donington, were not licensed. The returns do provide evidence for a Baptist presence among the Protestant nonconformists to the south-west of Lincoln for which no church records survive.*

Sources: Dec. of Indulg.; Orig. Rec.

Presbyterians. Its aims included the relief of 'the Poverty of Dissenting Ministers' of the 'many places' which were 'unable to afford them a meere Subsistence'. John Birkett's school in his native village of Billingborough attracted the patronage of sympathetic gentlemen. Establishments such as his nurtured an educated dissenting culture. All except three of the twenty-eight ministers in Lincolnshire who left the church had received a university education. Of the eleven who remained in the county and established nonconformist congregations all except one were graduates. Their departure from the Church of England deprived it of a group of able and learned divines, although their relatively small numbers meant that they provided no significant base on which to build any strong separate Presbyterian presence in the county, even less for the development of an Independent or Congregationalist tradition.[21]

Ten Presbyterian ministers and twenty-three Presbyterian meeting places in eleven towns and villages were licensed in Lincolnshire under the temporary suspension of the penal laws against dissenters offered by the Declaration of Indulgence of 1672. The distribution of this small body of ministers depended initially on the way in which they and the laymen who supported them had reacted to the Restoration settlement (Fig. 2). There were three types of Presbyterian meeting. One group under the patronage of gentry was regularly served by ministers, two of whom also had their own houses licensed for worship in the villages where they lived. Another group of ministers was less overtly dependent on gentry patronage and used their own houses for worship. A third group of meetings was held in the houses of laymen, but had no ministers specifically associated with them. Of the places under gentry patronage, Lady Jane Bury licensed her house at Linwood Grange in the parish of Blankney where John Wright officiated while still living in Leasingham. His home was also licensed as a meeting place where he enjoyed the patronage of more gentry as well as the company of other Presbyterian divines who lived in or near the village. Another gentleman, John Nelthorpe, had his house at Little Grimsby licensed, but there was no minister associated with it, while of the ministers not overtly under gentry patronage, Thomas Bonner, the former Rector of Lea, held services in his house at Brigg where he went through 'many Troubles and Straits'. The meeting places unconnected with any specific minister and licensed in the name of lay people also tended to be situated in towns. There were three in Grantham and another three in Spalding. One of another three in Stamford was connected with Joseph Cawthorne, who had been the Rector of St George's church in the town.[22]

The limited amount of longer-term growth that occurred in Lincolnshire Presbyterianism − and what there was tended to be hesitant and varied − was based on meetings that were able to develop within local communities on a broader basis than those that were more closely controlled by gentlemen. They offered an alternative to the fading and restrictive hope of comprehension within the Church of England. In 1689 Toleration gave a greater chance of success in efforts to bring these congregations together in a scheme of union. The creation of the Common Fund supported by both Congregationalists and Presbyterians in 1690 was a step towards cooperation between churches. Nine Lincolnshire congregations were listed in its survey of ministers and congregations, which included two of the seven – Spalding and Tetney – licensed as Congregational in 1672. Six had ministers associated with them in some way. Sleaford continued as a centre of nonconformity into the 18th century and beyond. Yet although William Scoffin, one of at least three ministers either living or preaching in the town after 1662, 'gained the esteem and respect of the whole neighbourhood' so that he was made annual presents by 'some of the principal inhabitants', they 'never attended his ministry'. On the other hand the Presbyterian church that was established in the rapidly growing non-corporate town of Gainsborough enjoyed the support of some of its well-to-do inhabitants. It was far better placed to survive and grow as it established a clear identity in the context of a long local tradition of religious dissent. Matthew Coates had been presented to the church courts for dissent in 1663 and 1664. His house was licensed as a Presbyterian meeting place under Indulgence and was still being used for worship in 1690. In July 1701 Coates, a mercer, conveyed the 'house or building lately erected in a place called the Ratton Row' and 'used or intended to be used as a Chappell or Meeting House ... for such Protestant dissenters ... to meet, assemble and worship God in, or distinguished or goe under the names of Congregationall Independents or Presbiterians'.[23]

Although churches such as Gainsborough used the title they were not part of a formal Presbyterian church order. The links that dissenting laymen such as Matthew Coates had with like-minded people, both within Lincolnshire and beyond, provided informal structures that sustained the town-based networks of which they were a part. When Eleanor Anderton, a spinster from the parish of St Mark in Lincoln, made her will in 1709 she was mindful of these associations. Matthew Coates and his family were beneficiaries, but as well as the £2 that she left to the dissenting congregation at Lincoln of which she was a member, she also left money to each of two congregations in Norwich. There were small cash bequests to ministers at Bulthrop and Sheffield, as well as to William Scoffin, the Sleaford nonconformist minister. Her bequests also drew in members of the Coates family living in Norwich, and there were legacies to Peter Finch and James Chorley, Presbyterian ministers in the city, as well as to Samuel Baxter, a minister at Ipswich.[24]

THE BAPTISTS

The Baptists already had a separate church organization by 1660 and looked for the toleration promised in Charles II's Declaration of Breda to enable them to worship in freedom. It was a hope undermined by the persecution that followed Venner's London rising in January 1661. By appearing to confirm a continuing association between religious dissent and political radicalism it was enough, as the Lincolnshire Baptists had asserted in addresses to the Crown for relief in 1660 and again in 1661, 'to render any man criminal to be called an anabaptist; or at least ground sufficient to question his loyalty and fidelity to the king's majesty'. A royal proclamation of January 1661 that linked Baptists and Quakers with the politically extremist Fifth Monarchy Men prohibited their meetings. The sufferings of Thomas Grantham, a leading figure in local Baptist life, show how persecution was meted out by the civil authorities as magistrates, fearful of rebellion, employed soldiers to make arrests and search for arms. Grantham's prominence rendered him vulnerable to persecution and his tribulations included imprisonment without trial for fifteen months at Lincoln and a further six-month period in Louth Gaol in 1664. Grantham's figures of a hundred imprisonments for attendance at religious meetings and a thousand fines which had 'weakened many poor men' during the period of persecution after 1660 had a rhetorically satisfying roundness. They also demonstrated that, despite their protestations of loyalty to the Crown, Baptists remained vulnerable because of what was perceived to be their radical sectarianism.[25]

Thomas Grantham described the institutions and practices of 'the Baptized Churches in Lincolnshire' in his *Christianismus Primitivus* written 'at their Importunity, and by their Encouragement'. Church members who had repented, believed, and been baptized were gathered into the church, meeting together for fellowship, the breaking of bread and prayer. Baptism by immersion was the distinguishing mark of believers and it was the occasion for the person to be baptized to profess their 'sense of Sin, and sorrow for it', their 'purpose to live holily', and their 'Faith in Christ'. Until chapels were built and pools provided, baptisms were necessarily held in the open air and were occasions for public witness, although Joseph Hooke's baptism in the river at Peterborough in 1677 was seen as inviting persecution. There was an average of nine baptisms each year in the Spalding and Bourne church between 1688 and 1700. John Cropper's was in a time of 'hard frost and deep snow' at Spalding in January 1694, but his unharmed health was seen as a sign that God protected his servants who obeyed his commandments. No one should 'be afraid to venture into the water when the season is cold, lest they be laid in their graves before the weather be warm'.[26]

Accounts of Baptist sufferings were frequently coloured by the credence that was given to signs of 'divine judgments against those who were forward in opposing this church'. Generalized accounts of the 'rude treatment from mobs composed of certain lewd fellows of the baser sort' were part of a vocabulary of harassment that stretched back to the Protectorate. It included stoning of windows, beating on the doors of meetings and sounding of horns, and it continued to be employed against religious nonconformists into the 19th century. This was the nearest Baptist sources generally came to giving any account of their tribulations in the specific context of the local communities of Lincolnshire. The atavism aroused by the burial of Robert Shalder, a prominent Baptist from Burgh le Marsh, one of the group from the parish who was excommunicated in 1664, conferred a notoriety on the event which masks its exceptionality. Shalder's body had been buried at Croft in 1666 but it was taken from the grave by some of the villagers and dragged on a sledge back to his home and left at the gate. Dissent was strong in Croft, but the use of its churchyard by a person who may also have been a Sabbatarian – departing from village norms to the extent of observing Saturday as the divinely appointed day of worship and rest – may have triggered the deep feelings which had been stirred by the burial of someone from outside the parish. Presentation before the church courts for failing to attend the parish church, for spurning its offices, and refusing to pay its dues is a clearer indication of the place Baptists occupied in individual parishes. Two men and three women from Croft, a community that was to become tolerant of dissenters within a few years, were excommunicated in December 1663 and a week later the penalty was applied to a further eight men from the neighbouring parish of Burgh le Marsh, another place with a strong Baptist presence. Other excommunications followed at Burgh in 1664 and 1667, and the churchwardens there continued to present for non attendance at church until the early 1670s. There were also twenty-two similar presentments from the parish of Donington on Bain in the early 1670s, although generally the number of church court cases involving Baptists declined in line with those that involved other dissenters.[27]

The resilience of the Baptist churches of Lincolnshire was strengthened by an organization and a leadership whose social and economic prominence provided a basis for their ultimate assimilation into the parish communities of the county. Baptist meetings were licensed in twenty-two places in 1672 (Fig. 2). As the largest group of dissenters in the county they constituted a considerable proportion of the nonconformists enumerated in the villages of Lincolnshire by the Compton Census of 1676 (Fig. 1). Licences under Indulgence were not, however, sought for all the places where there was a Baptist presence. There was no request from Coningsby, where Baptist church life was strong. Whether licensed or not the faith of

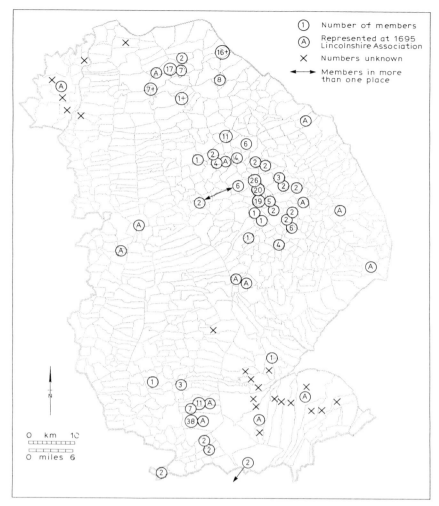

Fig. 3   Lincolnshire Baptist Members 1660–c.1700 showing the distribution of Baptist members in Lincolnshire. The clusters of members indicate the way in which they were spread in the area around their churches, and the extent to which their religious allegiance transcended parish boundaries. Their distribution can be compared with the Compton Census returns (Fig. 1) to show the numbers of Baptists who were included in the Protestant Nonconformists enumerated there. The lack of figures limits the usefulness of the material from the Spalding and Epworth church books, while no comparable material is available for Coningsby or the churches to the south-west of Lincoln.

Sources: Ast. & Don. Ch. Book; Bourne Ch. Book; Ep. Ch. Book; Killingholme Baptist Church Book (SHARO, T54) ; Sp. Ch. Book; Eng. Gen. Bapt. 1.

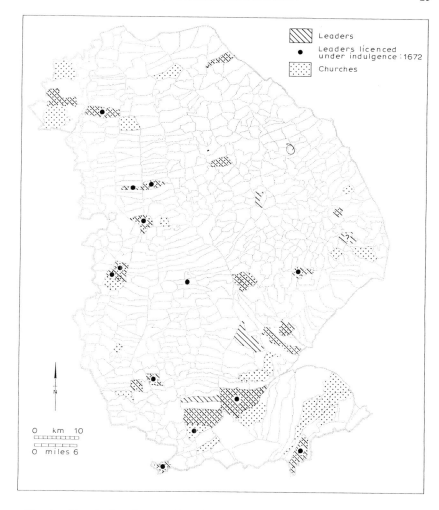

*Fig. 4   Lincolnshire Baptist Churches and their Leaders in the period 1660 to
c. 1700 showing the extent to which local Baptist churches were integrated into
wider Baptist affairs. As well as the places where local Baptist churches were based,
this map also shows those places in which there were church leaders who were
involved in Baptist affairs beyond their local churches. Individuals who sought
licences under Indulgence are also identified.*

Sources: Bapt. Min.; *Orig. Rec.*; G. F. Nuttall, '*Lyon Turner's* Original Records:
note and identifications', TCHR., *XIV (1945–48)*

the clusters of households and families that were at the heart of Baptist life was maintained by inclusion in a pattern of worship and discipline based on the self-governing congregations of individual churches. They were linked at county and national level through leaders who were involved in associations of churches (Figs. 3 and 4). Although these were voluntary, they provided a framework for Baptist identity from the 1650s and their ability to organize addresses and to join in national petitions was indicative not only of the level of organization among Lincolnshire Baptists, but of the quality of its leadership. The signatories of the addresses to the Crown in 1660 and 1661 included men from the church based on Asterby and Goulceby, from the Bourne area, Epworth, Frampton, Lincoln, Manthorpe, and Swineshead as well as the South Marsh. These churches were, with those from the Isle of Axholme, Coningsby, and Tattershall as well as Spalding and Marshchapel, represented at the Lincoln Association of General Baptists that met twice a year in Lincoln by 1695 and maintained a common fund. Representatives from it attended national General Assemblies in London. They included the Lincoln minister Thomas Paine who, like Thomas Grantham, was an ordained Messenger: a minister who sought to link local churches, 'taking all occasions to cause the Light of the Glorious Gospel to shine unto such as sit in Darkness, to plant Churches, to confirm or settle them in the Faith, to visit and comfort those who have believed through Grace'.[28]

Testimony under persecution and the reports of the fates that befell people who oppressed Baptists demonstrated the strength and validated the truth of Baptist witness so that the number of church members was said to have increased in the 1660s. There were reports of 'several who would not be otherwise convinced' who 'gave Glory to God, and were baptized' after witnessing the early deaths of individuals who had persecuted Baptists. Their fates provided ammunition for Baptist polemic, itself an important aspect of witness. Ralph James, from North Willingham, engaged in 'conferences' with Independents and Quakers in the 1670s. These disputations drew people from the area into fair and market day meetings in which an array of metaphysical evidence, including the thaumaturgic powers of the participants, was deployed in support of their positions. In the struggle between Baptists and Quakers for the soul of Richard Anderson of Panton, it was said that Anderson, acting with the authority of what he said was God's command, had pronounced James a leper, but it was one of Anderson's children who was covered in spots as a result of this supernatural battle of wills. Anderson, his wife and other children were smitten with 'a restless pain'. The pamphlets which reported these exchanges, such as James's *True and Impartial Narrative of the Eminent Hand of God that Befell a Quaker and his Family, at the Town of Panton in Lincolnshire, who affirmed he was commanded of God to Pronounce Mr*

with reluctance, although in those areas where the civil authorities chose to take action Quakers, like other dissenters, remained vulnerable. Five or more people were prohibited from assembling for worship under the 1662 Quaker Act, which was later extended to all dissenters. Actions under it were most frequent in the fens of south Lincolnshire and in the Isle of Axholme. Over eighty people from these areas were imprisoned for taking part in meetings in 1663, while Quakers at Beckingham and Honington were also targeted by the authorities. Six men attending a weekday meeting at Gedney in May were committed to Spalding prison and nineteen others were arrested and also imprisoned when they visited them and held a meeting at the gaol window. At Swineshead in 1663 the officers of the parish combined with the civil authorities of the area to make arrests. A 'captain' and constable broke up a meeting at the house of William Bladesmith and detained eleven men 'with swords and clubs and by force of arms'. At Gainsborough it was a parish officer, the constable Edward Laughton, who was said to be 'a very busy forward man' against Quakers in 1670. He often 'incensed' William Hickman against them. Hickman, a Gainsborough justice, used informers who were rewarded with a third share of any fines levied under the second Conventicle Act. Their activities strained local loyalties and Hickman's own servant boy was one. The Kesteven magistrates were more restrained and only five Quaker conventicles were proceeded against between 1676 and 1683, although the raid on a meeting at Joan Wray's house at Fulbeck was led by two justices, Christopher Beresford and John Thorold, who acted on the basis of information given, not by local inhabitants, but a 'rambling woman who used to stroll about the country begging, and blowing a horn'.[40]

One thousand one hundred and eighty-eight cases of the 'sufferings' of Quakers in Lincolnshire were recorded between 1660 and 1688. They included a number of types of harassment ranging in severity from imprisonment and physical violence to the seizure of goods of varying value from Friends of different levels of wealth. Some 335 individuals were imprisoned on writs relating to their excommunication 'and other penal laws' and a further 58 for refusing to pay tithes. In 1660 the 86 people imprisoned at Lincoln for refusing oaths increased the total number of cases of suffering in that year to 110, although the highest number in any one year was in 1670. In actions taken under the Conventicle Act, well over a third of the 117 cases reported were connected with meetings for worship in the Holland division. There was generally no physical violence associated with this particular surge in the harassment of Quaker meetings and the men and women at them were punished through fines and the distraint of goods. Over the whole period from 1660 to 1688 the value of goods seized for various reasons totalled slightly over £1,900 of which the majority was for tithe: £1,118 9s 9d. The 95 cases recorded in 1678 included three men and women imprisoned at the instigation of clergymen from Whaplode and Brant Broughton. Such incidents often had wider ramifications. Thomas Robinson was taken to Lincoln Castle from Brant Broughton for not paying tithe, but he was caught up in a more general campaign by the parish clergyman against the local 'conventicle'. In a confrontation in the church Robinson had denounced John Chapple as 'a false prophet and an hireling, who though he exacted great wages of the people, yet he profitted them not at all'. It was, however, a type of incident that was becoming less common by 1678, and the preponderance of seizures for small amounts of goods in the year is indicative of the extent to which the position of Quakers was changing. Tithe owed by Quakers from the Isle of Axholme and from smaller groups in Huttoft, Mumby, Sibsey and Spilsby, show them not to be engaged in confrontational witness with the whole of their parish communities, but at loggerheads over what were essentially issues relating to property with interests that included lay proprietors.[41]

Until Toleration Quaker meetings were mostly held in private houses, moving from place to place. A group from Tydd St Mary's, which was fined in 1670, was meeting in its customary silence at the house of Edward Tidsdall, 'a poore man'. Until the 1680s the first properties owned by the Society were burial grounds. One was created at Spalding as early as 1662, while that which served the Gainsborough Monthly Meeting was conveyed to five trustees by Thomas Fisher in 1668. His wife was already buried there, next to his homestead at Kexby. The trustees at Spalding and Gainsborough were representative of the men who were moving into positions of authority within the Society. At Spalding they were gathered from the town and its surrounding area: a tallow chandler, a tailor, a yeoman and a husbandman came from Spalding, while there was a yeoman from Crowland and a butcher from Weston. There was a similar mixture of trustees at Kexby, with a mercer and chandler from Gainsborough and a grazier and two husbandmen from nearby parishes. Although not as early as that at Spalding, the 1669 trust for the land on which the meeting house was eventually built in Lincoln had a wider social base redolent of the less structured life of the first phase of Quakerism. It included two labourers and exceptionally, three women trustees who were widows. The trustees for the meeting house and burial ground at Gedney Church Gate in 1689 were all, except one husbandman, described as yeomen. Yeomen made up nearly a third of all trustees of Quaker property in the late 17th century, although they were outnumbered by the forty per cent of trustees who were from trades and crafts based occupations. Another tenth were husbandmen, with a similar number of mercers.[42]

The influence of the Society's male office holders – who came to be known as 'weighty' Friends – increased from the 1680s, but the Society's membership was relatively youthful in the 1660s and 1670s. The number of marriages among Quakers in Lincolnshire reached a peak in the 1670s, when membership also reached its highest levels and there were between 1,300 and 1,400 Friends in the county. The absence of detailed membership figures mean that it is impossible to speculate on the extent to which the Quakers attracted converts. Earlier growth had not necessarily produced members with a strong commitment to the Society. The fears expressed at the Fulbeck Meeting in June 1680 that some Friends were spending 'too much time in the company of people of the world' and the high number of disownments taking place in the 1680s suggest that integration into lives of the local communities was becoming too far advanced for local leaders. Meetings for worship, discipline, and business were the main focus for Quaker life. After the Restoration John Whitehead is said for the most part to have conducted his ministry in them, but he also took part in the debates through which the Quakers, like the Baptists, asserted their position. In places where both Baptists and Quakers existed side by side confrontations between them developed into trials of strength in which they reached out to seek converts among people more convinced by signs of divine approval or judgment than by theological discussion. Reference back to issues in earlier debates turned them into a series of on going occasions. It was alleged that in 1669 Whitehead had convinced William Smith of Elsham , 'late a brother of the Baptists', of the Quaker view of the supremacy of the 'light of the spirit'. He was then drawn into the clash with the Baptist Ralph James of Willingham in 1672, while the debate over Smith also became linked to an encounter that took place at Wrawby in early 1673.[43]

The implicit support that Friends gained from people who refused to benefit from what were seen as their misfortunes was at best based on neighbourly values rather than a positive commitment to Quaker teachings. Although the justice of the peace who returned Thomas Robinson's goods in 1678 'was of a more generous disposition than to seek advantage to himself by the loss of his neighbours', this was not until they had failed to attract a buyer. When 'divers of the poor people' had goods distrained from Quakers distributed to them by the village constable of Beckingham in 1670 they 'returned their parts to the right owners ... saying that they would rather live of bread and water ... others saying they would begg their bread rather'. There was also an element of fear among those who would not buy the 'spoil of conscience'. Several people who bought goods belonging to Thomas Everett of Honington that had been distrained for fines for meetings held at his house in 1670, 'were so troubled in mind that they could not rest till they had restored them to the owner'. They had the example of 'the priest cald William Carter' before them. He had harassed meetings and 'bestirred himself much to cause such spoil', but had been taken sick coming home from the chief constable's house 'and in a short time was found dead in his bed'.[44]

There were considerable areas of Quaker life, and even discipline, that provided the basis for their integration into the lives of local communities. Their discipline stood as testimony against worldly values, but the importance of the household in their religious life meant that, like the Baptists, they conformed to the predominant structures of local life. Quaker concern with moral conduct was distinctive less for its substance than for its continuing and committed involvement in areas that were ceasing to be matters of official interest to the church courts. Those aspects of their discipline that sought to guarantee Quaker rectitude in business affairs enhanced the quality of their dealings with people from outside the Society. Such was the importance of their involvement in local commercial activity that members of the Garthorpe Meeting sought to move the day on which Gainsborough Monthly Meeting met to give 'their chapmens access to buy their goods and fatt cattell'. Quakers had sought initially to remove probate matters from the church courts. Wills and inventories were enrolled in minute books, but in 1679, since no religious principle was deemed to be involved, the Lincoln Quarterly Meeting decided to allow wills to be proved in the church courts. It continued to be concerned to ensure that Quaker executors fulfilled their responsibilities. In 1681 Lincoln Quarterly Meeting ordered that the will of Thomas Dereby, formerly of Ruskington, be obtained and Thomas Everett be summoned to give an account of his trusteeship.[45]

Quaker charity

Friends worked to relieve their poor through the monthly meetings. They distributed aid to the members of the local particular meetings, which meant that they transcended the boundaries of the parish-based poor law. In so far as their work lifted liability from the parish it was likely to stand them in good stead. There are no examples of Quakers refusing to pay their parish poor rates on the grounds that they already made provision through their own meetings, although poor relief was, after matrimonial matters, the most common concern of Quaker meetings. It came before Gainsborough Monthly Meeting 121 times between 1669 and 1689. Relief was given in both cash and kind. Contributions totalling £4 5s 8d were received from the meetings based at Gainsborough, Epworth, Winteringham, Garthorpe, and Brigg in 1678 and dispersed to four individuals, although the relief given to three of them included clothing and assistance with nursing as well as payment of rent. In 1681 the Crowle meeting paid for the funeral of Simon Ross. A house had been provided for him and his family in 1675, while the house where Widow Chapman and Widow Moseley lived in Crowle was repaired for them in 1682. Children

lesser amounts. Edward Crunkhorne of Irnham was excused as a pauper. At the same time another seventeen Catholics entered similar bonds at Sleaford. They were scattered in a number of villages with the largest number – three – from Scopwick. More recognizances were taken at Easter 1679, but the panic had begun to abate. Seventy-eight people from Lincolnshire were included in a warrant of pardon issued in early 1685.[52]

The effects of the Popish Plot were felt particularly hardly among the Catholic clergy. The reputation of the Jesuits meant that they suffered disproportionately, although their narratives of events had an eye to posterity. Thomas Jenison, the chaplain to Sir Philip Tyrwhitt of Stainfield, who was arrested by Titus Oates at the Tyrwhitts' London lodgings in 1679, was said to be 'inflamed with the desire to suffer for Christ'. He died later in the year in Newgate as a result of his confinement. Robert Kent, alias Neale, had spent all his missionary career in the county of his birth, but the panic of the times broke down any protection he enjoyed because of this. He was forced to visit Catholics by night and in disguise. Peter Hamerton was in a similar situation. He was in London in September 1678, but returned to the county and lived 'so retiredly' for over six years at the Comptons' house at Girsby that it was said that no Protestant neighbours knew he was there. Although he was much incommoded and in fear of his life, he was unharmed. Nearly all the priests in the area had fled and for two or three years he ministered to Catholics within a thirty mile radius, assuming the guise of a doctor, even entering houses through windows unbeknown to Protestant servants. The threat of an excursion into Lincolnshire by the priest-taker Sir William Waller led Hamerton to move to Clixby and then on to Twigmore. He once had to flee from the place where he was staying, although it was a winter's night and he was recovering from a fever. Hamerton feared to write down the exact numbers, but he estimated that 'above a hundred' were baptized, buried, assisted at their deaths, and reconciled to the church during this time.[53]

The anti-Catholic backlash that accompanied the accession of William of Orange in 1688 was the occasion of more disturbances. Like other Catholic places of worship and schools in towns and cities the Catholic chapel and presbytery at Lincoln were attacked and levelled. Peter Hamerton fled with two priests from the city into Yorkshire where they were arrested and imprisoned in York Castle for nine months. The books and furniture from the chapel were burnt and its stones and woodwork auctioned, but the providential dispensation that brought misfortune to those who benefited from the spoil of religious goods also protected Catholics. The warehouse built with the materials from the chapel quickly fell down. Chapels in the Lincolnshire countryside remained unmolested, protected by their gentry owners, and the 'Glorious Revolution' was, for many Lincolnshire Catholics, merely an uncertain episode in their lives.

Although the Toleration Act of 1689 applied only to Protestant dissenters, the number of Catholics indicted at Kesteven Quarter Sessions fell off for a time. At Michaelmas 1689 the only people presented were a couple living at Osbournby away from seigneurial protection. Indictments of recusants began again the following Easter when nineteen individuals were charged with being absent from their parish churches for three Sundays. Seventy-eight Catholics also appeared in the record of Bourne Midsummer Sessions in 1690 for not attending church, but these indictments were effectively lists that recorded recusants. Only four individuals were actually committed and only one fine – £20 but reduced to 5s – was recorded. When eight of the more prominent Kesteven Catholics were required to make their declaration against Transubstantiation and to swear the oath of supremacy they did not appear and there the matter rested. There was a relatively constant number of names appearing in the records of the Quarter Sessions. By the 18th century the Clerk of the Peace no longer troubled to copy these lists of Catholics into the book of proceedings. He simply noted that they were 'as in the last Sessions', although the bundles of Sacrament certificates that he held were a reminder that willingness to take communion in the Church of England remained a requirement for anyone who aspired to public office.[54]

Notes to Chapter II

1   I. Walton, *The Lives of John Donne, Sir Henry Wootton, Richard Hooker, George Herbert and Robert Sanderson,* Oxford, 1966 impr., pp. 400, 402; Rob. Sand., I, pp. 37–9; P. G. Lake, 'Serving God and the Times: the Calvinist conformity of Robert Sanderson', *Journal of British Studies,* 27 (April 1988), pp. 95, 104–5, 113–16; *The Works of Robert Sanderson, D.D., sometime Bishop of Lincoln,* ed. W. Jacobson, II, Oxford, 1854, pp. xxx–xxxiii.

2   LA, Reg. 32, fol. 1; P. B. G. Binnall, 'Bishop Sanderson's Ordination Book', *LAAS,* (new ser.) 9, part 1 (1961), p. 63; A. Whiteman, 'The Re-establishment of the Church of England, 1660–1663', *Trans. Roy. Hist. Soc.,* (5th ser.) 5, (1955), p. 114 ; Eccles. & Relig. Life, pp. 5, 51, 38–9; Rob. Sand., II, pp. 160–68, 176; K. Major, 'The Lincoln Diocesan Records', *Trans. Roy. Hist. Soc.* (4th ser.) 21, (1940), pp. 56–7; Ch. in Eng., p. 101; D. F., *Reason and Judgment: or special remarques of the life of the renowned Dr Sanderson, late Lord Bishop of Lincoln,* 1663, pp. 36, 41.

3   *Rest. Ch.,* p. 43; Eccles. & Relig. Life, pp. 5, 39–40, 59, 240–41; Ch. in Eng., p. 97.

4   *Rest. Ch.*, pp. 40–41; Rub., Ord. & Dir., pp. 44–6, 615–18; *Art. of Vis.*, passim; D. Cressy, *Birth, Marriage and Death: ritual, religion and the life-cycle in Tudor and Stuart England*, Oxford, 1997, pp. 2, 140–41.

5   LA, Vj 32, fols. 1–10; Ch. P. /L. /1664/ Christianity, 9 May 1664; R. Hutton, *The Restoration: a political and religious history of England and Wales, 1658–1667*, Oxford, 1985, pp. 177–8; Rob. Sand., II, pp. 151–4.

6   Lincs. Fac., p. 19; Rub. Ord. & Dir., p. 615; *DNB*, XXXII, p. 81; LA, Calendar of Red Book, pp. 205–7.

7   LA, Calendar of Red Book, pp. 192–202; N. Yates, *Buildings, Faith and Worship: the liturgical arrangement of Anglican worship, 1600–1900*, Oxford, 1991, pp. 66, 68; K. Lindley, *Fenland Riots and the English Revolution*, London, 1982, pp. 132, 232; *17th C. Lincs.*, p.154.

8   Lincs. Fac., pp. 19–22, 34–6, 41; Rub., Ord. & Dir., p. 656.

9   *Advice to the Clergy of the Diocese of Lincoln by the Right Reverend Father in God James, Lord Bishop of that Diocese*, London, 1697, pp. 21–2; *The Diary of Abraham de la Pryme the Yorkshire Antiquary*, ed. C. Jackson, Surtees Society 44, Durham, 1870, pp. 140, 142–3; *Spec.*, p. 147.

10 *The Answer of Sir Edward Lake Baronet, and Doctor of the Laws, Chancellor to the Lord Bishop of Lincoln, for the Diocese of Lincoln, to the Petition and Articles given in Against Him to the Honourable the Committee of Parliament for Grievances, that is of the House of Commons, by Edwarde Kinge of Grayes-Inne Esq.; as He Writes Himself*, pp. 1–2; *17th C. Lincs.*, p. 225; Lincoln Cathedral Library Bs/145, *To the Honourable the Committee of Parliament for Grievances, the Humble Petition of Edward King of Grayes-Inne in the County of Middlesex, Esq.*; LA, Inv. 157/2, 157/10, 157/55, 158/31, Stow Wills 1660–1663/22.

11 *Rest. Ch.*, pp. 209–10; Rub. Ord. & Dir., p. 635; *Art. of Vis.*, pp. 8–9; LA, Ch. P. /L/1663/2/9 October 1663/ South Holland, Ch. P. /L/27 April 1664; the figures for presentments are based on the calculations of Dr J. A. Johnston whose generous assistance in making them available is gratefully acknowledged.

12 Rub., Ord. & Dir., p. 636; LA, Ch. P. /L/Walshcroft/30 April 1666; *Min.*, I, pp cviii–cix, II, p. 311.

13 *Art. of Vis.*, pp. 8–9.

14 LA, Vj/32, Episc. & Archd. Vis.: Stow: 1662, fols. 61v, 64–65v, Vj/35, Episc. & Archd. Vis.: Lincoln: 1671–72, fols. 3, 137, 178v, Vj/33, Episc. & Archd. Vis.: 1663–1664: Stow, fols. 12, 20, Ch. P. /L/ Longoboby, 16 November 1671.

15 LA, Vj/33, Episc. & Archd. Vis.: 1663–1664: Stow, fols. 47v, 50, Vj/35/ Episc & Archd. Vis.: Lincoln, 1671–72, fols. 42v, 131v, 155v, Ch. P. /1674–72; *17th C. Lincs.*, p. 225.

16 LA, Ch. P. / Episc. Vis.: South Holland/ 2 September 1674, /25 August 1690, /Grimsby/1 September 1690.

17 Rel. Cen., pp. 100–104; *Min.*, II, pp. cxxii, 1, 3, 21, 41, 44, 57, 69, 84, 112, 130, 134, 137, 140, 159, 164, 172, 183, 187, 202, 205, 209, 219, 221, 251, 258, 261, 297, 305; LA, Ch. P. /4/Sleaford/15 October 1666/Lafford, Vj/34/Aveland and Lafford/1668, Vj/35/Episc. & Archd. Vis., Lincoln, 1671–72, fols. 4v–5, Ch. P. /L/1680/10/ Sleaford/Aveland and Lafford/19 October, Ch. P. /L/1687/1/ Sleaford/ Aveland/24 October; *Calamy*, pp. 76, 141, 170–71; *Kest.*, pp. 72–3; *17th & 18th C. Lincs.*, p. 35.

18 *CSPD*, 1671, p.427; *Calamy*, p. 59; *17th C. Lincs*, pp. 45–6.

19 A. C. Sinclair, *A History of Beelsby*, London, 1947, pp. 97–8; *Calamy*, pp. xii–xiii.

20 *Calamy*, pp. 316–17, 411, 549.

21 *Calamy*, pp. lxi, 1, 58–9, 453; *Free. After Eject.*, p. 223.

22 *Orig. Rec.*, pp. 726–30; *Dec. of Indulg.*, pp. xxxvi–vii, lxxii–lxxiii; *Calamy*, pp. 64, 106; *17th C. Lincs.*, pp. 244, 247.

23 *Free. After Eject.*, pp. 70–71, 173, 239, 330, 366; *Calamy*, pp. 64, 76–7, 385; *Orig. Rec.*, p. 729, *Sketches*, pp. 119–20.

24 *Free. After Eject.*, pp.152–3, 210, 263; LA, Wills 1709/2/4.

25 *Diss.* I, pp. 221–3; W. T. Whitley, *A History of the British Baptists*, London, 2nd edit., 1932, p 109; *Eng. Gen. Bapt.*, I, pp. 185–8; *The Second Humble Addresse of those who are called Anabaptists in the County of Lincoln*, London, 1660; *The Third Address of those Persons, known by the Name of Anabaptists, in the County of Lincoln, in All Due Humility and Uprightness, presented to Charles the Second, King of England, Scotland, France and Ireland, &c.*, London [1661]; *Bapt. Min.*, pp. xxv–xliii.

26 T. Grantham, *Christianismus Primitivus*,'Epistle Dedicatory', Book II, Part 2, London [1678], pp. 24–5, 50; T. Grantham, *Hear the Church: or, an appeal to the mother of us all. Being an epistle to all the baptized believers in England; exhorting them to stedfastness in the truth, according to the Scriptures. Together with some farther considerations of seven queries, sent to the baptized believers in Lincolnshire, concerning the judge of controversies in matters of religion*, London, 1687; Sp. Ch. Book; *Eng. Gen. Bapt.*, I, pp. 216–17.

27 *Hist. Eng. Bapt.* 1, pp. 82, 267–8, 288; 2, pp. 264–71, 288; *Eng. Gen. Bapt.*, I, p. 187–8, 202, 205–5; *Top. Acc.*, pp. 100, 141; B. W. Ball, *The Seventh-day Men: sabbatarians and sabbatarianism in England and Wales, 1600–1800*, Oxford, 1994, pp. 290, 328; J. Plum, 'Early Protestant Nonconformity in Lincolnshire', unpublished M.A. thesis, University of Sheffield, 1940, pp. 168–9.

28 *Orig. Rec.*, pp. 730–33; SHARO, Killingholme Baptist Register Book, 1686–1846; Ast. & Don. Ch. Book; Sp. Ch. Book; Ep. Ch. Book, fols. 1–3; Bourne Ch. Book, fol. 6; F. J. Mason, 'The Old Minute Book of Bourne Baptist Church', *BQ*, XV, 5 (January 1954), pp. 226–7; S. W. Bowser, 'A Note on Professor McGlothin's Baptist Confessions of Faith, *BQ*, (new ser.), II, 6 (April 1925), pp. 246–7; *Bapt. Min.*, pp. xxxv–xlii, 35; *Eng. Gen. Bapt.*, I, p. 203; Grantham, *Christianismus Primitivus*, Book II, Part 2, p. 64.

29 *Hist. Eng. Bapt.* 1, III, p. 79; T. L. Underwood, *Primitivism, Radicalism, and the Lamb's War: the Baptist–Quaker Conflict in Seventeenth-Century England*, Oxford, 1997, pp. 4–5, 11, 116, 164–5; *Eng. Gen. Bapt.*, I, p. 203.

30 Sp. Ch. Book; Bourne Ch. Book, fol. 8; Grantham, *Christianismus Primitivus*, Part Two, Book Two, p. 188, Book Three, pp. 45, 61–62, 66, 68, 94–6.

31 *Eng. Gen. Bapt.*, I, p. 203; Grantham, *Christianismus Primitivus*, Part Two, Book Two, pp. 94–6; Grantham, *Hear the Church*, pp. 28–30.

32 *Compt. Cen.*, p. 359; LA, Vj/35, 1671–72, fols. 57–8, LCC Wills 1675/41, 1677/70, 1681/i/197, 1691/ii/123, 1686/ii/152, Inv 177/18, 182/157, 219A/36.

33 S. W. Bowser, 'A Note on Professor McGlothin's Baptist Confessions of Faith', *BQ,* (new ser.), *II, 6 (April 1925), p. 247; Rec. Ch. of Christ,* p. 223; *Bapt. Min.,* p. xxxv; *Dec. of Indulg.,* p. xxxvi; LA, LCC Wills 1672/i/19; 1679/ii/545, 1690/125, Inv 182/390, 180 (2) /381; Bourne Ch. Book, fol. 8.

34 *Eng. Gen. Bapt.,* I, pp. 186, 188; LA, LCC Wills, 1674/221, 1692/ii/275, 1669/ii/402, Inv, 169/155, 177/166, 190/335; *Top. Acc.,* pp. 99–100.

35 Grantham, *Christianismus Primitivus,* Part Two, Book Two, pp. 70, 180–81; LA, LCC Wills, 1671/ii/406 and 7, 1692/i/177, 1693/ii/212, Inv 190/256.

36 CSPD, 1661–1662, p. 540; *Qu. in Lincs.,* p. 25; B. Reay, 'The Authorities and Early Restoration Quakerism', *J. Eccles. Hist.,* 34, 1 (Jan. 1983), pp. 70–73; *Gains. Min.,* I, p. 189, III, p. 135; *Tud. & Stu. Linc.,* pp. 177–8; FL, 132/15, Martin Mason, *Charles, King of England,* London, 1660, 132/17, Martin Mason, *A Loving Invitation, and a Faithful Warning to All People, who believe they must give an Account to the Righteous God for the Deeds done by them in the Flesh, That they speedily seek to make their Peace with the Living God, who made them, before the Stroak of his Justice come upon them,* London, 1660, p. 6; *Extr.* 3, p 255; L. Brace, *The Idea of Property in Seventeenth-Century England. Tithes and the Individual,* Manchester, 1998, p. 140; *Life & Writ.,* pp. 107, 119–21, 123, 153.

37 *The Journal of George Fox,* ed. J. L. Nickalls, Cambridge, 1952, p. 512; Quart. Min., fols. 532–3; *Gains. Min.* I, p. xvi, III, pp. xi, 171–3; *2nd. Per.,* p. 464; LA, SOC FR 154, Digest of Deaths and Burials in Lincolnshire: Quaker Registers, 1656–1837, 155, Supplementary Digest of Marriages, Births and Burials in Lincolnshire: Quaker Registers, 1618–1770.

38 LA, Ch. P./L /Longoboby, 1671, Vj/35, 1671–72, fol 26; *Gains. Min.,* III, pp. 134, 138, 139, 141, 142; Reay, 'The Authorities and Quakerism', pp. 78–9; Quart. Min., fol. 81; *17th. C. Lincs.,* p. 225; *Suff.,* p. 347.

39 *Gains. Min.,* III, pp. 149–50, 152–3; LA, Ch. P. /L/Longoboby, 1671; *Suff.,* p. 347; Quart. Min. fols. 37, 88, 491, 543; *Winteringham 1650–1760,* ed. D. Neave, Winteringham, 1984, pp. 23-5.

40 *Life & Writ.,* p. 201; Quart. Min., fols. 70–79; *CSPD,* January 1686 – May 1687, p. 389; *Gains. Min.,* III, pp. 160, 164; *Suff.,* pp. 356; *Kest.,* pp. 72–3.

41 Quart Min., fols. 44–6, 217, 226–7, 475, 491; D. M. Butler, 'Friends' Sufferings 1650 to 1688: a comparative summary', *JFHS,* 55, 6 (1983–89), pp. 180–83; *Suff.,* p. 354.

42 Quart. Min., fol. 101; LA, SOC FR 10/1, A/14/4, 18/1; Meet. Hou., p. 181; *Gains. Min.,* I pp. xviii, xxi, III, p. 154.

43 *Qu. in Lincs.,* pp. 48, 57; J. S. Rowntree, *Quakerism Past and Present being an Inquiry into the Cause of its Decline in Great Britain and Ireland,* London, 1859, p. 82; *Life & Writ.,* pp. 212, 272; T. R[udyard], *The Anabaptists Lying Wonder Attested,* 1672, pp. 1, 11; FL 107/37, J. Whitehead, *The Quakers Refuge Fixed upon the Rock of Ages, Though the Swelling Waters Lash near so Violently to Overturn it. Wherein is prov'd, that the Narrative of Ralph James is an absolute Lying-Wonder, according to his own Definition,* 1673, pp. 4–5; Underwood, *Primitivism,* pp. 41, 116; James, *A True and Impartial Narrative,* pp. 14–15.

44 *Suff.,* pp. 350–51, 354; Quart. Min., fols. 106–7.

45 *Gains. Min.,* I, pp. xx; Quart. Min., fol. 579.

46 *Gains. Min.,* I, pp. xix, 36, 62, 89, 92; Quart. Min., fol. 543.

47 Quart. Min., fols. 543, 552; *Gains. Min.,* I, pp. 18–19, 22, 71, 119–20, 125, III, pp. 49, 74, 186, 200.

48 *Gains. Min.,* I, pp. 49, 97; Quart. Min., fols. 547, 575–6, 584.

49 *Compt. Cen.,* pp. 341–64; HL, Main Papers/3 December 1680/321/ Lists of Papists in Several Counties, fols. 47–8; *Records*, II, pp. 648, 653, V, p. 621, VII, pp. xiii, xci, xcv, cii, cvii, cli; *Tud. & Stu. Linc.,* p. 66.

50 *Records* II, p. 617, V, pp. 599, 613, VII, p. clv; T. P. Trappes-Lomax, 'Bishop Leyburn's Visitation in 1687', *A Newsletter for Students of Recusant History,* 4 (1962), pp. 16–17.

51 J. Miller, *Popery and Politics in England 1660–1688*, Cambridge, 1973, pp. 51–6, 58, 64–6; *Records* V, p. 624; Rel. Cen., p. 100; *17th C. Lincs.*, pp. 248, 252; J. P. Kenyon, *The Popish Plot*, London, 1972, pp. 9–10, 13, 14–17; *Min.*, I, pp. cxv, cxvi, cxviii , 24; *Kest.*, p. 70.

52 *Min.*, I, pp. 93, 95; *Kest.,* p. 73; Kenyon, *Popish Plot,* pp. 236–7.

53 Kenyon, *Popish Plot*, p. 190; J. C. H. Aveling, *The Handle and the Axe: the Catholic Recusants in England from Reformation to Emancipation*, London, 1976, p. 215; *Records* V, pp. 20, 23, 613, 615–16, 624–6.

54 Aveling, *Handle and the Axe*, p. 240; *Records* V, pp. 621–2; *Min.*, I, p. cxix, II, pp. 352, 362, 371–2; Rel. Cen., p. 104; *Kest.*, pp. 73–4.

CHAPTER III
STABILITY AND CHANGE

The Church of England 1689–1830

CHURCH LIFE, PLURALISM, NON RESIDENCE, AND THE POSITION OF THE
CLERGY

The toleration of Protestant dissenters in 1689 constituted an
acceptance of the failure of the Church of England to achieve the
monopoly of religious practice envisaged for it in 1662. It also gave
legal recognition to a situation that had developed over a number of years in
those parish communities where dissenters already enjoyed the tolerance
of their neighbours. This led to concern among some of the clergy about the
position of the Church and an increasing, often defensive preoccupation
developed with what was seen as the decay of national morality and piety.
A result of this was the formation of Societies for the Reformation of
Manners that involved both clergymen and laymen and sought to use the
secular courts to control and discipline personal behaviour: 'putting the law
into operation against Prophaneness and Debauchery'. Although they were
primarily an urban phenomenon, the coercive aspects of the work of these
societies chimed with many of Samuel Wesley's instincts. He had preached
for one that existed in Westminster before he moved to Lincolnshire as
Rector of South Ormsby in 1691, and he claimed to have been working 'to
carry on the bussiness of Reformation' after he went to Epworth. Yet
despite his interest in the societies he remained reluctant to give up older
forms of discipline. As late as 1717 the bishop of Lincoln, Edmund Gibson,
stressed the need to present obstinate offenders to the spiritual courts.
There had been a slight, although hardly significant, increase in the number
of Lincolnshire parishes where penances were enforced in the first two
decades of the 18th century, although numbers were small: twenty-five in a
three-year period up to 1718, rising to thirty-six between 1718 and 1721.
The majority of them were for sexual offences where the interests of the
poor law guardians coincided with those of the churchwardens. They were
often the same people in many parishes. There were twenty-seven
presentments for sexual immorality in the archdeaconry of Stow between
1743 and 1750, but the context within which parish officers operated was

encapsulated in the response of the churchwardens of Winteringham at the archdeacon's visitation in 1757. They stated that all was well

> except that we don't say that there are no persons who do not neglect coming to church to hear divine service, or to the sacrament of the Lord's supper – neither do we say that there are no common drunkards or swearers in our parish nor any who do not follow their ordinary vocation or labour on the Lord's day – neither have the late churchwardens given up their accounts nor is our schoolmaster licensed.[1]

The frequency of services

The use of printed questionnaires addressed directly to the clergy at visitations in addition to the formal proceedings meant that bishops began to be concerned with what were essentially pastoral matters rather than breaches of church law. William Wake was probably the first bishop in the country to adopt this approach at his primary visitation in 1706. When Edmund Gibson, pleading 'an ill state of Health', separated the business of his Primary visitation in 1718 from the confirmation that was usually held at the same time, he increased opportunity to make 'Enquiries and Observations, and to attend to such Questions and Representations as the Clergy may have occasion to offer'. A major concern of the bishops was the due performance of worship. In 1706 Wake had stated that the duties of a clergyman included reading 'public prayers, if he could get a congregation, every day; but at least on Wednesdays and Fridays, Sundays, Holy-days and their eves'. By 1718 Gibson looked for two services on Sundays, but the one weekly Sunday service that was provided for the 225 people of the village of Dorrington with Holy Communion three or four times a year was more representative of the tenor of the church life in the county during his episcopate. This was the pattern of Sunday worship in 342 or 55 per cent of the parishes of Lincolnshire. In the next largest group – 173 or 28 per cent – two Sunday services were provided although they were sometimes reduced in the face of the mid-winter cold. This level of provision was often associated with additional weekday worship. At Luddington services were held on the feast days of the church, 'if any people are present, which rarely happens', but at nearby Haxey there were services at feasts and on Wednesdays and Fridays. In some places, such as Branston, the Wednesday and Friday services were a Lenten observance.[2]

Holy Communion was usually celebrated four times a year at the beginning of the 18th century in 39 per cent of the 604 parishes for which there is information. This was on the great feasts of Christmas, Easter, and Whitsun, with the fourth service usually at Michaelmas. As well as the others, where it was three times, there was a number of parishes with more frequent Communions: six times a year in 79 places, five times in 37, while another 21 and 22 had seven and eight celebrations respectively. Thirty-two places had monthly Holy Communions, and in some they were augmented by additional celebrations on the three feasts of Christmas, Easter, and Whitsuntide. In churches where Holy Communion was held at least once a month it was usually in conjunction with two Sunday services and weekday prayers. This was the case at Harlaxton. The regular round of services maintained by the vicar of Holbeach — two on Sundays, one on weekdays — included monthly Communion, while the two celebrations at each of the feasts of Christmas, Easter, and Whitsun accommodated the people of his large parish. Uffington, was exceptional in the 1720s for the weekly Communion services that were held there. There were also services there on the fourth and sixth days of the week as well as twice on Sundays.[3]

In the middle years of the 18th century the frequency of services was largely unchanged and while nearly a third of the parishes in the county had two Sunday services, over half had only one. Sunday worship was at fortnightly intervals, or less, in the rest. There appears to have been a marked decline in even this level of provision towards the end of the century. In the 171 parishes in the Archdeaconry of Lincoln for which there is information for the period 1788 to 1792, the proportion with only one Sunday service had increased to over 70 per cent. The number of places with a fortnightly service had risen to nearly 10 per cent, while there had been a decline to just under 13 per cent in the churches where there were two Sunday services. There was probably an element of under recording in the three returns that showed only three places as having weekday and holy day prayers. Yet despite the decline in the frequency of Sunday services there was a higher proportion of places in which Holy Communion was celebrated four times a year.[4]

Places where there was Communion four times a year had increased from 39 per cent of the total to just over 47 per cent by the middle of the century, with a corresponding drop from 26 to nearly 21 per cent in the number with three celebrations. By the late 1780s and early 1790s the proportion of places from the 147 parishes for which information is available that had Communion four times a year had risen to 72 per cent. The proportion wth a monthly celebration was unchanged, although the generally increased availability of the Sacrament did not mean that more people partook of it. The prayer book warned of the danger of 'destruction both of body and soul' to those who received it 'unworthily', while the authority that its rubrics gave ministers to exclude anyone who was an 'open and notorious evil liver' or who had wronged their neighbours, added to the high seriousness with which it was regarded. Indifference as well as fear kept people from the holy table, so that numbers of communicants fluctuated from place to place and returns from a total of 464 parishes in 1718 produced a range of responses. At one extreme there were places such as Sempringham where only 14 people from 60 families were communicants, while at the other there was North Elkington. It had 9 families whose members were said to have communicated 144 times. For all Samuel Wesley's rigour, and despite the frequent availability of the Sacrament at Epworth, there were said to be only 64 communicants from some 300 families – one of the lowest ratios of communicants to population in the county – and they may have each taken communion only three times a year, since Wesley reported in 1701 that he did not have above twenty communicants at his monthly Sacraments. The average attendance at Epworth had increased to seventy in the period between 1742 and 1762 although numbers were larger in the 1740s, particularly at Christmas. The largest number of communicants recorded at any one Communion service was on Christmas Day 1744 when there were 135 present.[5]

The fluctuating numbers of communicants at Epworth reflected the considerable freedom inhabitants of a large community had as to when they worshipped at their parish church, or if indeed they chose to worship at all. In other places the pressure for deferential conformity was stronger. The village of Careby had nine families in the early part of the 18th century. A resident rector diligently provided two Sunday as well as week and feast day services supported by his patron, Thomas Hatcher, who owned and lived in the parish. All the adults there were said to be communicants. At Apley in the early part of the 18th century all the parishioners were tenants of Sir John Tyrwhitt 'by whose order' they usually attended the church at Stainfield, but in an act respectfully deferential to the due order of the parish in which they lived, they made their communion on two 'Sacrament days' a year within its bounds and in its church. Epworth, Careby, and Apley represented part of a range of contexts within which attitudes to worship were shaped. In almost three out of five parishes an average of between one and two people for each household were said to be communicants. It was an indication of the hold the church retained on the loyalty of many of the people of the county, although there remained the large number of parishes in which even this limited expression of religious sentiment was not to be found. Whether the Sacrament was seen simply as an act of deference to the established order in church, state, and parish, or as an observance of high seriousness to be undertaken only after considerable personal preparation, it was not, despite the evidence for its increasing frequency towards the end of the century, a central part of the religious experience of the majority of the people of Lincolnshire. Just under a third, or 4,933 of the 15,042 inhabitants of a group of 79 parishes in the Horncastle area, were to be found in the 'ordinary' congregations of their churches at the end of the century, but less than a sixth of all adults aged fourteen years and over attended the Sacrament.[6]

Not all local gentry exerted the influence over religious provision on their estates that was evident at Apley and Careby. In 1721 the Rector of the Pelhams' parish of Brocklesby was said to be in London and had not been in the village for ten or eleven years. They appeared to be content with a non-resident curate, although he regularly provided services in the next parish of Great Limber. Yet the domestic chapels of country houses such as Grimsthorpe suggest that the personal piety of the owners of many of them was more than merely formal and the high level of religious observance that was often found in parishes associated with country estates, although it was not confined to them, was a product of the ordered lives of their communities. Another fourteen of the places in Lincolnshire with well-developed patterns of public worship in the early 18th century were market centres. In Grantham there were public prayers twice daily, except on Saturday market day, with Holy Communion on the first Sunday of each month and on the greater feasts. The patron of the living was the Prebendary of South Grantham, and over a third of the thirty-five parishes, urban and rural, where there was similar provision had ecclesiastical dignitaries or corporations as their patrons. Prominent landowners and members of the titled aristocracy were patrons of another fifth. Yet although patronage was an important influence on local churchmanship, it did not in itself determine its shape, and was more significant when combined with relatively valuable livings. There were eleven Lincolnshire benefices worth over £200 a year at the beginning of the 18th century, and they were marked by the frequency and regularity of the provision for worship associated with them. While Harlaxton and Waddington were the only ones with monthly communion, some had as many as eight celebrations each year, and there were two Sunday services and regular weekday observances in the majority. Like other incumbents in the same position, the resident rector of Great Coates, Edward Thompson, who had been presented to the rectory worth £250 a year by a gentleman patron, was able to exercise his clerical office with diligence, providing services twice on Sundays and on the feasts of the church, secure in the favourable patronage and the material security that it brought him.[7]

The nature and quality of the parochial ministrations of the Church of England were ultimately determined by the availability of clergymen to lead religious worship and the place that the clergy occupied in parish life. This was dependent on their presence in their parishes, which was, in its turn, related to the value of livings, although more strongly so at the beginning of the 18th century than at its end. Perceptions of the role of clergymen changed as their numbers diminished and the value of some livings increased as a result of agricultural improvement. Forty-six per cent of the 496 parishes of Lincolnshire for which there is evidence in 1721 were served by incumbents who resided in them, and a further 9 per cent were said to have resident curates. The proportion of parishes with resident clergymen had dropped to 37 per cent seventy years later, while nearly 8 per cent had resident curates. These later reports on residence, made between 1788 and 1792, come from only about half the parishes in the county, but they are in line with those from other counties in the late 1770s and early 1780s. In 1788 twenty-one clergymen in the archdeaconry of Lincoln served three parishes, another seven had four, while three were responsible for as many as many as five. One Sunday service in each of the places they served was as much as many clergymen could provide. John Thomas attributed the smaller number of candidates for the Petertide ordination in 1744 to the procedures he adopted in testing their aptitude and qualifications. They were kept at his residence at Buckden in Huntingdonshire for three days and he 'suffered none of them to gallop to and from Cambridge every Day as had been the Practice', but the diminishing number of ordinands which Thomas experienced was part of a national trend and owed little to his rigorous treatment of them. The average annual number of ordinations in the whole country reached a low point of 245 at about this time – 23 per cent less than in the first thirty years of the century – and numbers did not increase until into the 1760s.[8]

There is little direct local evidence of the extent to which the diminishing number of ordinations was related to the material rewards of the clerical life, but there were a large number of livings of relatively low value in Lincolnshire. From their foundation in 1704 the work of the Governors of Queen Anne's Bounty had a gradual impact on them, while changes in the basis of clerical taxation, introduced when the Bounty was established, had a more immediate effect. The Bounty Governors made a total of 520 augmentations to 226 livings in the county between 1714 and 1823. Their work gathered pace from the mid 1740s reaching its height between 1804 and 1813 when 78 livings were improved. While the standard augmentation from the Bounty was £200, utilized to purchase land that was then rented out for the benefit of the incumbent, private benefactors were given the opportunity to match or give more than this sum. Sixty-two livings were augmented in this way. Exemption from taxation of livings below £30 a year brought relief to 366 benefices in Lincolnshire, but much clerical poverty still remained at the end of the 18th century. Three hundred and twenty-three livings were valued at below £100 a year, and of these 78 were worth less than £30. Clergymen in poorly endowed livings sought to support themselves and their families by combining duties in more than one parish, and the shortage of clergymen meant that it was not only easier but also necessary for them to do this. The Rector of Sixhills, where he lived in 1721, was curate of West Torrington. Sixhills was worth between £36 and £60 a year. He noted that he would not 'desire to seek ... bread in so many parishes' if any one of them provided him with 'a competency'.[9]

Stipendiary curates who served in the place of non-resident clergymen received little direct relief from the augmentation of the livings of beneficed clergy. They were forced, because of their low and insecure incomes, into holding a plurality of curacies in an attempt to provide themselves with a reasonable level of income. It was not until 1813 that minimum levels of remuneration were laid down for them. Thirty pounds a year was the most common of the higher stipends for curates in the 18th century and in 1721 this was paid in places as diverse as Addlethorpe, Aswarby, and Ingoldmells, irrespective of whether the curates actually resided or not, although at Flixborough £30 was paid for two parishes. There was a tendency for the curates of larger places such as Spilsby to be remunerated at or above this rate. In the large fenland parish of Long Sutton the curate received £40 a year, while at Tydd St Mary his stipend reached £60. Other curates were far less well provided for. It was said at Coates by Stow in 1721 that one had served the parish for fifty years at £13 a year. While curates' stipends of less than £40 had been virtually eliminated in Lincolnshire by the 1830s, scattered references such as that to the £26 paid at Barnoldby le Beck, or the £25 paid by the Duke of Ancaster to the curate at Edenham in the late 1780s and early 1790s, suggest that this came late.[10]

As well as the gradual increase in clerical incomes that resulted from the work of the commissioners of Queen Anne's Bounty, the incomes of some beneficed clergymen grew as the value of their tithes and glebe were enhanced by agricultural improvement. This was particularly the case in the second half of the 18th century when drainage made livings in the fens some of the richest in the county. In the course of the century the value of the combined rectories at Leasingham rose eightfold, from £115 to £924. At Sutterton the increase was even greater: from £78 to £884. The commutation of traditional tithe payments into land holdings meant that the tensions and conflicts engendered by its collection came to an end, although this was not always achieved without friction. In 1829 the vicar of Langtoft and Baston struggled to try to correct an error that he felt had left him with half the property to which he was entitled. In Lincolnshire the value of tithes payable to both clergymen and lay impropriators – also considerable beneficiaries from the process – totalled £60,493 by 1812, a sum that had increased by 42.5 per cent since 1806. Yet the process of parliamentary enclosure and the tithe commutation that came with it only affected a third of the parishes of the county. Moreover, any value that accrued to livings was based on their existing assets so that, despite considerable increases in individual parishes there was no fundamental shift in the way in which resources were distributed between them, although there was a general tendency for the income from small livings to rise faster. The Rector of Benniworth received 406 acres in lieu of glebe, common right and, most importantly, tithes at the enclosure of the parish in

1771. The vicar of one of the smallest livings in the county, Skillington, worth between £20 and £30 a year, received just over 25 acres of land when his parish was enclosed in 1797.[11]

Clergymen who received large accessions to their benefices became important as property owners. As a result, not only was the nature of their position within their parish communities altered, but their place within the wider society of the area became defined in terms of their social role rather than their occupational function as clergymen. The considerable growth in the number of clerical J.P.s in the second half of the 18th and into the 19th centuries was indicative of the extent to which the social position of the more favoured group of beneficed clergymen was changing. In the reign of George II a quarter of the newly appointed acting justices were clergymen. By the reign of George III the proportion was a half. Such clerical magistrates were useful for their presence in areas where there was a shortage of active justices. Dr Cayley Illingworth, Archdeacon of Stow and rector of Scampton at the turn of the 18th century, was 'a very useful member of society, especially as an active magistrate'. His 'most strict and uncompromising' discharge of his duties meant that 'all the disorderlies in the neighbourhood stood in complete awe of him'. Fifteen of the seventy magistrates in Lindsey between 1740 and 1780 were clergymen. By 1761 they comprised 15 per cent of the Lincolnshire bench and by 1831 47 per cent of the county's active magistrates. Clergymen were also active in other spheres of local administration. The financial and social threshold for membership of the local land tax commission was less high than that for the commission of the peace, but although there was an increase in the number of clergymen who were tax commissioners, their generally smaller proportion reflected the tendency of those who were qualified for local administration to gravitate towards its upper echelons. Ten per cent of the 60 commissioners for Lincolnshire in 1723 and 16 per cent of the 184 in 1775 were clergymen. They were also to be found in the less socially elevated roles of turnpike trustee or even commissioners in parliamentary enclosures, but here they were proportionately even less prominent. Only three out of 115 commissioners acting in 71 parliamentary enclosures in the second half of the 18th century, mainly in north Lincolnshire, were in holy orders.[12]

The High Church clergymen of the earlier part of the 18th century, whose toryism had often denied them a place in public life, had used the livings they had acquired through the fortunes of patronage to maintain the diligent resident ministries that were apparent among early 18th century visitation returns. A newer breed of clergymen, unencumbered by the political patrimony of their predecessors but also fortunate in their access to patronage, were able to use their livings as stepping stones to a place in local public affairs. The patronage they enjoyed led to increased pluralism as they enhanced their incomes and hence their social standing through an accumulation of livings. All three of the clerical justices active in the Kesteven division in 1757–58 were pluralists with influential patrons. John Bland had become curate of Rippingale in 1724 and was also vicar of Edenham. He was active as a magistrate from at least 1746 and lived mainly at Edenham, near the seat of the Duke of Ancaster who, as lord lieutenant of the county was responsible for making recommendations for appointments to the bench. Bland also for a time held the living of Withcall, and then Aby with Belleau, Theddlethorpe St Helen, and Mablethorpe St Peter. They were all benefices in a web of patronage connected with the Duke. Although Bland gave up Aby when he became rector of Willoughby in the Marsh, he retained the other livings until he died in 1761.[13]

The problem of non residence was frequently linked with inadequate housing for the clergy, but the rebuilding of parsonage houses in the course of the 18th century, funded from the increasing value of benefices and aided from 1776 by grants under the terms of Gilbert's Act, was as much an expression of the changing status of the clergy as an attempt to solve the problems of non residence. The visitation enquiries of Edmund Gibson had shown seventy parishes in the county with no house for the clergyman in 1718 and 1721. As many more had property that was said to be ruinous or

Fig. 7 Bigby Rectory, built shortly before 1790 on an imposing hillside site, provided a stylish domestic setting for the lifestyle of a well-to-do country parson with a role in local society that extended beyond his country parish.

unfit for an incumbent's residence. These included Leasingham which had 'No house except a Cottage', while that at Aslackby was small and unhealthy because of underground water. In 1704 Alexander Scot lived at Tetney, but he served his living in the neighbouring parish of North Cotes and had no other preferment. Said to be 'rich enough' to repair the ruined rectory house, the work was done by 1720. Scot was able to move and become resident in a house that fitted his personal needs and lifestyle as a well-to-do clergyman. John Calthorp, the vicar of Boston, had a new house built in 1751 with a contribution from the town's corporation. He was the nephew of an alderman of the borough, but was himself rich, well connected, and had a wife who was 'a lady of very large property'. A justice of the peace and in touch with the oligarchy that ruled the town, his parsonage house matched his social status. A new vicarage at Grantham cost the Revd Joseph Hall £801 12s in 1789, including the demolition of the old house. Not only town parsons built in this way. The 'surprisingly urbane' rectory in the small rural parish of Bigby was similarly conspicuous. It was built on an imposing hillside site shortly before 1790 and with its 'cool dignity' and stylish stables it provided a suitable setting for the lifestyle of a prosperous clergyman. Lack of a suitable parsonage house became as much as a symptom as a cause of non residence while the stipendiary curates, on whom the upper echelons of the parish clergy became increasingly dependent, needed at best only one house from among the places where they ministered. Their pretensions were usually more modest than those of the clergymen who employed them. In 1833 approximately half the stipendiary curates in Lincolnshire lived in the 270 parishes they served, but only 87 used the glebe house. Another 51 were living elsewhere in the parish.[14]

The relationship between clergymen who were extended each Sunday over a number of parishes and the people they served came to be based on only the relatively formal exchanges surrounding the performance of Sunday duty and the necessary occasional services that marked the rites of passage. This meant that parish communities were able to express their religious identities within a context of loose clerical control. The situation constituted a minimal basis for religious practice, while what was being asked of the clergy was no more than they were either able or even wanted to provide. John Bird, who despite his great age and physical incapacity was still serving as a curate at Hibaldstow in 1845, looked back with relish to the period of his youth at the end of the 18th century when he served three curacies from Brigg and was able to balance his weekday interests with his Sunday duties. With 'two capital horses', which he also used for hunting, he said that he rode 75 miles each Sunday to conduct services, providing one in each place. In 1833, the parish clerk of Mavis Enderby coped with a similar situation by only beginning to ring the final bell for

Sunday service after he had sight of the curate spurring towards the church. It was a well-understood, almost official arrangement and in some communities parishioners played a more active part in what were in effect semi-official transactions to determine the terms of the church's ministrations. In 1755 the church wardens of Sibsey laid out 2s on a bottle of wine when they took advice on 'How to Petition for a Proficient Curate'. The implicitly minimalist arrangements in which both clergy and people were complicit broke down when parishioners began to look for different types of religious experience. The people of Mavis Enderby were no longer prepared to wait for between half an hour to an hour on Mr Swan's convenience and the 'flourishing' dissenting meeting-house in the village was said to provide the 'sympathy and comfort' which 'the poor people who are religiously disposed' found lacking at the established church.[15]

CHURCH BUILDINGS, THEIR MAINTENANCE, FITTINGS, AND PLACE IN PARISH LIFE

Although standards of church maintenance often also reflected the minimalist approach that characterized the arrangements for worship which had developed in the majority of parishes in the county, the work that was carried out on church buildings and their fittings in the 18th and early 19th centuries also showed the extent to which they still represented a focus for the loyalties of parish communities. This included the provision of new churches, and considerable rebuilding, repair, and ornamentation. Briefs authorizing collections towards repair or rebuilding were granted for at least fourteen Lincolnshire churches between 1711 and 1824. The amount of the first, for Market Rasen in 1711–12, where the church was said to be 'ruinous from age and from its sandy foundation', is not known. The largest for the whole period was £3,420 1s 11d for Wainfleet All Saints in 1821 and 1824. The largest amount authorized in the 18th century was £1,757 for Grimsby in 1720–1721. Most briefs were for between £1,000 and £2,000. Seven town churches were rebuilt in the course of the century, six of them – St Botoph, St Michael, St Mark, St Peter in Eastgate, St Paul, and St Peter at Arches – in the city of Lincoln and All Saints, at Gainsborough. None of them was aided by a brief, although in 1805 one for £777 8s 2¼d was authorized for St Swithin's, Lincoln.[16]

The direct links that existed between Lincoln corporation and the church of St Peter at Arches meant that the common council was active in arranging finance for the work on the church which began in 1719. This was said to be at a cost of £3,373, although the enterprise was not funded exclusively from municipal sources and a large body of trustees including members of the nobility, clergy, gentry, and citizens was set up to administer the building fund. Civic identity and pride were less evident in the rebuilding of the decayed parish church at Gainsborough where accommodation was needed for the town's rapidly expanding population. A committee was appointed in 1734, but it was unable to gain support for a general rate to pay for the work. Where the local community failed, Parliament prevailed, and a tax on coal landed in the town was authorized by Acts of Parliament in 1736 and 1741. It was a measure that had been extended to a number of provincial ports after being used to fund the rebuilding of St Paul's cathedral and other churches in London, although nothing had come of a petition to Parliament in 1713 to impose a similar duty for the repair of Boston church.[17]

The work carried out on other Lincoln churches reflected the differing aspirations of their parish communities. The congregation at St Mary Magdalene, where the church was rebuilt in 1695, came from the houses of the richer gentry, but in 1721 the more lowly vestry of St Botolph's rejected the bishop's proposal that material from their church should be used to rebuild St Peter at Gowts. They asserted their independence by having a new church built. Their venture was regarded by the church authorities as unrealistic, but loans were raised, subscriptions collected, and in 1731 a burdensome rate of 5s in the pound was levied. The church was completed

Fig. 8   All Saints' church, Gainsborough. This replacement for the medieval church nave was built between 1736 and 1744.
One of seven town churches built in Lincolnshire in the 18th century, it was financed from a tax on coal landed in the town.

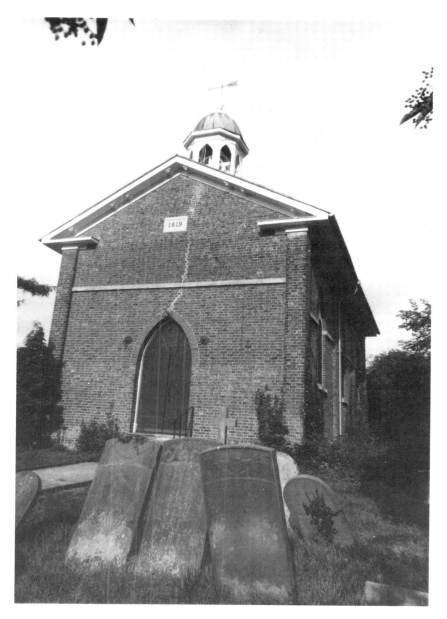

Fig. 9   St Peter's church, Midville, built in 1819, was one of the six churches
built to serve the scattered population of the newly drained fens
under the terms of the Fens Churches Act of 1812.

for £481 8s 4d. Although the corporation gave £50 towards the 'very handsome tower' added to the Lincoln church of St Martin, the rebuilding of the church also owed much to parochially based sentiment. The antiquary and cathedral officer Thomas Sympson said that it would never have been rebuilt had it not been for 'an honest gardener that happened to be churchwarden'. The rebuilding of St Michael's in 1739 was less widely supported. Sympson was churchwarden and here he provided the leadership to push the work forward, with £20 from the city towards the cost, although four bells, said to be unused for fifty years, were also sold. The church was in the area of the city where the expanding households of the gentry and cathedral clergy were located. The need to provide church accommodation for them also lay behind work on St Paul's in 1786, although when St Peter's in Eastgate was built in 1781, the pews in it had been assigned to subscribers. In the lower city work was begun on a new St Mark's in 1740. In the different urban context of Louth the church interior was restored for £500 in 1720 with 'new seats for the inhabitants'. Subscribers were spared pew rent, but there was a consciousness that they deterred the poor from attendance. Madam Sarah Ellis provided lofts for the 'batchelors to sit in' in Grantham church at her own expense.[18]

Church building in the countryside

The sense of pride in and identification with their parish churches that moved the inhabitants of urban parishes to works of rebuilding or reedification were also evident in a minority of places in rural Lincolnshire. This often reflected the aspirations of landed proprietors, although a more broadly based feeling for church buildings was not totally absent in country parishes. A number of churches built in Lincolnshire in the 18th century have been destroyed, but some thirty survive from between 1710 and 1760. Major works were carried out on others, while six chapels were built under the terms of an Act of 1812 to serve the newly drained fens. At least sixteen rebuildings are known to have been effected through the generosity of individuals. That at Castle Carlton was built 'at his own proper costs and charges' by Sir Edward Smith in 1707. Matthew Humberstone's ambition to consolidate his position in the Lincolnshire village which had his name led him to provide for the rebuilding of the body of its church and restoration of its tower. The work was eventually carried out after his death in 1709 and noted on the fine monument with which the church, like others with similar gentry associations, was adorned. The Lincoln lawyer Thomas Becke laid out the fortune he had acquired 'without the sordid means of avaricious Parsimony' on a landed estate in Cherry Willingham and was buried in the church which he rebuilt in 1753. St Helen's at Saxby, rebuilt 1775, remained as an impressive statement of the interest of the family of the Earl of Scarborough in the area. The church was isolated from its

earliest pieces date from 1692, bear the names of their donors. They are evidence of some of the loyalties that the town's parish church evinced even though they were not strong enough to secure its rebuilding without outside help. Spalding church had a collection of plate which was constantly augmented from the 16th century. New chalices were provided in 1721 and 1736 and a wine strainer in 1799. At Louth the church plate was enhanced by the addition of an alms dish in 1724.[23]

The afternoon sermons at St Peter at Arches in Lincoln attracted 'a great concourse of people', but although the support that was given to preaching in towns is better documented it was not an exclusively urban interest. Thomas Townsend, Vicar of Gosberton and curate of Surfleet, preached a sermon every other Sunday in each of his churches. The attention paid to the provision of seemly pulpits in furnishing Georgian churches, such as that at Old Leake, with its fluted Ionic columns, is an indication of the emphasis that was laid on preaching. Samuel Wesley preached regularly to his Epworth parishioners and, despite a painful fall from a waggon preached twice and administered the Sacrament on Whit Sunday 1731, which was towards the end of his life. A sermon was part of the long Sunday morning services in Louth parish church in 1791, although the vicar was reported by visitors to be 'inaudible and unimpressive'. Services were also enlivened by music and singing in many places. In 1748 a gallery was built at the east end of Whaplode church to accommodate parishioners who were 'skilled and experienced in Psalmody'. The choir of village artisans and tradesmen from Epworth with 'their present parochial way of singing', was part of a robust rural musical tradition which was available to serve the church, while at Pinchbeck the choir was strongly associated with the youth of the parish. In some places choirs from other villages were occasionally employed by churchwardens, and in 1732 the Caythorpe singers were paid 5s 0d to sing at Digby. As many as thirty people accompanied by musical instruments sang the psalms in Bourne parish church in 1791. Bassoons are the instruments most frequently mentioned in churchwardens' accounts. They were used with oboes in the crowded singing loft of Folkingham church. The music was 'loud and shrieking', although the arrangements included a notable lady singer. The musical provision at Boston church, where a new organ was installed in 1716, was more sophisticated. The organist appointed to play the new instrument was contracted to provide three voluntaries at the Sunday and holy day services and when there was a sermon. There was another voluntary after the sermon on Communion days, and he accompanied the psalms. Even this clear agreement did not prevent a quarrel between vicar and organist. The adjustments and compromises that were made between clergymen and choirs were part of the nexus of relationships through which various groups in parish communities identified with their parish church and its worship.

The need to reconcile the independent spirit of village choirs and orchestras with orderly worship is seen in the agreement that was drawn up for the arrangement of the seating for Epworth choir in 1732.[24]

PARISH AFFAIRS AND CHRISTIAN PHILANTHROPY

The complex and varied transactions which sustained parish churches and worship were part of the wider process through which the civil as well as the religious life of the parish was maintained. The duties and observances of the Easter season were a pivotal point in them. The annual vestry meeting of the parish provided a time of reckoning in the secular affairs of the parish, as well as in more specifically religious matters. The use of the church as a meeting place was a clear statement of the extent to which religious and secular aspects of parish affairs were intertwined. It reinforced the symbolic position of the church in parish life, although the extent to which meetings were adjourned from it meant that parish politics, even those most concerned with church affairs, were not totally enveloped in its sacred space. When 'the Townsmen' met in 1718 to discuss the seating arrangements for Sibsey church, part at least of their proceedings were held in a local inn. The business of Easter Vestry meetings was frequently adjourned in this way, and while such arrangements might be conducive to harmony and good fellowship, alcohol also inflamed feelings. In 1787 the business at Horncastle was interrupted by drunken altercations. The use of committees, such as those appointed at Gainsborough in 1734 and Stamford St Mary's in 1787 to supervise work on the church fabric, gave greater control to smaller groups of rate payers. The delegation of powers to select vestries was a development that reflected fundamental changes in the nature of the lives of at least some of the larger parishes, including the beginnings of a more marked division between the sacred and secular aspects of their lives.[25]

The select vestries for poor law administration, such as that which met fortnightly at Hundleby towards the end of the 18th century, were a sign of the separation that had begun to develop between the fulfilment of the parish's statutory responsibilities and the duty of charity enjoined on all Christians. The rubrics for Holy Communion formalized this duty with the provision that the alms collected at the service be distributed to the poor. Samuel Wesley had used three-quarters of the collections made at the monthly services at Epworth for the parish charity school. The rest was given to relieve the poor who had no regular parish relief. Since it was only given to those who came to the Sacrament, an explicit connection was made between charity and religious observance. By the 1740s a proportion of the money was distributed immediately and the balance put into the poor box for later use, including medical help. There were also more permanent charities for the poor, but because this kind of provision was made through the generosity of individuals its incidence was uneven. A large town such as Gainsborough had charities of only £4 to £8 a year, but there was £80 a year available in Grantham, a place of comparable size. The £2 dole distributed to the poor of Barton at Christmastide was part of a general pattern of seasonal benevolence, but the association of the church with the more organized acts of parochial charity continued in so far as its distribution took place on holy days. Pre-Christmas almsgiving was generally associated with St Thomas's Day, 21 December, but charities were distributed at Easter at Harlaxton or St Andrew's Day at Manton. Charities vested in the clergyman and officers of a parish, and the use of the church building for their distribution, were further skeins in the web of parish life which perpetuated the association between the church and charity, despite an increasing perception of poor relief as a separate secular function of the parish. Where parish offices were confined to a small and overlapping group of men, the temptation to use charitable income to reduce the poor rate was strong. Charity boards in churches, such as those in Gainsborough and Grantham, were a permanent reminder of the purposes for which charities had been ordained. They also set philanthropy in a Christian context. Single gifts by will, such as the legacy of twenty shillings left by John Prudence to the poor of Clee in 1724, were only known of in the immediate context of their distribution, but his bequest, however transitory, was another part of the network of Christian sentiment that enveloped the people of Lincolnshire parishes and that linked both recipients and donors to their parish church in its more formal manifestations.[26]

CHRISTIAN EDUCATION

Despite the growing neglect of Holy Communion by a sizable proportion of the adult population of the county during the 18th century, large numbers still continued to qualify themselves for admission to the Sacrament through confirmation. They continued to do so into the 19th century. It was a paradox best explained in terms of the place the rite came to play as marking the passage between childhood and adolescence. At Grantham in 1706 the numbers to be confirmed comprised nearly twelve per cent of the total population of the deaneries of Grantham and Loveden. By 1712 when Wake visited eleven churches in Lincolnshire and held four confirmations in the cathedral, the number of candidates in the county had more than doubled to 11,207 with some 2,000 in Spalding alone. Even after Gibson deliberately reduced numbers at each of his confirmations there were still about four hundred candidates in every place. These large numbers meant that people were frequently confirmed on their own terms rather than those imposed by the church. Samuel Wesley admitted to Wake that 'great numbers' of the 800 at Epworth in 1712 had been confirmed before, 'some of them twice or thrice over'. In the 19th century this was said to be because the bishop's touch brought medical relief. Whatever attempts were made by the church authorities to control proceedings at confirmations, the sense of occasion that surrounded the bishop's visit meant that the service continued to be a public event when large numbers of young people aged between fourteen and sixteen gathered to mark what was essentially a point of transition in their lives.[27]

The requirement that children brought to the bishop for confirmation should be able to answer the questions in the prayer book catechism, which included a knowledge of the Creed, Lord's Prayer and Ten Command-ments, meant that, if only for a short time and even if the knowledge they imparted was largely formulaic, the clergy were able to exert an influence on the religious beliefs of the 'Children, Servants and Prentices' sent to them for instruction. Wake's enquiries in 1721 had shown that 89 per cent of Lincolnshire parishes had some catechizing. The bulk of it was in Lent. Thirty-one per cent of the parishes for which details are provided for the period 1705–21 had catechism then. It was extended into the summer months in nearly as many more. In another 21 per cent catechism was said to be held frequently. This left 76 parishes where it was in the summer only and a mere handful in which it was held at other times. In 22 this was infrequently and in 10 not at all. The position remained largely unchanged during the period 1744 to 1761 and catechism continued to be held in 31 per cent of the 483 parishes in the Lincoln archdeaconry in Lent, while in another 24 per cent it was held in both Lent and summer. There were 77 places where it was held only in the summer. In two it was said to be in the winter, in another for half the year, for between three and four months in four places and monthly in three. This left only nine places where catechism was said to be 'now and then' with another 13 where it was 'seldom' held. In the archdeaconry of Stow the situation was generally similar. Lent or Lent and summer were the periods in which catechizing took place in well over half the 87 parishes for which there is information on its practice.[28]

Catechism remained important in the late 18th century, but there had been a decline in its general incidence in parishes in the archdeaconry of Lincoln by the late 1780s and early 1790s. Lent remained the most common time for it. Forty-two per cent of incumbents said that it was held then, but the proportion of places where catechism took place in both Lent and summer declined to just over 4 per cent. It was frequent in only 10 places, some 7 per cent of the total. At Aslackby it was said to be held before confirmation, and its more general association with the rite meant that in nearly 7 per cent of the parishes for which there is information it is mentioned as being held either in this context or, as at Anwick, before visitation. If the association with confirmation was strictly maintained this

Arrangements for Mass at centres such as West Rasen were even more clearly so. The Constable family continued to be responsible financially for the provision of services on their estate at West Rasen, and £2 10s 0d was paid through their steward every six months between 1737 and 1756 for monthly duties by a priest who also served Hainton. Brigg began to be visited by Robert Newton as part of his travelling ministry, and even after he had started to reduce his activities in country centres he continued to visit the town monthly to say Mass in the top floor of a house in Bigby Street. A further sign of the increasing importance of towns in the development of Catholicism in Lincolnshire was the opening of the first chapel in Market Rasen in 1784 where the number of Catholics had increased from 14 to 33 in the fourteen-year period between 1767 and 1781. It was built behind a house purchased by the Jesuit priest, Richard Knight, in the town centre on the north side of Queen Street. He belonged to the Knight family of Kingerby, but his work in Lincoln, where he served from 1764 until his death in 1793, had brought him into contact with urban Catholicism, which he worked to preserve and develop. Knight was able to provide and adapt the Market Rasen house from his own means, and while he contributed handsomely towards the priest's stipend there was also money from old Jesuit funds.[47]

The move into the town of Market Rasen was completed in 1782 when the Jesuit James Leslie left Kingerby to occupy the new premises there, although he continued to say Mass in the village. At Lincoln, where there had been a continuous Catholic presence throughout the 18th century, a house near St Swithin's and, from 1750, a garret in Bank Street were used for worship after the destruction of the uphill Catholic chapel in 1688. Richard Knight was succeeded there by a French priest exiled by the Revolution, Guillaume Beamont, who stayed until 1818. He was one of the six out of a total of some 7,000 emigrés who came to Lincolnshire and were available to serve the new town churches. They also filled the gap left as the number of priests coming from Continental seminaries decreased because of the disturbance of the French Revolution. The suppression of the Jesuit order between 1773 and 1813 also put further pressure on rural Catholic missions. There were French priests in Barton, Brigg, Louth, Market Rasen, and Grantham. Jean Froment was at Louth and Brigg, and also baptized in Barton and Worlaby. He was a former confessor to Louis XVI of France, but it is difficult to gauge the effect that their past experiences had on the work of these emigré priests. Beamont's period in Lincoln coincided with an upturn in Catholic life in the city. A new chapel was opened in Silver Street in 1799. The number of people confirmed rose from a low point of 3 in 1805 to 15 in 1809, and while there were only 10 in 1821, the number reached 30 in 1831.[48]

Notes to Chapter III

1   *Rest. Ch.*, pp. 234–5; J. Spurr, 'The Church, the Societies and the Moral Revolution of 1688', in *Ch.of Eng.*, pp. 127–8; G. V. Portus, *Caritas Anglicana or, a Historical Inquiry into those Religious and Philanthropical Societies that Flourished in England between the Years 1678 and 1740*, London, 1912, pp. 29, 39, 50; T. Curtis and W. A. Speck, 'The Societies for the Reformation of Manners: a case study in the theory and practice of moral reform', *Literature and History*, 3 (1976), pp. 48–50; *200 Years*, p. 88; *Reas. Enthus.*, pp. 14, 53; [E. Gibson], *The Charge of Edmund Gibson Lord Bishop of Lincoln at his Primary Visitation, begun in the year 1717*, p. 19; *Spec.*, pp. 178–85; Archd. Vis., p. 154.

2   W. J. Sheils, 'The Bishops and their Dioceses: reform of visitation in the Anglican church 1680–1760', unpublished paper, pp. 39–40; N. Sykes, 'Bishop Wake's Primary Visitation of the Diocese of Lincoln, 1706', *J. Eccles. Hist.*, II, 2 (1951), pp. 194, 195; *Spec.*, p. ii–iii, iii–iv, vii, 21, 41, 94, 162, 164–5; *Wake*, p. 177.

3   *Spec.*, pp. iv, xx, 65, 133, 159.

4   Spec. 3; Spec. 4.

5   Spec. 4; LA, GIBSON, 13–15; *Ep. Par. Life*, pp. 19–20, 50–51.

6   *Spec.*, pp. 4, 29, p. 6; *Vindic.*, p. 18.

7   *Spec.*, pp. xvi, 33, 53, 60, 80, 112 ; LA, GIBSON 14, fol. 359; Pevsner 2, p. 351; *Lay Peop.*, pp. 98–100.

8   LA, GIBSON, 13–16; Spec. 4; *Ch. in Age of Neglig.*, pp. 186, 193; F. C. Mather, 'Georgian Churchmanship Reconsidered; Some Variations in Anglican Public Worship, 1714–1830', *J. Eccles. Hist.*, 36 (1985), p. 266; HMC 10th Report, part 1, p. 439.

9   C. Hodgson, *An Account of the Augmentation of Small Livings by the Governors of the Bounty of Queen Anne*, London, 1826, pp. 371–83; I. Green, 'The First Five Years of Queen Anne's Bounty', in *Princes and Paupers in the English Church 1500–800*, ed. R. O'Day and F. Heal, Leicester, 1981, pp. 232–4; G. F. A. Best, *Temporal Pillars: Queen Anne's Bounty, the Ecclesiastical Commissioners, and the Church of England* , Cambridge, 1964, pp. 30–34, 207; LAa GIBSON 15, fol. 449.

10   Archd. Vis., p. 148; *Ch. in Age of Neglig.*, pp. 228–30, 239; Spec. 4, fols. 4, 24.

11   E. J. Evans, 'Some Reasons for the Growth of English Rural Anti-Clericalism *c.* 1750–*c.* 1830', *P & P*, 66 (February 1975), p. 98; *Ch. in Age of Neglig.*, pp. 73, 270; *Spec.*, pp. 79–80, 121; N. Sykes, *Church and State in England in the XVIIIth Century*, Cambridge, 1934, pp. 212–13; E. and R. C. Russell, *Parliamentary Enclosure and New Landscapes in Lincolnshire*, Lincoln, 1987, pp. 50, 174; R. C. Russell and S. Bennett, 'Parliamentary and Older Enclosure in Lincolnshire', *Atlas*, p. 82.

12   A. Burns, *The Diocesan Revival in the Church of England, c.1800–1870*, Oxford, 1999, pp. 102–3; *Ch. in Age of Neglig.*, p. 119; *Stow Visitat.*, p. 74; P. Langford, *Public Life and the Propertied Englishman 1689–1798*, Oxford, 1991, pp. 258, 416, 423, 427; Russell, *Parliamentary Enclosure*, p. 27; E. and R. C. Russell, *Making New Landscapes in Lincolnshire*, Lincoln, 1983, pp. 117–18.

13   *Kest.*, p. 89; B. J. Davey, *Rural Crime in Nineteenth Century Lincolnshire: north Lincolnshire 1740–80*, Hull, 1994, pp. 59–60.

14 *Spec.*, pp. xiv–xvi, 6, 33, 79 ; *Hist. & Antiq.*, p. 215; A. M. Cook, *Boston (Botolph's Town)*, pp. 93–4; G. S. Bagley, *Boston: its story and people,* Boston, 1986, p. 133; Pevsner 2, p. 144; A. Savidge, *The Parsonage in England: its history and architecture,* London, pp. 96, 97, 110; Bish., Cler. & Peop., p. 383.

15 *Stow Visitat.,* p. 55; Kaye Corr. 4/114/5; *17th & 18th C. Lincs.,* London, 1940, p. 112.

16 *Ch. Briefs*, pp. 1, 303–61; Pevsner 2, pp. 65, 293.

17 *Georg Linc.,* p. 64; *Lay Peop.*, pp. 186, 188; *18th C. Ch.*, pp. 9–10; *Build. 18th C. Ch.,* pp. 92–3, 217, 218; *Hist. & Antiq.*, p. 166.

18 *Lay Peop.,* p. 189, 190–91; *Tud. & Stu. Linc.,* p. 202; *Georg. Linc.*, pp. 41–2, 49, 64–6, 147; *Build. 18th C. Ch.*, p. 22; *Hist. Louth*, p. 200.

19 Pevsner 2, pp. 64–5, 568, 401–2, 622; *Build. 18th C. Ch.,* pp. 68, 119; A. E. Kirkby, *Humberstone: the story of a village,* Lincoln, 1953, pp. 44, 97–8; *Georg. Linc.*, p. 57; T. W. Beastall, *A North Country Estate: the Lumleys and Saundersons as landowners, 1600–1900,* Chichester, 1975, pp. 84–5; *Torr. Diar.*, p. 365; *Ch. Briefs*, p. 308.

20 *Build. 18th C. Ch.*, pp. 120, 152, 171; Yates, *Buildings*, pp. 54, 109; Pevsner 1, p. 510; Pevsner 2, p. 247; *18th C. Ch.*, p. 9; Archd. Vis., pp. 150–51; LA, Faculty Papers, Fac 3/41, 10/21.

21 *Georg. Linc.,* p. 63; Cook, *Boston,* pp. 84–5; G. Jebb, *A Guide to the Church of St Botolph,* Boston, 1903, p. 88; *Lay Peop.*, pp. 10, 186, 188.

22 Hill, *Georg. Linc.*, pp. 64–5; Cook, *Boston,* pp. 86–7, 90, 92; Jebb, *St Botolph*, pp. 75, 79; *Lay Peop.*, pp. 213, 214; *Stow Visitat.*, p. 60.;

23 *Lay Peop.*, pp. 216–17; Pevsner 2, pp. 294–5, 319, 673; Jebb, *St Botolph,* pp. 82–3, *Hist. & Antiq.*, p. 166; J. Veale, *All Saints, Gainsborough: a guide and short history,* [Gainsborough] 1968, p. 21; *Stow Visitat.,* pp. 60–61; *Hist. Louth*, p. 200.

24 *Spec.*, pp. 52, 80–3, 121; Pevsner 2, p. 594; *Torr. Diar.*, p. 383; *Ep. Par. Life,* pp. 11, 22–4, 35–6; *Reas. Enthus.*, p. 21; Mather, 'Georgian Churchmanship', pp. 265–6; *17th & 18th C. Lincs.*, p. 117; Cook, *Boston,* pp. 86–7, 91.

25 *17th & 18th C. Lincs.*, pp. 54–6, 59.

26 *17th & 18th C. Lincs.*, p. 59; *Spec.*, pp. 11, 54, 60, 157, 159, 165; *Ep. Par. Life,* pp. 19–20, 49–51; Pevsner 2, p. 402; *Lay Peop.*, pp. 156, 160–61, 214; LA, LCC Wills 1724/265.

27 *Wake*, pp. 246–9; Sykes, *Church and State*, pp. 121, 123, 133; *Examples*, p. 108; *Relig. & Rur. Soc.*, pp. 131–2.

28 *Spec.*, p. xx; Spec. 3; I. Green, *The Christian's ABC: catechisms and catechizing in England, 1530–1740*, Oxford, 1996, p. 141.

29 Spec. 3 and 4; *Spec.*, pp. xx, 26, 90, 109; Green, *The Christian's ABC*, p. 103.

30 T. Isaacs, 'The Anglican Hierarchy and the Reformation of Manners', *J. Eccles. Hist.,* 33 (1982), pp. 391–2, 400–403; *Ep. Par. Life*, pp. 13–20; *200 Years*, pp. 8, 87, 89–93; *Lay Peop.*, pp. 77–82; SPCK Archives, London, Wanley MSS C5 3/1, fols. 145, 151.

31 *200 Years*, pp. 87, 89–93; *A Chapter in English Church History: being the minutes of the Society for Promoting Christian Knowledge for the years 1698–1704 together with abstracts of correspondents' letters during the same period,* ed. E. McClure,

London, 1888, pp. 1–2, 4, 5, 6, 10, 221, 319; Portus, *Caritas Anglicana*, pp. 114–15.

32 SPCK, Abstract Letters 4, 1712–13/ CR. 1/4, fol. 56, Abstract Letter Book 7, 1716–1717, 5133, CR 1/4 Abstract Letter Book 4, 1712–1713, fols. 56–7, 196, Sm/02, Standing Committee Minutes, 1713–1718, fols. 255, 258, FT 8/1, Ledger of Carriers, 1719–1726; FT 8/1, Ledger of Carriers, 1719–26.

33 M. Spufford, *Small Books and Pleasant Histories*, London, 1981, p. 119; C. J. Sommerville, *The Secularization of Early Modern England: from religious culture to religious faith,* Oxford, 1992, pp. 172–3; D. W. Bahlman, *The Moral Revolution of 1688,* New Haven, 1957, pp. 78–9; D. M. Valenze, 'Prophecy and Popular Literature in Eighteenth-Century England', *J. Eccles. Hist.*, 29 (1978), p. 77; B. Capp, *Astrology and the Popular Press: English almanacs 1500–1800,* London, 1979, pp. 52, 242–3.

34 D. H. Webster, 'A Charity School Movement? The Lincolnshire Evidence', *LHA,* 15 (1980), pp. 39, 42, 43, 44; *Wake,* pp. 68–9; *Georg. Linc.,* pp. 71–2; *Spec.,* pp. xxii–iv.

35 *200 Years,* p. 91; Webster, 'Charity School Movement', pp. 41–2; *Spec.,* pp. xxii–xxiv, 17, 118, 157; *Ep. Par. Life,* pp. 49, 51–2; Spec. 3, fol. 54, Spec. 4; F. West, 'The Charity School in Wrangle', *LH,* 2 (1963), p. 6; C. Ellis, *Carre's Grammar School Sleaford, 1604–1954,* Sleaford, 1954, p. 44; G. S. Bagley, *Floreat Bostona; the history of Boston grammar school from 1567,* Boston, 1985, p. 47.

36 Lincs. Cler., pp. 33–4, 38–9, 40; G. Tomline, *A Charge Delivered to the Clergy of the Diocese of Lincoln, at the Triennial Visitation of that Diocese in May, June and July, 1812,* London, 1812, pp. 9–19; *Georg. Linc.,* pp. 282–3; *Hist. Sch.* 3, pp. 13–15, 16, 19, 22.

37 J. N. Clarke, *Education in a Market Town: Horncastle 1329–1970,* London, 1976; *Georg. Linc.,* p. 71; Spec. 4; *Hist. Sch.* 2, pp. 12–13, 17, 91–2.

38 *Hist. Sch.* 1, p. 11; *Georg. Linc.,* p. 299; J. Walsh and S.Taylor, 'The Church and Anglicanism in the "Long" Eighteenth Century', in *Ch. of Eng.*, pp. 19–20, 50–51.

39 *Ch. Miss. Soc.,* pp. 23, 24, 25, 350; *Wesley,* 23, pp. 215, 217; *Gran. Wes. Meth.,* pp. 291–9.

40 [J. Stillingfleet] *Private Thoughts on Religion, and Other Subjects connected with it extracted from the Diary of the Rev. Thomas Adam, to which is prefixed a Sketch of his Life and Character,* London, 1822, pp. x, xi, xiv–xvi, xl; *Wesley* 22, pp. 148–50, 343; *DEB,* p. 603; J. D. Walsh, 'The Yorkshire Evangelicals in the Eighteenth Century with Special Reference to Methodism', unpublished Ph.D. thesis, University of Cambridge, 1956, pp. 34, 122–3, 373; J. Le Neve, *Fasti Ecclesiae Anglicanae 1541–1857,* IX, *Lincoln Diocese,* compiled by J. M. Horn and D. M. Smith, p. 23; G. Tomline, *A Charge Delivered to the Clergy of the Diocese of Lincoln,* London, 1812, p. 5; W. R. Ward, *Religion and Society in England, 1790–1850,* London, 1972, p. 52.

41 *Ch. Miss. Soc. Proc.,* I, pp. 364, 371, 378; *Ch. Miss. Soc.,* pp. 24, 431, 480–81, 517; E. Elbourne, 'The Foundation of the Church Missionary Society: the Anglican missionary impulse', in *Ch. of Eng.,* pp. 258, 263; *DEB,* p. 161.

42 *Georg. Linc.,* pp. 298–9; W. Canton, *A History of the British and Foreign Bible Society,* I, London, 1904, pp. 479–81; *Ch. Miss. Soc. Proc.,* IV, pp. 690–91; *Ch. Miss. Soc.,* p. 547; *DEB,* p. 255.

43 *Names*, pp. 65–9; Spec. 4, fol. 40; LA, Kesteven Quarter Sessions Papists' Estate Rolls, 1717 Register Roll.

44 *Names*, p. 67; *Returns of Papists 1767*, 2, *Dioceses of England and Wales, except Chester*, ed. E. S. Worrall, CRS Occasional Publication, 2, 1989, pp. 70–72; HL, Main Papers, Return of Papists, 1781, fols. 415–16; W. M. Brady, *The Episcopal Succession in England, Scotland and Ireland A.D. 1400 to 1875*, III, p. 212; Market Rasen, Holy Rood Presbytery, Baptisms at the Catholic Chapel, Osgodby.

45 D. I. A. Steel, *A Lincolnshire Village: the parish of Corby Glen in its historical context*, London, 1979, p. 8; LA, GIBSON 15, fol. 58; *Spec.*, pp. 28, 32, 146; *Records*, VII, pp. cxxx, cxxxv, cxxxvii; Father Thaddeus, *The Franciscans in England, 1600–1850: being an authentic account of the second English province of the English Friars Minor*, London, 1898, pp. 154, 182, 188–9, 210; Brady, *Episcopal Succession*, p. 212; Joseph Gillow, 'The Rev. Pierce Parry's Private Baptismal Registers at Claxby and Oscott, 1755–1766', *Miscellanea*, 8, CRS, 13, Edinburgh, 1913, pp. 28–9; Reg. Book, p. 195; LA, MCD 1065, Photocopy Typescript, Holyrood Roman Catholic Church; 'Market Rasen Missions' by George Young of Kingerby, 1811–1884, complied and extended by Arthur Young, 1960, pp. 1, 3, 4, 18, 20–21, 58; F. Edwards, *The Jesuits in England: from 1580 to the present day*, Tunbridge Wells, 1985, p. 116; *Eng. Cath. Com.*, pp. 337–8.

46 Reg. Book, pp. 194–5; LA, MCD 1065, 'Market Rasen Missions', fol. 47; Oscott College Manuscripts, Claxby: A279, A686, A698, A711, A731, Osgodby: A735, by courtesy of Fr Philip Bayley.

47 LA, MCD 1065, 'Market Rasen Missions', pp. 1, 3, 5, 6, 7, 8, 9, 44–6; M. E. Finch, *Richard Knight and the Founding of the Catholic Chapel at Market Rasen, 1782*, Market Rasen, 1982, pp. 10, 14–18.

48 *Georg. Linc.*, pp. 66–7; *19th C. Brigg*, p. 49; *Eng. Cath. Com.*, p. 356; A. Bellenger, *The French Exiled Clergy in the British Isles after 1789: an historical introduction and working list*, Downside Abbey, 1986, pp. 142, 147, 149, 183, 186, 225, 256, 259, 260, 261, 268, 269, 274, 280; B. Bennett, *The Catholic Church in Lincoln*, Lincoln [1982], p. 38.

CHAPTER IV

THE TRANSFORMATION OF DISSENT

GROWTH AND LOCATION

The Baptists were the largest group of Protestant dissenters in Lincolnshire at the beginning of the 18th century. Most of their 57 congregations were the theologically Arminian General Baptists. There were also 28 Quaker, 12 Presbyterian and two congregations described as Presbyterian or Independent. Eleven had no specific denominational identity. A sixth of the parishes of Lincolnshire had dissenting meetings and their general distribution remained basically as it had been in the 17th century, clustering in the Fens and fen edge villages in the south of the county, in the Isle of Axholme, the marshlands of the north-east Lincolnshire coast, the parishes of the south Wolds and in a group of places to the south-west of Lincoln (Fig. 13). Yet despite their presence in the same areas, there were few places outside the towns and the large parishes of the Fens and Isle of Axholme where there was more than one type of dissenting meeting. By 1851 when the number of dissenting congregations had increased to 123, there was still considerable continuity in their general location, but the main change was in the type of dissenting church that was favoured by the people of Lincolnshire (Fig. 14). The Presbyterian interest had all but disappeared, superseded in some places by Unitarian congregations. There were only nine Quaker meeting houses, but the Baptists had consolidated their position, particularly in the Fens and some of the villages of east Kesteven. The increase in the number of their meetings to 63 – some churches had more than one meeting associated with them – was also due to the establishment of places of worship in the developing towns of Holbeach, Horncastle, Grantham, Grimsby, and Louth from the second half of the 18th century; but it was the growth in the number of Independent places of worship to 38 that accounted for much of the overall increase in dissenting meetings by 1851. It was situation that remained largely unchanged until the last quarter of the 19th century. While 59 churches and associated meetings either belonged to the New Connexion of General Baptists or were described as 'Evangelical Baptists' in 1871, the Lincolnshire Association of Independent Churches, later the Lincolnshire Congregational Union, had 41 churches and out stations associated with it. By 1900 the number of Baptist churches or meetings had

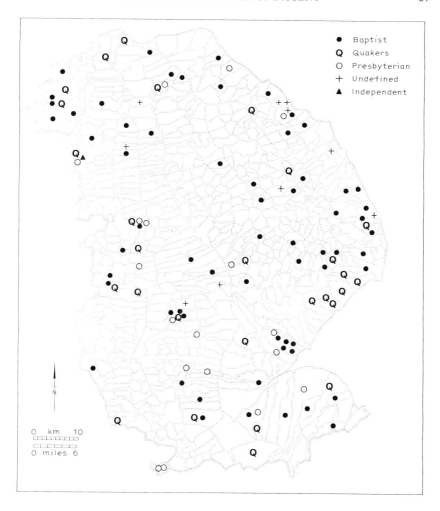

Legend:
- ● Baptist
- Q Quakers
- O Presbyterian
- + Undefined
- ▲ Independent

Fig. 13 Protestant Nonconformity in the 18th Century. The distribution of Protestant Dissenters remained largely as it had been before Toleration, although the presence of Dissenters in parishes stabilized as permanent meeting houses were built. The period was generally one of stagnation and even decline until the new impetus given by the Evangelical Revival. Baptists were more closely identified with rural parishes than the Presbyterians, whose meeting houses became located in towns. There were few places outside the towns and some of the larger villages of the Fens and Isle of Axholme where there was more than one type of dissenting meeting.

Sources: Spec.; Bapt. Min.; *Evans List; Thomp. List.*

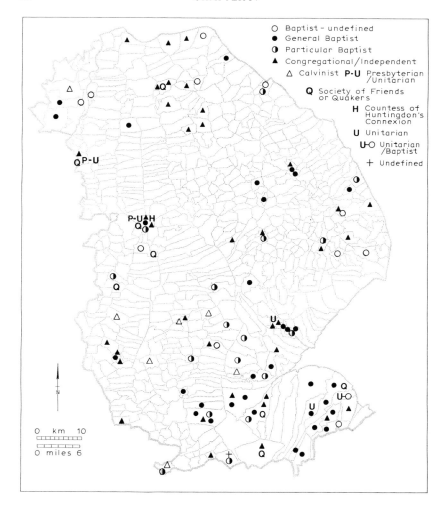

Fig. 14 Dissenting Churches in 1851 showing the growth in the number of Protestant dissenting churches from the end of the 18th century. The development of the New Connexion of General Baptists had led to an increase in the number of General Baptist chapels (see also Fig. 19) while a number of Particular Baptist chapels had been established. The Independent and Congregational churches that had appeared in the county by 1851 were largely the result of the activities of the preachers associated with the Countess of Huntingdon in the later 18th century and the student preachers supported by Thomas Wilson. The number of Quaker meetings had declined (see also Figs. 5 and 13). The small number of people still associated with them by 1851 were grouped in areas where the Society had always been relatively strong.

Source: Rel. Wor.

dropped to 54 and those of Congregationalist persuasion to 35.[1]

The dissenting churches of early 18th century Lincolnshire were supported by between 4,278 and 5,381 people. There were 2,362 General Baptists, between 1,041 and 1,762 Presbyterians and Independents, and between 875 and 987 Quakers. Lincolnshire had the third largest proportion of Baptist members to its population among the English counties, but the lowest proportion of Presbyterians. The proportion of Quakers was, at 0.51 per cent of the population, still in the bottom half of the English counties. There were significant differences in the average number of people linked to each dissenting congregation. This meant that the influence of the churches varied within the local communities where they were established. The 12 Presbyterian and Independent churches, which included large churches in Boston, Gainsborough, and Lincoln had a maximum average affiliation of between 74 and 151, while the 30 or so Quaker meetings were much smaller with between 29 and 33 Friends attached to each of them. There was an average of 131 people belonging to each of Lincolnshire's 18 General Baptist churches, but an average of just over 40 people in each of their meetings. There were dissenting churches in only some sixth of the parishes of Lincolnshire, but their concentration in certain areas of the county meant that their local influence was more significant than could be inferred from their general strength.[2]

The Toleration Act of 1689 gave Protestant dissenters the freedom and security to build places of worship, although the Spalding Baptists anticipated its provisions and acquired a burial ground and meeting house in 1688. There may have been a Baptist meeting house in Lincoln as early as 1695. One had certainly been built at the Brayford Head in St Benedict's parish by 1701. New meeting houses were often built first in the places that gave their names to churches and became centres for other meetings belonging to them. That at Lincoln acquired the status of 'a kind of metropolitan for the baptized churches of the general faith in Lincolnshire'. Despite its importance, its situation, down a narrow passage and hidden from public view, reflected the insecurities of an earlier period of Baptist life. The meeting at Monksthorpe was safe from the urban mob, but it was perhaps as much a convenient centre for scattered groups of Baptists as a refuge for a persecuted minority. Licences under the Toleration Act also gave recognition to meetings in houses or outbuildings and strengthened the networks of church life. Although they might move later into more permanent meeting places, most of the dissenting congregations of Lincolnshire still met in temporary premises at the beginning of the 18th century.[3]

The effect that the challenge of the fresh spiritual perspectives of the Evangelical Revival had on the existing structures of the dissenting churches and their institutions can be gauged from the number of licences

*Fig. 15   Gosberton Baptist chapel. Now stripped of later additions,
the chapel is an example of the modest style of building
adopted by dissenters into the 18th century.*

granted for worship by the bishop between 1740 and 1844. They covered
1,961 places in some 500 parishes. Nearly half were said to be for the use of
congregations of either Independents or Protestant Dissenters. This was a
heading that frequently included early Methodist meetings, but for
whatever body they were made, the registrations were symptomatic of the
vigour of life within the dissenting churches in the period, although this
differed from church to church. While there were 127 Baptist registrations
there were only three for the Presbyterians, and four for the Quakers. Many
licences were for relatively humble meeting places, vulnerable to pressure
from without and to disagreement and dissension from within, although
some continued to maintain a distinctive religious witness for long periods.
Premises such as the barn used for worship at Goxhill from 1787 were a
stage in the development of a local church before the congregation moved
into permanent and purpose-built chapel buildings.[4]

PRESBYTERIANS AND INDEPENDENTS

Presbyterians living in the towns of Lincolnshire accepted the reality of
their position as dissenters from the Church of England after 1662 more
quickly than the few village congregations under gentry influence. They

tended to cling to an ever-fading hope of some degree of comprehension within the Church of England. That which assembled in the township of Birthorpe in Sempringham parish used the ancient manorial chapel building. It was incorrectly perceived by contemporaries to be a parish church and a comparatively high proportion of gentlemen –15 out of 115 hearers – attended it into the 18th century. This meant that it had the quality of a local establishment. In the ambiguous configuration of the parish of Kirkstead a congregation drawn from 228 people also worshipped in a medieval chapel building. Although it was outside the jurisdiction of the bishop, its ministers kept its registers and described themselves as curates. The Kirkstead church included no gentlemen and the largest occupational group in it were yeomen with nine tradesmen, the rest farmers and labourers. They were supported by one family of substance, the Presbyterian Disneys, who owned but did not live in the parish. Between 1715 and 1733 Daniel Disney settled land to maintain the minister and conveyed the chapel to trustees. Dr John Taylor, the first minister to benefit from these provisions, wrote some forty-five years later of the 'perfect peace' that he enjoyed under their patronage.[5]

In 1800 seven out of ten of the Lincolnshire Presbyterian congregations were in towns, where meeting houses had been built. That at Lincoln was for a congregation which had met in the house of Daniel Disney. He was, with three others who are described as gentlemen, one of ten trustees who purchased the land for it in December 1725. William Cappe, another gentleman trustee, was from Coleby where the Presbyterian conventicle in the village had ceased to meet. The Lincoln meeting house trust also included two tanners, a carrier, a maltster, and a brazier, all of whom came from the city. The deed to which they subscribed lacked a formal doctrinal statement, but adopted the language of religious Independency and referred to the Lincoln meeting as 'that separate congregation or Church of Christ'. Although the church continued to be loosely identified with national Presbyterian bodies, its government owed nothing to Presbyterian church order. The Gainsborough church, with which it was linked, continued to use the title Presbyterian down to the middle of the 19th century, but it was in contact with Congregational churches in London about the supply of a new minister in 1696. It was described as Independent in the early part of the 18th century.[6]

The Presbyterian churches continued to retain an openness about their membership that embodied the instincts of a body of churchmen that had aspired to be a part of the religious establishment. In the absence of a potentially exclusivist discipline exercised by church officers and members, their ministers came to occupy a central position in church life so that their personalities, ideals, and theological positions were crucial to the development of the churches they served. Long tenures of office such as

the thirty-year ministry of George Ault at Boston, ending with his death in
1733, together and with the freedom that ministers enjoyed from external
ecclesiastical authority, left them with the liberty to pursue new theological
perspectives. There was also the danger of stagnation and decline. While
there had been 253 'hearers' at Boston in 1717 it was only necessary to
provide space for 60 people when a new meeting house was built in 1738.
The Gainsborough church was already being described as theologically
Arian by the early part of the 18th century and Jeremiah Gill, its minister
for over forty years, was 'not an orthodox preacher'. The theological
development of his successor Jacob Brettell typifies the changes taking
place in the English Presbyterian churches in the period. Brettell had
abandoned the Calvinism of his youth and, freeing himself 'from the gloom
of a system he had been taught to revere' also 'rejected the doctrines of the
Trinity and the atonement as "derogatory of the true character of God"'.
Brettell, and ministers like him, were rendered more secure in their
speculations where there were endowments for their maintenance, such as
those that existed at Gainsborough, Kirkstead, and Lincoln. Long
ministries did at least bring continuity. Churches without them often
disappeared. There were 116 hearers at the Presbyterian chapel in Sleaford
in 1717, but no minister for five years after the death of William Scoffin in
1732. Two who came later were unable to restore the fortunes of the church
and the meeting house was demolished.[7]

QUAKERS

As Quaker membership grew to reach 1,107 during the decade between
1720 and 1729, a level only exceeded in the 1670s, the number of their
meeting houses increased. Nine had been set aside for worship by 1700 and
seven more by 1727. Those which survive at Lincoln, Brant Broughton in
south Lincolnshire, and Gainsborough are evidence of the way in which
Quakers eschewed forms and ceremonies in worship. That at Lincoln had
special importance because it was used for the Quarterly Meetings for
Lincolnshire and its cost was shared over the county. Other meeting houses
were opened after Toleration: at Brigg in 1690, where an existing building
was adapted, as well as at Carlton le Moorland, Gedney, Sibsey, Thealby,
Tumby Woodside, West Butterwick, Waddington, and Winteringham.
Meetings continued to be held in private property when needed, but in 1696
Anthony Westoby, a mercer, and his son Mordecai renounced control over
their premises in Winteringham when they transferred the copyhold to
trustees. It was a measure of the influence that individuals could exert in
such situations that it continued to be referred to as 'Anthony Westabys
Meeting House'. The transaction marks a period of transition in the
Society's affairs in which leadership through the power of personality and
the personal gifts of an individual was giving way to more clearly based

Quaker registers and by 1788 the couple had been admitted into membership. Other people who were not members, but who were attached to the Society through family connections, are also evident in Quaker registers from the 1780s. Joseph Bourn of Gainsborough was the child of a runaway marriage between the Quaker Deborah Maw and William Bourn, an Anglican. His mother's death when he was born in 1798 meant that his parents had hardly been married long enough to establish their position, and the registration of his birth in the Quaker records is evidence of their cordially ambiguous relationship with the Society of Friends. Nor was Joseph's case necessarily exceptional, since the births of all the six other children of his father's second marriage to another Quaker were also recorded as non-members in Friends' registers. While scruples about the burial of the unbaptized in unconsecrated ground may have made his interment in a Quaker cemetery necessary Samuel, one of the children of Joseph Richardson, whose turbulent relations with the Society had ended with his disownment in 1705, was still found a place with it in death twenty-three years later, when he was buried among the Winteringham Quakers.[15]

Tithes

The special legal arrangements made for Quaker marriages meant that Friends were able to maintain their internal discipline without the need to compromise with statutory provisions on marriage. This left their refusal to pay tithe as the most substantial single area of their lives in which they remained in conflict with the law of the land after the Affirmation Act of 1696 had dealt with the bulk of Quaker grievances over oath taking, and the demise of the church courts had further reduced possible areas of friction and confrontation. In the first two decades of the 18th century disputes over tithe constituted almost all the cases – usually some 130 or 140 a year – that injured Quakers in Lincolnshire. The value of the goods distrained in pursuit of payment was often an indication of the vindictiveness with which cases were pursued rather than the real value of tithe that was being refused, but the money still had to be paid out of Quaker pockets. Solomon Ashbourn, the High Church vicar of Crowle, chose to use the more punitively expensive Exchequer proceedings to recover £2 3s 6d for tithe and Easter dues that he was owed by Thomas Winder. This meant that an order for £33 to include the costs was made against Winder. It resulted in his imprisonment at Lincoln from 1705 until 1709. Arrangements were made for a 'convenient room' to be rented by the Society of Friends for him during his time in prison and he and his wife also received financial support.[16]

Other Quakers were less resolute than Winder and found themselves called to task by the Society for their faltering witness. Joshua Reeder was reported to the Gainsborough Monthly Meeting for 'disorderly walking' in 1703 and it was felt desirable that Friends 'should have an eye over him as to his conversation' and 'to diswade him against the payment of tythes'. Such cases are rare, yet not all tithe cases were the clear matters of principled confrontation that their inclusion in Quaker records appears to make them. When John Chantry, a Boston Quaker, was imprisoned for eleven months in 1703 for not paying what was said to be a small amount of tithe, no specific religious issue was at stake since the suit had been initiated by a lay impropriator. In 1727 it seemed necessary for the Yearly Meeting to stir up 'zeal and faithfulness' by recirculating a minute of 1703 against the payment of tithes 'by kindred or neighbours'. The Gainsborough Monthly Meeting recorded in 1777 that almost all its members bore faithful and Christian testimony against tithes, 'yet some others are deficient therein'. The arrangement by which William Burtt of Low Hall, Fulbeck, gave a tithe owner a large arable field in Brant Lane to extinguish the payments due from his farm illustrates the possibilities that existed for local arrangements on this point. Nonetheless, tithe remained as an irksome issue for Friends and, although families such as the Burtts continued to farm in Lincolnshire, the greater freedom from tithe that could be enjoyed by urban tradesmen increased the attractiveness of town life. It was a further factor in the decline of rural Quakerism.[17]

Quakers were tenacious in the steps that they took to hold errant members within their discipline, but while attendance at worship was deemed to constitute membership in the early and expansionist phase of the Society's development, this was modified in the early part of the 18th century. After forty years of discussion, the 1737 Yearly Meeting consolidated existing practice and Society legislation into a ruling that tied membership to settlement. It was the same concept as that used to define eligibility for parish relief, but based on a Quaker meeting. The rule, which remained in use into the 19th century, implicitly subsumed the already familiar and long-standing concept of membership through right of birth by including the children of members in settlement arrangements. It also provided a formal basis for the administration of poor relief and mutual help that was already embedded in the Society's practice, although a relatively well-understood working relationship appeared to continue to be maintained with parish authorities.[18]

Matters relating to relief came before the Gainsborough Monthly Meeting on a total of 202 times in the 30-year period between 1669 and 1699 and the apprenticeship of poor or orphaned Quaker children 149 times. There were 328 occasions on which poor relief was discussed and 144 on which apprenticeship matters were before the meeting in the next 20 years. The meeting was willing to contribute towards the cost of the education of the orphaned children of Appelline Brown in 1689, a charge that would otherwise have fallen to the 'inhabitants of Crowle'. The transfer of the widowed Esther Barrow to the care of the Monthly Meeting in 1696 was a matter for negotiation between representatives of the Society and the parish authorities in Haxey. The amount of time spent by Gainsborough Monthly Meeting on the discussion of poor relief and apprenticeship matters increased in the early part of the 18th century. Like the overseers' accounts for the parishes of Lincolnshire, Quaker minute books contain names that appear with a regularity which arose from the long-term nature of their needs.[19]

As Quakers left the countryside the Society's affairs passed increasingly into the hands of a town-based elite. The testimony of urban Quakers was muted by Toleration and a greater involvement in trade and commerce, while the prosperous farmers and their families that remained were not immune to the attractions of a life of less distinctive witness. Although the refusal to pay tithe remained one of the single most important concerns of Quaker Meetings for Sufferings after 1689, the value of goods in these cases declined after 1720 as Quakers ceased to be dependent on the land for their livelihoods. The exercise of the Society's discipline also passed into the hands of a diminishing body of leaders. As the distinctive piety of the Quakers came to be more narrowly based, their spirituality became increasingly Quietist in its tone in the course of the 18th century. Gainsborough Friends had noted in their minutes as early as 1675 the warnings of the Yearly Meeting against 'immoderate' spirit-inspired acts such as 'serious sighing' 'sensible groaning' and 'reverent singing'. Corporate silence became more important. The ambience of Quaker worship was summed up in a report to the Gainsborough Monthly Meeting in which no unbecoming behaviour was noted 'except some little drowsiness'. A more restrictive emphasis on the maintenance of patterns of personal behaviour and the assertion of identity through distinctiveness in areas such as dress ran up against the inclination of a new generation to conform more closely to the world outside their Quaker homes and meeting houses. The negative aspects of marriage discipline also became increasingly irksome as the number of potential Quaker partners declined. In 1717 the Gainsborough Monthly Meeting recorded the advice of the London Yearly Meeting which condemned the pride of young people who had forsaken the 'Yoak of Christ'. Men had cut off their hair and put on 'long extravagant & gay wiggs' while women had adopted 'that unseemly & immodest appearance of their high heads & wearing their gowns set up like the proud fashon mongers of the world'.[20]

THE GENERAL BAPTISTS

By the 18th century the dominant pattern of discourse among the General
Baptist churches was based on a literal reading of the Bible. In the
rapprochement that the Lincolnshire Messenger Joseph Hooke effected
with the Lincolnshire Association in 1712 after a dispute over his
ministerial authority, he 'acknowledged the authority of the scriptures, in
opposition to articles of human composition'. They were, it was asserted in
another exchange with the Association in 1718, 'the only foundations of a
true faith'. Asterby and Donington on Bain church had expressed their
support for Hooke in 1710 by questioning the soundness of his opponents'
doctrinal views on the nature of the Incarnation and Christ's pre-existence,
distancing itself from the South Marsh church who were castigated as 'a
disorderly people'. The Scriptural warrant that was deployed in these
divisive controversies was deemed to extend to practice as well as to the
content of belief. Used pedantically, without much regard for either context
or contemporary relevance, it became a shibboleth that both divided and
defined the churches. Discussion of matters of practice was not as evident
in Lincolnshire during the 18th century as it was in other parts of the
country. The contemporary relevance of the dietary laws enunciated in the
fifteenth chapter of the Acts of the Apostles and the necessity for the
imposition of hands on newly baptized people had been matters that had
concerned the Lincolnshire churches in the past. Nonetheless such issues
had not disappeared totally and a member of the Asterby and Donington
church was charged in 1708 with eating blood contrary to Acts 15.[21]

Baptist 'good order'

The preoccupation with internal matters that characterized the General
Baptists in the first half of the 18th century was paralleled by a concern
with 'laxity in discipline and conformity to the manners of the world'.
Baptist church books constitute the main source for the administration of
the disciplinary proceedings that defined and controlled the conduct of
church members, but they are frequently made up of material transferred
selectively from older sources, based on partial assessments of its
usefulness and coloured by the memories of past disagreements. Little can
be deduced about the criteria adopted in the selection of material for
inclusion in them, about its representativeness and whether its inclusion
constituted a complete record or merely recorded a precedent. The
Coningsby Church Book, that had been bought in London by Joseph
Lupton in 1657 'to keepe in memory such thinges as are of much
concernment and of spetiall note hapninge to the baptised people and
churchis', had two pages removed in 1707 at a time of dispute with the
South Marsh congregation.[22]

Baptist churches of Lincolnshire became increasingly preoccupied with their internal lives. The Evangelical Revival brought both a numerical and a spiritual transformation in the 1790s to those churches that were influenced by it. The Boston General Baptist church was comparatively large, but the number in full membership had dropped to 'about 40' in 1762. There had been 73 members in 1738, but only a committed core of 27 men and 12 women attended the church meeting to appoint a new Pastor and Elder. Absence from these deliberations indicated a more tenuous commitment by members, while beyond them there was a wider circle of people, many of whom were connected to the church through birth but not baptism, attended its worship to a greater or lesser extent, and looked to it to provide a religious dimension at the turning points of their lives. They were often invisible in the official records, but in 1766 they were recorded as coming to it for funerals and thanksgiving after childbirth.[32]

It was through this outer circle of less fully committed people that the General Baptist churches melded into the lives of of the communities of which they were a part, not only in towns such as Boston, but in smaller and more inward-looking rural churches. Throughout the 18th century the registers for the Baptist church at Fleet record burials in the graveyards of parish churches at Fleet, Gedney, Holbeach, and Lutton of people who were not not members of it but for whom the Baptist church provided an alternative to the establishment. They still found a place among the rest of the parish community in death. While the Baptist churches appeared to create what were, in the imagery of the Song of Solomon, enclosed gardens, the metaphorical walls with which they were surrounded were rhetorical devices which, while of significance to the committed membership within them, were straddled by people who were associated with the churches but not baptized into them, and open to the influence of their discipline but not bound by its sanctions. These people were a bridge to the wider world. They formed a link on which the growth that came with revival could be built.[33]

In his *Epistle to the Baptized Churches in Lincolnshire* of 1729, John Hursthouse, the member of a family prominent in the Spalding church and who ministered at Boston and Monksthorpe, had looked for a return of the 'former prosperous condition' of the Lincolnshire churches. As their members endeavoured to find a greater sense of God's love in their hearts the 'unhappy divisions' that had driven His presence from the churches would be healed under an active and well-organized ministry. Hursthouse had served at Boston on a part-time basis between 1729 and 1738. This brought him into contact with a church which, while not immune to membership loss, had remained open to change. William Thompson became its minister in 1762 at the end of one of its lowest periods. There is an element of hyperbole in the account of its condition then, when it was said to have 'scarcely forty nominal members' of whom many were 'irregular and ineffective', gathering with a few people 'composed chiefly of the lowest classes of society' in a 'ruinous' meeting house. Nonetheless Thompson exercised an effective ministry in which the church was revivified through religious revival.[34]

The relatively open structures within which he worked meant that Thompson was able to realize the potential of a gathered church whose members were seeking to accomplish their personal salvation in covenant both with God and with each other. It became an instrument for the salvation of others and by 1770 its membership had grown to 76. Public worship was held twice each Sunday with an evening meeting for prayer and the recollection of sermons. There was 'frequent preaching' in the neighbourhood and a week-night meeting for prayer and singing at which, in the manner of Wesleyan class meetings, people communicated their religious experience to each other.[35]

Ministers and church growth

In 1745 the Lincolnshire Association of General Baptists had condemned Methodism as 'contrary to the holy scriptures and the peace and welfare of the societies'. It threatened disciplinary action against members who attended Methodist meetings. Churches where members exercised a theologically introverted discipline were far less receptive to revival than that at Boston. Nor did all ministers welcome it. Although the Baptist Messenger Gilbert Boyce and John Wesley had 'confirmed their love towards each other' when they met in 1748, Boyce continued to hold an inward-looking and conservative position rooted in Biblical literalism. Evangelically orientated ministers, such as William Thompson, needed to be sure enough of where they stood to ignore the more introverted tendencies of church discipline and build on links that transcended the exclusiveness of internal debate. Boyce was, in fact, more secure in his position than many, and the possession of an adequate stipend was an important influence on the local standing of ministers with their churches. The yearly payment from a legacy of £400 that had been left in 1784 by Richard Turner, a Bourne gentleman, to support the Baptist minister at Coningsby, was exceptional. While several Lincolnshire General Baptist churches were 'pretty large' in the 1770s, the ministers in other small churches were obliged to 'labour hard to support their families, making their own hands to minister to their necessities'. Many were 'persons exercised in trade'. The continuity provided by ministers of the more prosperous churches was another important influence on their development, although there was period even at Boston between 1751 and 1762 when it lacked a properly ordained pastor. Ministers whose positions were less secure needed to be more watchful of the churches they served and wary of making statements that could entangle them in the sort of proceedings with which Isaac Hinman, a deacon at Spalding church had been afflicted between 1708 and 1722. He was alleged to have used 'cloudy expressions' on the divinity and pre-existence of Christ.[36]

REVIVAL – CALVINIST ITINERANTS AND CHURCH GROWTH

The authority that Presbyterian and Independent ministers carried within their churches meant that they played a central role in determining the ways in which their churches responded to change. A succession of ministers of Unitarian persuasion at Gainsborough maintained the church in this position from the 18th century to the 20th. There was less continuity at Kirkstead after the sale of the Disney estate when the congregation lost the use of the chapel there. Israel Worsley, who became minister at Lincoln in 1806, recovered the endowment. A new chapel was built and what was in effect a rural Unitarian mission had been established under Richard Wright by 1827. It was described as an English Presbyterian chapel by 1851 when it had a congregation of some 30 people. Worsley also secured the Lincoln meeting house for the Unitarians after it had been used by groups of Calvinists from the 1760s. Boston Presbyterian church, which had Calvinist ministers, survived the formation of a separate Unitarian church led by John Platts, 'a mechanic', in 1804, but did not grow and had ceased to exist by 1825 when the meeting house was pulled down.[37]

Stamford Presbyterian church lacked the institutional continuity and doctrinal stability of the Boston church, but although its congregation had little ministerial leadership they were untrammelled by discipline and so responsive to change. When another minister was needed the church appointed him from the Academy at Hoxton in Middlesex. After he had preached in the town during his summer vacation in 1814 George Wright was invited to settle in Stamford. As a result of his ministry an Independent church was formed in 1817. It was a development that epitomized that of Protestant Dissent in the county. Full-time and professional ministers became the main agents of religious revival working within wider organizations – unions, societies, or even a connexional arrangement like the Methodists – to revivify or to establish the gathered churches that were the bedrock of Protestant Dissent. In Lincolnshire they included theologically Calvinist preachers supported by the Countess of Huntingdon as well as the Independent preachers, first from Hoxton Academy and later from Highbury College, who were part of the 'apostolate by remote control' exercised by the wealthy former silk merchant Thomas Wilson. Some local ministers also began to cooperate in arranging itinerant preaching under the aegis of the national Societas Evangelica.[38]

Fig. 17   Boston Unitarian chapel. In the 18th century many Presbyterian churches became Unitarian in their theology, but at Boston a separate Unitarian church was established in 1802. This chapel was opened in 1820.

The Countess of Huntingdon's Connexion

The greater ultimate size and extent of Methodism in Lincolnshire and the importance of the New Connexion of General Baptists has meant that the work of the Calvinist itinerant preachers in the 18th century revival of religion has been underestimated. George Whitefield, John Wesley's erstwhile associate, and who like him was in priest's orders in the Church of England, may have preached at Gainsborough in 1767. Although Whitefield's personal influence in the county was minimal, it was the infusion of Calvinist theology with the concern for practical evangelism which characterized his ministry that became the means through which the isolation of the old dissenting congregations was surmounted and their affairs were transformed. The Connexion financed and controlled by Selina, Countess of Huntingdon, Whitefield's patroness, did not formally secede from the Church of England until 1782, but by then her preachers were established in Lincolnshire. Cradock Glascot visited the county in

1774 and was joined in a summer preaching tour by four students from the college maintained by the Countess at Trefeca in Brecon. Glascot was, like other ministers supported by the Countess, an ordained Anglican clergyman. He established, with his companions, a rudimentary circuit system, reminiscent of that employed by the Methodists, and divided into Gainsborough and Stamford 'sides'.[39]

In June 1776 Glascot undertook a hundred-mile circuit in the county. This itinerancy challenged existing parochial structures and the Countess's preachers met opposition when they entered Lincolnshire communities as outsiders. They were tolerated or even given positive support in others where their work resonated with local sympathies. The mayors of Lincoln and Stamford offered Glascot protection, but he was pelted with 'serpents made of powder and rotten eggs' at Grantham, where he had to retreat before the mob. The small estate village of Bloxholm became a centre for evangelical preaching under the patronage of Lady Manners and this was extended into Sleaford. In 1776 Henry Peckwell, a man of 'zeal and eloquence', 'absolutely owned by God in the conversion of souls', who had been a close associate and adviser of Lady Huntingdon, was presented to the living of Bloxholm and served there for eleven years. On the other hand aristocratic influence carried little weight in the large village of Haxey. The Countess of Huntingdon's family owned the patronage and presented James Glazebrook, the first student at Trefeca, to the living in 1780, but his influence was limited to curtailing John Wesley's efforts there.[40]

The Countess of Huntingdon's Connexion was highly dependent on her personal direction and support. Its most permanent achievements were in towns where its preachers were able to gather congregations and open chapels, building in some cases on older traditions of Calvinistic piety. Ten chapels were opened in Lincolnshire. They were at Alford, Brigg, Gainsborough, Grantham, Grimsby, Louth, Morton near Gainsborough, Pinchbeck, and Sleaford, together with a congregation that used the Presbyterian meeting house in Lincoln until they moved into Zion Chapel in Silver Street. Cradock Glascot had preached in Grimsby at the invitation of several people. A room and later a barn were opened for worship, supported by a local committee. The foundation stone of a chapel was laid in 1779. To John Wesley the Countess's preachers were 'striplings' who had 'crept' into the town and were 'striving to divide the poor little flock'. The sudden departure of the preacher at Grantham, where there had been threats to pull down the chapel in November 1793, was said to have led to rejoicing among the Arminians who attacked the Connexion's doctrines as leading to licentiousness.[41]

With support from Bloxholm the Countess's preachers at Sleaford were able to build on a tradition of dissent in the town that reached back to the 1660s. Despite the demise of a properly constituted church and the failure to maintain a meeting house, families such as the Fawcetts had maintained a connection with the mainstream of dissenting life while attending, for their public worship, what was for them the 'formal and lifeless' Church of England. Family 'reading, praise and prayer' had filled the spiritual vacuum in their lives and provided a seed bed for revival based on the Calvinist tradition. The Countess's preachers were the means through which this occurred and the town's Zion Chapel, where they preached, was built in Hen Lane in 1776. Its subscription list included Cradock Glascot and the congregation of Whitefield's Tabernacle in London, links that were sustained for a long time. The Sleaford chapel was still being supplied in the 1820s from the college at Cheshunt in Hertfordshire that had succeeded Trefeca, although by 1851 Zion Chapel in Lincoln was the only place in Lincolnshire that retained at least a nominal allegiance to the Countess of Huntingdon's Connexion in Lincolnshire. Its congregation of between 40 and 50 adults and 40 Sunday scholars, was said to have become a 'gathering of the poor' that had long lost its evangelistic momentum.[42]

The Societas Evangelica and Thomas Wilson's preachers

The Societas Evangelica which promoted a limited amount of itinerant preaching in Lincolnshire from the 1790s into the 19th century was a link through the Independent churchman, Thomas Wilson, with efforts to develop Calvinist itinerant preaching on a permanent basis. Although the Society used full-time evangelists, the Grimsby minister William Smellie received grants from the Society in support of his work 'to spread the Gospel in some of the darkest parts of Lincolnshire'. He had gone to the town as one of Lady Huntingdon's preachers in 1782 but remained committed to itinerant preaching after he seceded from the connexion and settled into an Independent ministry there. The Revd Mr Norris of Alston in Cumberland was given a grant of £10 in 1805 and spent 7 weeks in the 'dark and unvisited' parts of the county, travelling 743 miles, visiting 25 places, and preaching 42 sermons. He returned in other years as part of a larger programme of evangelism on behalf of the Society. In 1805 the 'associated ministers in Lincolnshire' were in touch with the Society to thank it for supporting Norris's work. An association for Lincolnshire and Nottinghamshire ministers 'of Calvinistic persuasion' had been formed in March 1799 and in June of the same year it held its half yearly meeting at Smellie's Grimsby meeting house. While bringing together existing but isolated congregations, and revivifying ones that were dormant if not extinct, the association sought to encourage its members to preach actively in the villages near where they lived and to involve gifted lay brethren in the work. Chapels were either rebuilt or opened at Swineshead, Walcot near Folkingham, Barton-upon-Humber, and Mablethorpe, while ministers from Billinghay and Caistor were present at Association meetings.[43]

Thomas Wilson's support for itinerant preachers until his death in 1843 gave ministers a central role in the work of revival. Just as the Countess of Huntingdon's preachers had been dependent on her, ministers prepared through undenominational training at Hoxton Academy and later at Highbury College worked on Wilson's direction and were financed through his munificence, but their achievements were more permanent. Wilson appreciated the importance of a firm local base for the continuing success of their work. This was often most secure when it contained a strong middle-class element who were largely townspeople in Wilson's own mould, as entrepreneurial in their religious as in their business lives. At Boston, where the church was planted by ministers from Long Sutton and Wisbech, and where members included the local banker Joseph Claypon, a chapel was built in Grove Street at a cost of £1,200. Like the Fawcetts of Sleaford, the aspirations of these middle-class men and women for deepened and quickened spiritual lives were not necessarily being met by the routine ministrations of the parish church. This was particularly true of places where patterns of ministry perpetuated the sort of disengaged accommodation between clergy and people that had developed in the 18th century. It was found necessary at Boston to enquire whether members of the Church of England who did not wish to become dissenters, but worshipped at the church, could be admitted to occasional communion. The break between the Independents and the parish church at Long Sutton was more decisive and the Independent church that was established there in 1818 was centred on a group of parishioners who had seceded from the church in support of a curate dismissed for his enthusiasm. He had acted 'too much in accordance with the Articles of the Church, and in too earnest and energetic a manner', challenging settled patterns of worship. The psalms and hymns of Isaac Watts had been used, he had taken his Bible into the pulpit and held weekly prayer meetings in a house kitchen.[44]

Lincoln's Independent church, formed in 1820 after a Hoxton student had preached by invitation of a group of people who sought a revival of religion in the city, also found support among the city's more prosperous inhabitants. It had some twenty members and a considerably larger congregation. About a hundred had worshipped at the Countess of Huntingdon's Zion Chapel, but the distinctively middle-class character of the new Independent church was confirmed when a proposal that the congregations should unite was rejected. There was an element of social exclusiveness in the move that left a rump of poor worshippers at Zion. The well-to-do congregation at the Independent chapel in High Street was vulnerable to financial pressures of a different order from those which afflicted the people of Zion. The minister reported that religion was 'extremely flat' in 1830 when there had been a number of financial failures in the congregation – one for as much as £30,000. Support for the Hoxton student preacher who was sent to Spalding was also said to include some respectable and wealthy people, although it was in fact a fairly heterogeneous group with farmers, grocers, weavers, clock case makers, millers, boatmen, boat builders, carriers, servants, carpenters, and drapers. When their chapel was opened they had no benefactor like Joseph Claypon to extinguish the debt, although the spirit of the market economy informed their deliberations to the extent that they took a four per cent loan from him.[45]

The development of Independency and Congregationalism

The position that the Independent churches of Lincolnshire established for themselves in local towns was not always easy to maintain. As they worked to assert their distinct identities their congregations were vulnerable to the attractions of other, more securely established churches. In Louth preaching was begun with the support of a gentleman 'of considerable opulence' whose wife had belonged to an Independent church in Lancashire. It was in response to what the Boston minister saw as 'a very extensive desire' for the Gospel among people who were 'respectable and lovers of the Church'. As the Independent church developed, between the Church of England and the Methodists, the clergy were reported to begin to 'rave' against it while the Methodists were 'unremitting in their opposition'. Churches had to establish and maintain their position in what was essentially a free market where their ministers earned their salaries from the people who chose to attend the services that they provided. The church at Louth was said to need a minister with the talent to attract people and then the ability to build up the ties of 'affection' that attached people to it, but the need to concentrate on these aspects of the work limited opportunities to practice the itinerant evangelism for which ministers were trained and through which the Independent cause was built up. The financial problems at Market Rasen, where the church only survived for eight years, were a brake on the its work in Tealby and other villages in the area. Thomas Wilson's practice of sending a succession of students to a particular place for a month also engendered instability. Any assistance that he was able to give was short term. When James Munro resigned from Long Sutton church it was because of the financial situation and the 'very unhandsome' conduct of the local committee towards him and his wife. Yet the competitive ethos in which the churches developed also drove their ministers, and any ministerial vacancy that arose was usually contested. In 1828 some half a dozen candidates offered themselves for a vacancy in Louth.[46]

The practical leadership provided by college-trained ministers, the embodiment of moderate evangelical Calvinism, gave substance to the development of the Independent churches of Lincolnshire. The impulse towards association that had been present in the collaborative evangelistic enterprise of the late 18th and early 19th centuries was developed into cooperation in support of wider initiatives. The North Lincolnshire Association of Independent Ministers supported the national Congregational Union from its inception in 1832, but only half the eighteen churches in the county joined the reorganized and extended Lincolnshire Association of Independent Ministers and Churches in 1859. The other churches entered it gradually and by 1869 there were twenty-eight churches in association. Grantham and Grimsby remained outside, while Barton and Barrow on Humber were part of the Hull and East Riding Association. The situation remained unchanged when the Association became the Lincolnshire Congregational Union in 1872, although Grantham church was a member by 1878.[47]

The 38 Independent places of worship enumerated in Lincolnshire at the 1851 Census of Religious Worship attracted 5,142 people to their best-attended services on Sunday 30 March. These were in the morning, and the fact that they coincided with the best-attended services of the Church of England demonstrated the extent to which the Independent churches had developed a distinctive place in the local communities where they had been become established. Well-attended evening services also showed that they attracted people when there were fewer Church services. Their predominantly urban base had been confirmed by the end of the 19th century when the twenty Congregational churches in the county had a total of 2,175 members. Nearly 72 per cent of them were concentrated in seven places: Boston, Gainsborough, Grantham, Grimsby, Lincoln, Spalding, and Stamford. The largest was Newland in Lincoln with 481 members. Churches in the market towns made up the next layer of Congregational life and that at Holbeach had 52 members, while Bourne, Brigg, Caistor, and Horncastle all had some 30 members each. Helpringham continued to be an exceptionally strong village church with 27 members, while the village mission at South Witham had 20 church members. There were twelve at Market Deeping, but it was the two and five at nearby Langtoft and Tallington that typified the general failure of Congregationalism to make much headway in the villages of Lincolnshire.[48]

Local lay leadership in the Independent and Congregational churches of Lincolnshire was the most middle class of all the nonconformist bodies in the county, with 78 per cent of its trustees coming from their own ministers and people described as gentlemen, from the professional classes, or from among middle-class town shopkeepers. The minister of Lincoln's Newland church, the Revd J. Williamson, speaking at the annual meeting of the Church Aid and Home Missionary Society in 1882, said that the country churches of Lincolnshire offered 'the Gospel of the grace of God in connection with freedom of thought in connection with political freedom'.

*Fig. 18 Brigg Independent chapel 1813 (extended at the front in the 1870s)
reflects the confidence of the dissenters of Brigg. The position of the
Church of England in this market town, which did not become a parish
in its own right until 1872, was contested from the 17th century.*

It was an approach that had greater relevance in towns and places where there was a climate of religious choice. Independents and Congregationalists were active in the disputes over church rates that divided parish communities. The anti church-rate party at Brigg was led by the Congregationalist druggist Thomas Ball in the 1840s. Its watchword included 'Independence' and 'civil and religious liberty'. Brigg's professional and middle-class Congregationalists also found political self-expression in their attempts to free the management of the town's affairs from the anomalous parish structures that bound them. When Brigg's first local board was elected in 1874 its political cast was said to be Liberal with a majority of its members from people who attended the Congregational chapel. There was little mileage in such issues for rural congregations and, in the last analysis, a system which, in the words of the Revd J. Williamson, placed a clerical pastor over one small church and left him 'with nothing to do but preach two small sermons a-week ...and to starve on £80 a-year' was largely incapable of further development.[49]

REVIVAL – THE BAPTIST CHURCHES AND THE DEVELOPMENT OF CONNEXIONALISM

When the New Connexion of General Baptists amalgamated with the Baptist Union in 1891 it had nineteen churches in Lincolnshire, although the church at Burgh le Marsh and Monksthorpe had always remained outside it. Most of the other seventeen Baptist chapels associated with the Union had been established in the course of the 19th century although five, including Mint Lane, Lincoln, were the products of the revival of Calvinistic dissent in the late 18th century. This meant that there was a total of some 37 Baptist churches of all traditions in Lincolnshire by 1900. The theologically Unitarian General Baptist church at Lutton, a remnant from debates that had divided Baptists in the 18th century, had closed in 1865, but an associated church at Long Sutton was reopened in 1877 and enjoyed a certain degree of evangelistic success. It was connected to the old General Baptist Assembly which did not wind up until 1916.[50]

William Thompson's evangelically orientated ministry at Boston made him something of an exemplar and early in 1763 Daniel Taylor, a Halifax collier who had experienced evangelical conversion under the Wesleyan Methodists, attempted to contact the Boston church. Taylor had gathered a congregation at Hebden Bridge in Yorkshire, but although he had been influenced by the teachings of the Particular Baptists on believer's baptism, his Arminian theology precluded him from being baptized by them. Nor did a local ministry to a gathered church suit Taylor's quest for a more vigorous style of evangelism. He renewed his attempts to contact the Lincolnshire General Baptists and attended their Association in May 1763. His instinct for association, coupled with a sense of the need for order in church affairs, meant that he was more than an individualist driven by the imperatives of revival. Thompson and Taylor visited each other's churches and after a visit to Boston in 1764, when he preached at the opening of the new chapel, Taylor undertook a preaching tour, collecting money for a new meeting house that he was having built in Yorkshire. This took him to a group of five Baptist churches in Leicestershire which, while being theologically Arminian and Independent in their church government, were actively evangelistic. Attempts to bring them into formal contact with the Lincolnshire Association of General Baptists failed, and the New Connexion of theologically orthodox Arminian, but evangelistically orientated General Baptists, was established. Boston and Fleet were among

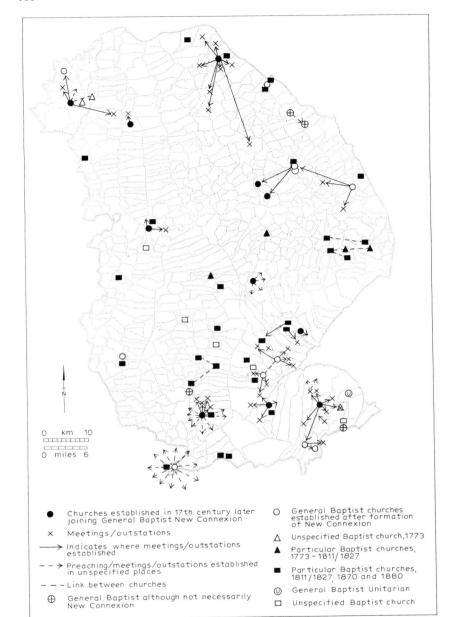

● Churches established in 17th. century later joining General Baptist New Connexion

×   Meetings/outstations

⟶   Indicates where meetings/outstations established

− − ➤ Preaching/meetings/outstations established in unspecified places

− − − Link between churches

⊕   General Baptist although not necessarily New Connexion

O   General Baptist churches established after formation of New Connexion

△   Unspecified Baptist church, 1773

▲   Particular Baptist churches, 1773 − 1811/1827

■   Particular Baptist churches, 1811/1827, 1870 and 1880

Ⓤ   General Baptist Unitarian

□   Unspecified Baptist church

*Fig. 19   The Growth and Development of the Baptist Churches, 1773–1880.
Where the Baptist churches were able to expand, particularly in the
large parishes and scattered communities of the fens,
the churches created from subsidiary meetings and outstations
were vulnerable to the effects of rural decline from the 1870s.*

*Sources: Thomp. List; MNCGB; 'A List of Particular Baptist Churches and
Ministers in England', BM, III (1811), p. 460; 'List of Particular or Calvinistic
Baptist Churches', BM, XIX (1827), p. 81; BH, 1870; 1880.*

the fourteen churches represented at its first Association at Whitechapel in
June 1770.[51]

Membership

The churches at Boston and Fleet brought 126 members to the New
Connexion and its membership in Lincolnshire reached a high point of
2,006 in 1877. Thereafter it fluctuated downwards. There were 1,693
members in 17 churches in 1890 and by 1892 the total membership of
former New Connexion churches had at 1,518 reached its lowest point
since 1849. The proportion of New Connexion members to the population
of the county reached 0.31 per cent in 1831 and 0.45 per cent by 1871,
dropping to 0.32 per cent in 1900; but these figures do not reflect the
importance of their churches in areas of the county where they tended to be
concentrated. Moreover, their impact was increased further by the number
of people who attended services without becoming full members. The
largest aggregate attendance at General Baptist services in Lincolnshire at
the Census of Religious Worship, when membership of the Connexion's
churches in the county totalled 1,556, was 3,460. This was at evening
services in 30 separate places of worship, the time when nonconformist
attendances were generally at their best. There had been only slightly fewer
worshippers in the morning with 3,385, while there had been 1,479 in the
afternoon. In the Spalding and Holbeach areas of the south Lincolnshire
fens New Connexion services attracted a quarter of all worshippers. In the
Boston and Bourne districts their share was between fourteen and sixteen
per cent.[52]

      The foundation articles of the New Connexion had maintained the
centrality of believer's baptism. No person 'ought to be received into the
church without submission to that ordnance'. Attitudes changed over time
and differed between churches, but despite moves towards more open
membership, repentance, belief in the gospel and baptism by immersion in
water remained the conditions for reception into them. The baptism of Mrs
Alice Andrew and her husband took place when they were admitted to the

church at Fleet in 1803, although they had actually experienced their
conversion among the Wesleyan Methodists. At about the same time, John
Peperdine, a farmer from Fosdyke, and his wife became members of the
church at Sutterton when they were baptized in response to the preaching of
the minister there. Mrs Kemp, a regular attender at Louth, was received
into church membership at the same time that she was baptized in 1821, yet
when a church was formed at Stamford in 1829 only six of the thirteen
people who were baptized were accepted as church members after
examination by ministers appointed for the occasion. By 1845 a tripartite
initiation rite of baptism, admission to the church, and participation in the
Lord's Supper had been developed at Kirton in Lindsey, while ten years
later a public baptism in the River Thorn at Crowle, witnessed by some
1,500 people, was followed by more private reception into the church and
the Lord's Supper. A more liberal concept of membership was associated
with an urban context where the church was in direct competition with
other evangelical bodies. At Lincoln the practice of open communion for
all, whether baptized or not, was adopted in 1861.[53]

The varying conceptions of what constituted church membership in the
New Connexion meant that, despite buoyant attendance figures, it was
possible for churches to give less optimistic reports on membership. A
report from Spalding in 1817 referred to large congregations and yet a lack
of converts for the 'too much neglected ordinance of baptism'.
Nonetheless, the importance to church life of people who attended worship
without being members was recognized in the reports of churches to the
annual assembly of the Connexion. In 1882 John Chatwin Jones, the
minister at Spalding, advocated open church membership. It should, he
said, be based on commitment rather than more rigidly defined criteria, so
that the common life which bound the churches together was so visibly
attractive that members were won to them rather than bound 'by the iron
hand of law'.[54]

Church development

Different ideas on church membership arose out of the ways in which the
New Connexion and its churches had developed in local communities.
Especially in the early part of the 19th century membership of the
Connexion as a whole increased as churches, some of which had been in
existence a long time, joined it, while the churches themselves grew mainly
either by gaining people from outside the circle of church attenders, or by
continuing to attract the members of families already associated with them.
At the beginning of the 19th century there were seven Lincolnshire
churches in the Connexion, at Boston, Bourne, Gosberton, Killingholme,
Kirton in Lindsey, Maltby, and Spalding. The number increased to thirteen
in the first quarter of the century of which four were new, the result of the

missionary enterprise of older churches. Even when the number of churches was at its greatest in 1888, and there were twenty-one in the county, only nine had been newly established in the 19th century. A number of them were in growing towns such as Grantham and Grimsby.[55]

Local churches had developed in a number of different ways. Sixteen had twelve additional chapels or preaching places associated with them in 1837, although some that were long established still continued to be based on only one place. It was not until 1879 that an outstation of Kirton in Lindsey was established at Cleatham in the neighbouring parish of Manton. Boston had some members living in neighbouring villages in the 1760s and this contact continued into the 19th century, but its main presence was in the town. A Sunday school was established in the Witham Green district in the 1840s and in due course a 'commodious' meeting house was built in this 'much neglected' but densely populated area. Other churches had much more highly developed networks of chapels and subsidiary meeting places. One of the largest was based on Bourne church where there were six chapels and outstations in 1838 embracing older centres of Baptist life at Hacconby and Morton. Houses had been licensed for Baptist worship in these villages since the 1790s; but it was the large parishes and scattered communities of the fens of south Lincolnshire, with their thinly spread levels of overall provision and a general absence of the sort of opposition which might emerge in parishes where patterns of authority were more tightly structured, that presented distinctive opportunities for church growth based on central churches and outstations (Fig. 19). Fleet church developed in this way. There had been preaching at Gedney Hill since the 1790s, but the separate church that was created there in 1820 had grown out of a meeting held by members of a family who had originally attended and become members of the church at Fleet. They were visited occasionally by a minister and when numbers grew a meeting house was built. By 1840 Gedney Hill had established a branch at Sutton St Edmund, where a chapel was built and remained associated with it until 1887. Fleet church also responded to population movements in the area and initiatives by preachers from the church led to a room being hired in Holbeach in 1841. In 1844 a chapel was built in a newly developed part of the town.[56]

Not all the churches that entered the New Connexion came in a flourishing condition. When Spalding sought to be admitted in 1798 it was said to be a 'decayed interest'. On the other hand the accession of the church at Maltby le Marsh came as the result of the initiative of twenty-two of its members, ten of whom were women. They covenanted together in 1772 to promote 'the power of vital, experimental religion'. The Old General Baptist church at Coningsby entered the New Connexion as a mature church of ninety-nine members in 1830; but whatever their origins the churches in the Connexion were united in their appreciation of the importance of a full-time, professional ministry. When it was at a low point in the 1830s the Spalding church was advised to find a lively young minister to revive it. Although the initiative to join the New Connexion did not stem from direct ministerial leadership at Maltby, the church members pledged themselves to advance their aims by encouraging those ministers who preached 'the essential doctrines of the blessed Gospel of Jesus Christ'. The church's great need for a minister was noted at the annual Association of the Connexion. After one was settled there in 1775 it became a centre for active evangelism when he began preaching in Alford and Theddlethorpe.[57]

Great differences remained in the type of ministry that each church was actually able to support, although it was through professionally trained and college-educated ministers that the shared values and standards which gave a common sense of purpose to the Connexion's work were ultimately realized. John Birch, the ordained pastor of the church at Gedney Hill from 1820, continued to work as 'a daily labourer'. James Kiddall began to assist the minister at Louth and in the surrounding villages on an occasional basis from 1824 and then to preach regularly at Maltby, where he was ordained pastor, in 1829. He also opened chapels in Alford and Louth. For all this time he worked successively as a draper, in the government stamp office at

Fig. 20   Boston General Baptist chapel, 1837. The date stone from an earlier chapel of 1763, and incorporated into the façade of the present building, links it with the establishment of the New Connexion of General Baptists of which the Boston church was a founding member.

Alford, and as a bank clerk in Louth, making the Gospel 'free of charge' until his death in 1862.[58]

The ministerially led approach that opened up the General Baptist churches of Lincolnshire to the full effects of the evangelical revival was personified in the leadership given by the Revd John Chatwin Jones in the development of Spalding church. College trained and with a degree from the University of Glasgow, he served for sixty-five years as the minister at Spalding. The outstations of the church were served by voluntary lay preachers who were organized in support of his work and seven out of the thirty-four lay preachers active in the New Connexion churches of the county in 1875 were at Spalding. The plans that give details of their deployment had clear affinities with those of Methodist circuits. That for the half year from October 1885 had seventeen preachers, all except two of whom lived in Spalding and moved out from the central church to conduct over 150 services in the outlying settlements of Pode Hole, Spalding Common, Mill Green, and Guthram. This was an entirely male effort and the general absence of Baptist women preachers of any type in Lincolnshire is indicative of the extent to which its churches reflected the conservative mores of the local communities in which they were located. Women's 'preaching gifts' were said to be 'readily recognized' and opportunities were said to be 'freely afforded' them in some places, but their employment was a matter left to the 'discretion' of individual New Connexion churches.[59]

Revival meetings came to be used to supplement the efforts of ministers and lay preachers in stimulating church growth. They were held in Spalding in 1839 and again in the spring of 1853. Those that were held at Fleet in 1860 were not only intended to stir up the people of the neighbourhood, but to arouse the church itself from its 'lethargic state'. In 1885 an American revivalist was employed at Louth's Eastgate church. He was reported as having added twenty members, but the majority of his converts came from members of the congregation and Sunday scholars. As candidates for baptism came from among the families of existing members, churches were renewed from within themselves rather than making converts from the outside world. One of the people baptized at Louth North Gate in March 1857 was from the fourth generation of her family to belong to the church. At special revival services held at Spalding for a month in the spring of 1888 there was 'hearty singing' by the choir, 'pointed' addresses, and earnest prayers offered for the conversion of the young people who belonged to the Sunday school as well as for members of the congregation who sat 'under the ministry of the word'. The majority of the twenty-eight people baptized at the conclusion of the cycle of services, whose ages ranged from ten to seventy, were children.[60]

Decline

The significant contributions made by their Sunday schools to the churches at Bourne, and to a lesser extent Spalding, demonstrated the importance of their well-developed institutional life in staving off numerical decline. Their central town churches, together with village chapels and the meeting associated with them gave a broader base than was the case in churches such as Boston. Although it was the largest church in Lincolnshire for most of the period between 1770 and 1900 Boston had no extensive network of outstations and did not move beyond its mission in Witham Green into the industrial area of Mount Bridge area of the town until 1883. Its membership declined from 1881. The Baptist churches within the towns of Grimsby and Lincoln did expand into the Freeman Street area of Grimsby and on to Monk's Road at Lincoln, although even here the churches failed to grow at the same rate as the populations of the towns.[61]

The General Baptist chapel that was built at Sutton St Edmund in 1840 was firmly rooted in local life. All the trustees, except a tailor, were farmers and graziers from the surrounding fenland settlements of Gedney, Lutton, and Parson Drove, but while this meant that it was closely identified with the local community it was left vulnerable to its economic vicissitudes. As agricultural depression began to deepen in the last quarter of the 19th century, the depopulation of rural areas not only affected the numerical strength and financial viability of churches, but cut across the affective relationships which cemented local church communities. These feelings were often expressed using the vocabulary of bereavement. In 1882 the church at Crowle was said to have 'suffered awfully' and experienced the loss of several 'dear friends', including a fifth of its members. Small churches faced with these strains, and preoccupied with survival, became less attractive to people whose association with them did not extend to full membership. As J. T. Atton of Spalding argued in 1884, they could also be dominated by the foibles of their small membership: 'oddly angular souls', 'crochetty people, vain and self righteous folk', narrowly focused on the immediate needs of their churches. The fundamental weaknesses of many churches founded in periods of expansion and in optimistic expectation of further growth had caused concern as early as 1859 when a special meeting of the New Connexion had drawn attention to 'feeble' churches in small towns and villages that were unable to sustain the 'official' ministry which provided effective pastoral oversight and leadership in the larger churches. Excessive reliance on unpaid preachers, without the benefits of planned provision of the properly organized local preachers that were to be found in Spalding, exacerbated these problems and left churches to 'uneducated brethren'. While they were 'men of ardent piety and devoted zeal and worthy of all honour and respect' their 'self-denying labours' needed to be supplemented by 'the teaching which men of higher culture can alone supply'.[62]

Faced with declining overall membership the New Connexion sought to strengthen its churches through reorganization and to create the broader base that characterized its more successful churches. The marked weaknesses of the rural churches of the fens and Isle of Axholme meant that attention was focused on these areas, although ones which were long established in other areas, such as Asterby and Donington on Bain, were drawn into the process. In 1881 plans to group some of the fenland churches were discussed, although the distances between them created problems. The 'union for pastoral purposes' of the three churches at Butterwick, Crowle, and Epworth meant that they were able to pay a college-trained minister to attempt to restore their evangelistic momentum. Moves of this kind curbed the continuing decline of the average-sized churches, but there was tension between the demands that settled churches made on their ministers and the need for missionary work to bring in new members. The past glories of the rural Baptist churches were extolled in an attempt to make a claim on the Connexion for a solution to their problems. It was a claim likened to that of parents on 'strong and well-to-do lads to prevent them from going into a parish-workhouse'; but the constraints of geography and the rigidities engendered by what were ultimately autonomous churches meant that this debt of obligation remained unpaid.[63]

After its reorganization in 1831 the national Baptist Union included both General and Particular churches as well as those from the New Connexion. The issue of the full fusion of the New Connexion with the Union had been discussed from 1857 and was accomplished in 1891. The East Midland Baptist Association, which included nearly all the General and Particular Baptist churches of Lincolnshire, was formed to coincide with the reconstitution of the Union. The common nature as well as the extent of the concerns of the Lincolnshire Baptist churches had become more evident as churches that were not part of the New Connexion also experienced a decline in membership from 1885, although this came eight years later. The Particular Baptist churches had some strong town churches, but none of them had developed a wide base in town and countryside. Victoria Street church in Grimsby continued to grow until 1887, when it had 399 members, while Mint Street in Lincoln attained its highest membership of 260 in 1880 and 1881. Both these churches had managed to develop outstations in the suburbs of the towns. The Grimsby church had one in New Clee and there was a church with 74 members in Monks Road, Lincoln. The new seven-hundred seat St Paul's Baptist chapel in Skegness, where a church was first established in 1894, catered for the needs of vacationing East Midland suburbanites. The Particular Baptists of Boston were divided into two churches. Both Salem and Ebeneezer chapels were located in Liquor Pond Street. They had managed only limited expansion in the countryside around Boston. Salem had 'country members', but had only established a more permanent presence in the fenland settlements of Cowbridge and Holland Fen by 1885. Ebeneezer's only outstation was in Wyberton.[64]

Mint Street in Lincoln held a prominent place among the city's dissenting churches throughout the 19th century. Its first meeting house was built in 1818 and when its trust was renewed in 1871 and again twenty years later it included a spread of Lincoln tradespeople and some craftsmen. Attracting visiting preachers of the calibre of Charles Haddon Spurgeon, who visited the church in December 1883, it maintained its Evangelical Calvinistic position, but reports of decreasing membership, the 'depressed' state of the church, and financial deficits in 1886 and 1887 made its affairs seem more akin to those of the rural Baptist churches. It had withdrawn from its limited commitment in the village of Waddington in 1882. The 'very dilapidated' premises were sold and the money applied to the extension of the church's city-centre premises. Mint Street church still continued to maintain its place in the religious life of Lincoln up to the end of the century and on Sunday 14 March 1903 it had a total attendance of 394 at its services, making it the sixteenth best attended church in Lincoln, but there were nearly half as many people – 136 – at the new church in Monk's Road. It was still in a far more comfortable position than the General Baptists at the Thomas Cooper Memorial Church. Even at its best-attended service on the evening of 14 March 1903 their church was only slightly under a third full.[65]

Notes to Chapter IV

1   *Spec.*, pp. ii–iii, ix; *Bapt. Min.*, p. lxii; Evans List; 1851 Tab. Ret., fols. 69–81; *1851 Census Ret, passim; CYB*, 1871, p. 183, 1899, pp. 283–5; *GBYB*, 1871, pp. 22–5; *BH*, 1871, pp. 138–9, 1900, pp. 294–5.

2   *Spec.*, pp. viii–ix; Evans List, fol. 58; *Diss.*, I, pp. 497, 509.

3   Sp. Ch. Book; LA, Bapt 6, A Statement Relative to the General Baptist Chapel, Lincoln; EMBA Deeds, Ts 189, Coningsby; *Eng. Gen. Bapt.*, II, pp. 112–13; Linc. G. B. Ch.; *Tud. & Stu. Linc.*, p. 194.

4   J. Varley, 'Dissenters' Certificates in the Lincoln Diocesan Records', *LH*, 4 (1949), pp. 172–3, 175–6; F. Baker, 'The Beginnings of Methodism in Lincolnshire', *JLMHS*, 4, 1 (1988), p. 4.

5   J. C. Warren, 'The Folkingham Classis', *TUHS*, II (1919–22), pp. 49–51; Memoir, p. 82; *300 Years*, p. 27; Hunt. Coll., fols. 356, 358, 362, 363; *The Gentleman's Magazine and Historical Chronicle*, XLII (November 1772), p. 502.

CHAPTER V

THE DEVELOPMENT OF METHODISM

JOHN WESLEY'S METHODISM

In June 1742 John Wesley visited Lincolnshire for the first time in 'many years'. It was the beginning of a series of some thirty-seven visits to the county that he recorded in his *Journal*. The last was in the July before his death in March 1791. New places were added to what developed into a regular round of preaching and visits to local Methodist societies, usually beginning and ending at Epworth. The accounts Wesley gave of these visits have tended to dominate the historiography of the Methodist revival, but they need to be read as material that was specifically prepared to provide a public statement of his activities and opinions. The *Journal* served to provide Methodists with an account of Wesley's stewardship, but it also had an apologetic and propagandist purpose. Certain motifs appeared with regularity. One of them was the turbulent crowd, such as the 'rude, wild multitude' that went to hear Wesley preach in Gainsborough Old Hall in August 1759, and were held quiet by his words. Opposition to him in Lincolnshire never reached the levels of fury and violence that he encountered in Cornwall and Staffordshire, although the mob his brother Charles faced at Grimsby in 1747 was dangerous enough. John noted in 1770 that Louth was no longer a 'den of lions', but the people of Horncastle remained a 'wild, unbroken herd' in 1774.[1]

Other deliverances from danger were celebrated in the *Journal*, and often interpreted in terms of the miraculous. In common with many of his contemporaries from all social groups Wesley had a sense of what was perceived to be the providential dispensation that guided his life, but more highly developed in his case because of his rescue as a child from the Epworth rectory fire of 1709. It was evident in the account of his escape when crossing the Trent at Owston Ferry during an October storm in 1743: the more remarkable in his eyes because his brother Charles had also been preserved from wreck while crossing the Severn on the same day and 'as near as we could judge the same hour'. Such occurrences were a justification for his work and people perceived to be opponents were often dismissed without due weight being given to their achievements. The

Countess of Huntingdon's preachers, whose Calvinism Wesley implacably opposed, were stigmatized in his account of Grimsby in 1779 as 'striplings' who had 'neither sense, courage nor grace to go and beat up the devil's quarters in any place where Christ has not been named'. Wesley's dismissal of the parochial ministry of Thomas Adam, the evangelical rector of Winteringham, was a riposte for Adam's rejection of Methodist itinerancy.[2]

It was only gradually that Wesley began to acquire the patriarchal status that he had achieved by the end of his life, when he was frequently invited to preach in parish churches. On his last visit to Lincolnshire he worshipped at Epworth church where there were five times as many at the service and 'ten times as many at the Lord's table, as usual'. He then preached in the market place to 'such a congregation as was never seen before'. By this time he was moving in a world of established local societies, meeting the preachers from the area and visiting the new 'preaching-houses' such as those that had been built recently at Gainsborough and Lincoln. There were some 2,500 Methodists in Lincolnshire by the 1790s and they had built eighteen meeting places, although they were often inadequate for the large numbers who flocked to hear Wesley himself. In the parishes where they existed and were used for Methodist worship the place that they occupied in local religious life was still developing. It was to remain ambiguous until Wesley's death. On his last Epworth visit he had gone to the parish church for Holy Communion, not merely as a gesture towards his upbringing as the son of a former Rector, but as a clergyman who remained committed to the church of his birth. Two years earlier he had found it impossible to persuade the Methodists of the town to attend the Sacrament administered by a curate who had preached against them, while as early as 1747 members of the society at Hainton had been 'repelled from the Sacrament' by the parish clergyman. Local circumstances like these meant that, although many Lincolnshire Methodists continued to communicate in their parish churches, the links that others had with them became more tenuous and their meeting houses more important in their religious lives.[3]

Wesley's visits to towns and villages are invested with considerable significance in local Methodism, but while his later journeys in the county took him around the societies that had been established, there was no systematic plan of evangelisation for even his earliest activities. They were often to meet the requests or needs of existing Methodist societies and it was through his responsiveness to emerging opportunities based on a clear appreciation of the potential inherent in them, that John Wesley made his distinctive contribution to both the evangelistic and the organizational needs of the emerging Methodist movement. He had been at North Scarle in 1759 following contact with the members of a local society established by one of his Moorfields converts, but important though Lincoln was in the life of the county, he did not preach in the city until 1780. On the other hand, he made twenty visits to Grimsby over a period of 45 years from 1743, although he had gone there initially only after he had sent one of his assistant lay preachers, John Nelson, to the town at the request of William Blow, a local cordwainer. While he did not ignore the 'little houses' of Cleethorpes when he visited the village during a local revival in 1781, Wesley was also conscious of the need to work, as far as was possible, within the patterns of authority in local communities. His contacts with sympathetic clergymen such as John Pugh of Rauceby and William Dodwell of Welby gave him a limited purchase within parochial life. In April 1745 he had responded to invitations to visit George Clark, the Rector of East Barkwith and George Lilly, who was then Rector of Hainton. His failure to preach in Lincoln was based on a realistic appreciation of the extent of clerical influence in the city that created a soil 'ungrateful to the tiller's toils'. Contacts with the aristocracy were also limited. Wesley's dismissive comments on the Pelham mausoleum at Great Limber in 1788 reflect his dislike of rich and fashionable society. His association with Robert Carr Brackenbury of Raithby Hall, near Spilsby, was as exceptional for him as Brackenbury's commitment to evangelistic activity was among the Lincolnshire landed gentry. Brackenbury's influence 'commanded both large and respectable congregations' and Wesley's awareness of the importance of the more middling sort also meant that he called on the authority and influence that they exerted. George Stovin of Crowle, a local Justice of the Peace, dismissed Methodist preachers brought before him in 1742, while in July 1748 he allowed Wesley to use his garden so that he could preach undisturbed.[4]

THE MAKING OF LINCOLNSHIRE METHODISM

Structures and membership

By the end of the 1740s the basic structures on which Methodism was to develop had begun to emerge out of the organizing work of John Wesley. An annual conference that he held with the travelling preachers stood over the societies of members that were the bedrock of local Methodist life. Membership figures for the circuits into which societies were grouped began to be returned on a systematic basis to annual conferences from the 1760s. England and Wales were initially divided into seven circuits and in 1746 Lincolnshire was part of one known as Yorkshire, but which also included Cheshire, Lancashire, Derbyshire, Nottinghamshire, and Rutland. The county was designated a circuit in its own right in 1753, but it had a considerable portion of Nottinghamshire attached to it. Full-time travelling preachers were stationed on circuits for a period and when Robert

Costerdine was appointed to what he described as the Epworth circuit in 1764 it took six hundred miles of travelling over a period of twelve weeks to visit the places in it. After he had spent twelve weeks on the Epworth side he moved over to Grimsby. By 1766 there were two Lincolnshire circuits known as Epworth and Grimsby, with 665 and 700 members respectively. They were returned as Lincolnshire East and West from 1770. Each had two travelling preachers who followed the other in turn around them. While there were some fluctuations, their membership grew steadily. By 1801 the area they covered had been divided into six circuits based on Grimsby, Louth, Horncastle, Epworth, Barrow, and Gainsborough. The number was further increased in response to growth in membership, so that while there were ten circuits by 1811, there were 25 by the end of the 19th century.[5]

As they became established the other branches of Methodism set up their own circuit structures in their turn. The first, the Methodist New Connexion, had little direct impact in Lincolnshire. It maintained a limited presence in the Epworth area from its creation in 1797, but Boston was its only Lincolnshire circuit. Largely based on the town it had a continuous existence from the 1830s, although there was a minister there from 1827. The impact of the Primitive Methodists was far greater and they grew to be the second largest branch of Methodism in Lincolnshire. In 1822 their first circuits were based on Scotter, Grimsby, Lincoln, and Louth, but the Ranters, as they were known, ranged over wide distances, driven by the imperatives of revival as much as by any clearly conceived logistical plan. Their over-extended revivalist preachers initially failed to build up the organizations that were needed to sustain their work and the four years from 1825 were said to be a period of 'depression and crisis'. This was followed by recovery and growth so that eight circuits had been created by 1848. The number had grown to 20 by the 1850s. With the addition of others in the second half of the 19th century there were 22 by the time Scunthorpe became head of a circuit in 1896, while the third Grimsby circuit was created in 1899.[6]

A small branch of what became the Wesleyan Methodist Association – a body that had split from the Wesleyan Methodists over what were essentially constitutional grievances in the 1830s – had been established in Louth and Alford in 1836. It was hardly a circuit and it reached its greatest geographical extent in 1838 when it had five places of worship. Its fate after 1847 is obscure, but it was important for the way that it anticipated the later development of Wesleyan Reform. Not all parts of the county were affected equally by the Reform movement of the 1850s, but by the end of the 19th century there were circuits of the United Methodist Free Churches, as most of the Reformers became known, based on all the main and market towns of the county except Bourne, Spilsby, and Stamford. Reports were made to the first assembly of the United Methodist Free Churches in 1857 from Lincolnshire's earliest Reform circuits at Spalding and Lincoln. Those based on Grantham and Louth were established in 1859, at Alford, Boston, and Market Rasen in 1861, and at Stamford for a year, in 1862. After the establishment of a Grimsby circuit in 1869 there were no changes to the structure of United Methodist Free Churches circuits in the county until Lincoln was divided in 1880. Holbeach circuit was created in 1883 and another begun at Gainsborough in 1900 giving the United Methodist Free Churches a total of 12 circuits in the county. The Reform interest was represented in Sleaford by the Wesleyan Reform Union and there was a circuit based on the town from the 1850s. There was also a small Reform Union presence in Grantham until 1880.[7]

Methodism as a whole grew at a greater rate than the population of Lincolnshire until the 1860s (see Table). While Wesleyan Methodist members made up just under 2 per cent of the population of the county when it was virtually the only branch of the Methodist movement in 1801, the combined membership of Wesleyan and Primitive Methodists, with the United Methodist Free Churches, the Wesleyan Reform Union, and Methodist New Connexion was just over 8 per cent of the population of Lincolnshire by 1861. It never reached such a high point again, and while the number of Methodist members continued to grow into the 1880s, it was not at the same pace as the general growth of the county's population. By 1900 the overall level of Methodist membership had fallen back to just under 34,000, comprising 6.8 per cent of the people of Lincolnshire. This was the same proportion as in the 1840s.

There had been fluctuations in Wesleyan Methodist membership, but it was not until the Reform movement of the 1850s, when there was a 30 per cent drop in membership from 22,639 to 15,626 between 1850 and 1854, that the general growth of Wesleyan Methodism was checked in any significant way. The rapid growth of the Reform churches did not make up for Wesleyan losses, so that when the proportion of all Methodist members to the population of the county reached 8 per cent by 1861 this was due to the recovery of the Wesleyans and the continuing growth of the Primitive Methodists.

Membership of the Primitives had fallen back after their initial revivalistic success in the early 1820s, when they gained some 2,000 members in Lincolnshire. There were 1,263 members in 1829, and with fluctuations in the 1830s and 1840s their number reached above 5,000 at the end of the 1840s. The 1850s were a period of considerable growth. Some of this may have been because of the instability engendered by the Reform movement so that Lincolnshire Primitive membership was over 9,000 by 1861. Their numbers continued to increase, again with fluctuations, until they reached a peak of 11,224 in 1884. The ratio of

Primitive Methodist members to the population of the county was at its height in 1891. Membership stood at 10,294 by 1900 when it comprised 2.06 per cent of the county's population.

The Reform movement brought considerable disturbance to those circuits where it took hold, but its overall impact in Lincolnshire was more limited. Although United Methodist Free Churches membership was well over half that of the Primitive Methodists in the 1860s and 1870s, it was nearer a third by 1900. There were 1,725 United Methodist Free Church members in Lincolnshire in 1857 and by 1859 their numbers had more than doubled to 4,118. They reached a peak of 5,952 in 1870, but by 1900 their membership had fallen back to the 3,616 it had been in the late 1850s and 1860s. The small Wesleyan Reform Union, which in the 1860s included circuits such as Alford and Market Rasen, added another few hundred to the number of Reformers and achieved its highest membership of 687 in 1864. Although there were years of recovery, notably in the late 1870s, when its numbers moved again to over 500, there was a general decline in membership of the Union so that by 1899 it had 181 members. Taken together and at their best in the early 1860s, the Reformers had a membership that was 1.4 per cent of the population of the county.

Local societies and their development

Methodist members were grouped within local societies into classes consisting of people who had either undergone a personal conversion experience or were earnestly seeking it and met regularly together to share their spiritual experiences. James Booth of Louth had been 'deeply awakened' to a 'sense of his lost state', and after it had 'pleased God ... to turn his mourning into gladness, and to fill him with joy and peace in believing' he joined the society at Louth in the 1770s. The 'pardoning love of God' was revealed to the soul of Anne Dalton of Keal soon after she joined the local society in 1783; but the influence of Methodism extended beyond these committed members. The visitation returns made by the clergymen for 200 parishes in the 1780s and early 1790s reported a total of 4,162 people who were described as Methodists (Fig. 21). While many are clearly rounded estimates, they indicate that there were nearly twice the number of people identified with Methodism than there were in full membership. One of the largest groups was in Heckington where there were said to be 250 Methodists, but there were other places such as Helpringham where there was said to be only one person in a village associated with the Methodists. The average size of groups in Lincolnshire was just under 20, although the presence of Methodists in a parish did not necessarily mean that there was a society there. When Elizabeth Richardson moved to Ravendale sometime in the 1760s she had to walk the three or four miles to Waltham or Binbrook for class meetings.[8]

Methodist members as a percentage of the population of Lincolnshire 1801–1900

Year	Population	Wesleyan Methodist	%	Primitive Methodist	%	UMFC & WRU	%	Methodist New Connexion	Total Methodists	% Total Methodism
1801	208,625	4,112	1.97						4,112	1.97
1811	235,224	6,316	2.69						6,316	2.69
1821	283,058	11,164	3.94						11,164	3.94
1831	317,288	13,211	4.16	1,642	0.52				14,853	4.68
1841	362,602	20,233	5.58	4,553	1.26			143	24,929	6.87
1851	407,222	19,945	4.90	7,068	1.74			126	27,139	6.66
1861	412,246	18,636	4.52	9,090	2.20	5,758	1.40	126	33,610	8.15
1871	436,624	19,323	4.43	9,383	2.15	5,986	1.37	60	34,752	7.96
1881	469,947	20,341	4.33	10,372	2.21	5,087	1.08	52	35,852	7.63
1891	472,907	20,331	4.30	10,695	2.25	4,504	0.95	68	35,548	7.52
1900	498,808	19,684	3.95	10,294	2.06	3,818	0.77	131	33,927	6.80

UMFC = United Methodist Free Churches   WRU = Wesleyan Reform Union

At the time of John Wesley's death there were Methodists in only just over a third of Lincolnshire parishes, but they were not spread evenly throughout the county. There were said to be as many as 100 among the 32 families of the parish of Raithby where Robert Carr Brackenbury provided local leadership. His influence also meant that there were people connected with Methodism in a cluster of neighbouring parishes. The Raithby class included members from Aswardby, Hagworthingham, Hundleby, and Sausthorpe. Methodism had also spread along the Marsh and in the north of the county there was hardly a parish on the south bank of the Humber that did not have some sort of Methodist presence. In some places numbers were large both in absolute terms and in proportion to the size of the population. There were said to be 40 Methodists from 42 families in South Ferriby. The large numbers in the Isle of Axholme and the Trentside villages to the east were undoubtedly related to looser social structures that had enabled religious dissent to flourish there since the 17th century, but Methodism was less strong in the similar environment of the south Lincolnshire fenland parishes. There were said to be as many as 70 Methodists in the parish of Swineshead, but none in Holbeach. Apart from a group of places that included and lay to the immediate north and east of Sleaford, the majority of which were in the fens or on the fen edge, Methodists were thinly spread in the parishes of Kesteven where the authorities exercised a firm control over parish affairs. The situation was similar to the north of Lincoln. A small knot of places in the Market Rasen and Tealby area had a more substantial Methodist presence, as did a group of parishes around Brigg. As many as 75 Methodists were returned from Elsham, a place with a long dissenting tradition.[9]

Methodism did not necessarily become established in places because of the weakness of other churches, but rather because of its ability to find a niche within the structures of parish life, whether these were the product of landlord influence or the attitudes that developed in less ordered communities. If the presence or absence of a resident Anglican clergyman is taken as an indicator of the pastoral strength or weakness of the Church of England, this was of little significance in the overall growth of Methodism. The incumbents of 136 of the Lincolnshire parishes in which there were Methodists between 1788 and 1792 were not resident, but there were another 66 in which Methodists coexisted with a resident clergyman. Although there was some confusion as to the composition of the groups that were said to be Protestant Dissenters from the Church of England their distribution was, like the Methodists, also unrelated to the diligence of the parish clergy. There were 4,129 Protestant Dissenters recorded in the 1788 to 1792 visitation returns, making them as strong as the Methodists. This was indicative of the extent to which the other dissenting bodies, influenced in their various ways by the Evangelical Revival, represented an

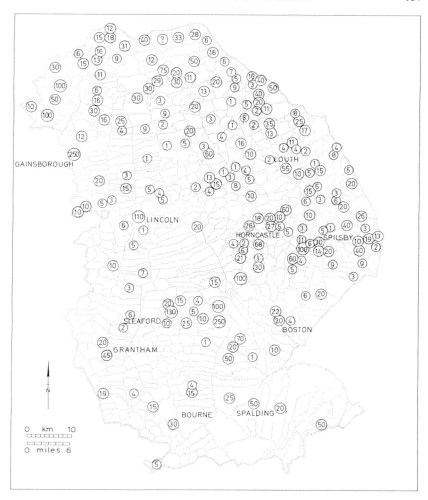

*Fig. 21   The Distribution of Methodists in the late 18th Century. The returns of
Methodists made by clergymen at visitations between 1788 and 1792 is indicative of
the spread of Methodism in Lincolnshire parishes during the period. While the
accuracy of the returns for individual parishes was dependent on the clergyman who
made them, the figures give a general impression of the growth of Methodism in the
county by the time of John Wesley's death in 1791. While Methodism became well
established in areas where the Protestant dissenters had been strong, it was not
universally successful in them. Nor did Methodism only flourish at this time in a
particular type of loosely structured local community. While there were reported to
be no Methodists in fenland parishes such as Holbeach, and while they were more
thinly spread in the more tightly controlled parishes of Kesteven, their presence in
the cluster of south Wold parishes, where the influence of the Methodist sympathiser
and preacher Robert Carr Brackenbury was strong, shows the importance of
influential local leadership in the development of Methodism.*
Source: Spec 4

*Fig. 22   Gainsborough Wesleyan Methodist chapel opened in 1804.
One of the large chapels often built in prominent positions in towns
to serve increasingly prosperous congregations.*

alternative to the Methodists at this period. Wesley's tetchy attitude to
Calvinistic dissenters and the suspicion that the Methodists elicited among
the Baptists demonstrated the extent to which the various groups of
evangelical Protestants were perceived, at least by their leaders, as being in
competition within the general context of revival.[10]

There were 66 parishes, often larger places such as Horncastle, in which
there were both Methodist and Protestant dissenters, but in most parishes it
was one or the other at this date. In 82 places Protestant Dissenters had no
competition from the Methodists while in the majority of places – 134 or 67
per cent – where Methodists had been able to establish themselves there
were no other dissenters. In a fluid situation individuals moved relatively
easily between the various religious groups. A lodger of 'exemplary life'
and 'holy conversation' who was a member of the Countess of
Huntingdon's Connexion, but who attended Horncastle Methodist chapel,
stirred the interest of the parents of Thomas Edman, the Methodist
travelling preacher. After Edward Wilson of Grainthorpe was awakened by
Methodist preaching in the 1770s he was 'beset' by some General Baptists
who tried to persuade him that he was deceived on the matter of adult

baptism.[11]

The applications that were made to the diocesan authorities to license premises for worship in Lincolnshire between 1770 and 1813 are further evidence of the fluidity that characterized this formative stage of local Methodist life. As well as the 591 applications made specifically for Methodists a number of their registrations were included among the 825 applications made between 1786 and 1824 for groups who described themselves as Protestant Dissenters. They were also included in another 239 applications for Independents made between 1749 and 1844. Most of them were for private houses. Death, disaffection, and the movement of families meant that these meetings were forced to move from house to house. Until a chapel was opened in 1810 six houses were used at various times in Laceby and Aylesby. Other Methodist societies achieved a measure of permanence by meeting in the same house for a number of years, but until they were fixed within the walls of legally secure chapels, the circumstances of local Methodist societies often remained insecure.[12]

Three generations of the Cheeseman family were said to have sustained Wesleyan Methodism in Apley and later meetings were held in their carpenter's shop. Yet despite the tolerance, even encouragement of some landlords, house meetings in tenanted properties remained susceptible to pressure from above. The society in the village of Irby-upon-Humber remained for nearly half a century in a 'thatched cottage near the church'. Although they had suffered some harassment, complaints about them to the steward of the Brocklesby estate fell on deaf ears. He pointed out that Methodists were 'some of the best tenants Lord Yarborough had'. The possession of a freehold property gave some degree of independence to people who made their homes available for Methodist worship, but it did not confer immunity from mob action. Thomas and Grace Emery of Great Gonerby had their windows broken frequently, while dead animals and 'various kinds of filth' were thrown at the people who met there.[13]

The movement of preachers, and the people who went to hear them, made Methodists appear as 'a wandering tribe of fanatical teachers'. Their disregard for the boundaries that structured the parochially based Church of England aroused the distrust and hostility that motivated some of the fiercest persecution they faced. The periodic visits of the circuit travelling preacher – the 'Methodist Parson' – a person seen as one who was 'not of their way', 'one of a strange tongue, and from a strange country', increased the sense that Methodism alienated its adherents from the local communities to which they belonged. Methodists also threatened the comfortable accommodation between clergy and people that left parishioners relatively undisturbed in matters of religion. Local narratives of the growth of Methodism are often stereotyped but, although the relative importance of its various components varied from parish to parish, they

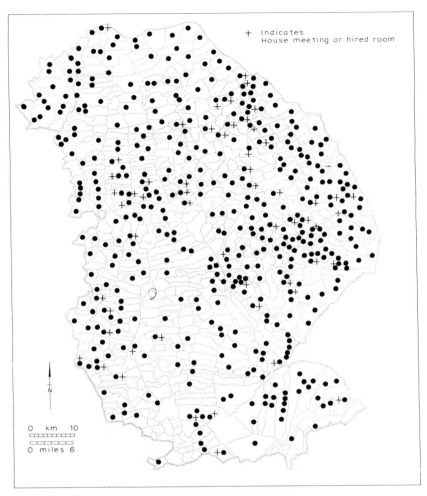

*Fig. 23   Wesleyan Methodist Places of Worship, 1851. By the middle of the 19th
century Wesleyan Methodism was established as the leading nonconformist
denomination in Lincolnshire. There were chapels or meeting houses in the majority
of Lincolnshire parishes, and it was only in the gentry dominated villages of the
Bourne, Sleaford and Stamford areas that the Wesleyan Methodists, in common with
the other branches of Methodism, were less successful in finding or building
premises in which to worship. Not all of their meeting places were purpose built
chapels, but this was only the case in a minority of parishes. These tended to be
concentrated in areas where local influence, principally that of unsympathetic
gentry or clergymen, made it difficult to obtain land on which chapels could be built.*

Source: Rel. Wor.; 1851 Census Ret.

delineate the main elements of the opposition that was encountered. This depended on the ways in which the affairs of communities were ordered. In some it was the 'squire of the parish', who supported action against Methodists. In others it was said to be 'a blustering influential farmer' or 'not unfrequently the clergyman himself' who either directly or tacitly conferred a measure of local legitimacy on anti-Methodist mobs. The absence of a resident clergyman would leave the religious affairs of the parish under the influence of local lay people.[14]

The involvement of individuals varied according to the place they occupied within the parish community. The constables of Wrangle took part in action against the travelling preacher Thomas Mitchell in 1751, holding him captive and seeking the advice of 'the minister' as to what to do. The extreme violence that marked the attacks on Mitchell came after he was released into the hands of 'the mob', but when they had finished, they deferred to the clergyman, followed his advice and took him '"out of the parish"'. At Navenby the influence of Mr Hazard, 'a gentleman of independent fortune', was not suffficiently strong to protect the Wesleyan preachers when they went to the village in 1792. An 'abundance of strong drink' given by 'rich farmers' added an air of the carnivalesque to the 'depredations' of the local mob.[15]

The Church of England and the development of Methodism

The 38 Methodist meetings said to exist in the 100 Lincolnshire parishes covered by a report from Lincolnshire clergy made in 1800 included an unspecified number of places where Methodists remained close to the Church of England. The first Methodist presence in the Grantham area, at Great Gonerby, grew out a small society of poor people whom the curate, Dr Palmer, had gathered in the parsonage house for 'religious conversation and prayer' in the 1760s. Two of its members, a baker and his wife, later opened their house for Methodist preaching and maintained it in the face of local opposition. Their own route into Methodism and the contacts the Gonerby Methodists made with the society at North Scarle linked them to that part of the Evangelical Revival that developed from the older religious societies in which John Wesley himself had experienced conversion. The society at Skillington was also identified with individuals who had experienced evangelical conversion as members of the Church of England. Clergymen like Pugh of Rauceby and Dodwell from nearby Welby maintained contact with converts of this kind, while Dr Ford of Melton Mowbray crossed the county boundary from Leicestershire to join Dodwell in 'planting the seeds of piety' in several parts of what became the Grantham Wesleyan circuit. During his short ministry at Waddington, which ended in 1816, Waldo Sibthorpe, then in his evangelical phase, took over the Methodist society, but when he left 'his sheep were ... without a shepherd'.[16]

While individual clerical sympathizers were important, they were not widespread, and the main influence of the Church of England on local Methodism was more general. A central element was the Christian education that it provided. This gave a foundation on which the evangelical experience offered by Methodism could be built. The catechizing that was carried out among the large numbers of young people who were presented for confirmation was the basis for the development of their religious understanding, while the 140 parish schools that existed in Lincolnshire by the beginning of the 19th century not only provided religious instruction, but produced people whose levels of literacy enabled them to further their personal spiritual development and theological understanding through reading, discussion, and debate.[17]

The future Methodist travelling preacher George Shadford, who was born in 1739 and brought up in Scotter, was sent to be catechized every Sunday and was confirmed at the age of fourteen. Shadford deviated from this path when he began to read 'books that were entertaining to youth ... such as Ovid's Metamorphoses, and his Art of Love', but the education that he received served him well when he turned to less 'carnal' matters. Isabella Belton imbibed 'certain Calvinistic notions' from the teacher of the school that she attended at Barrow on Humber in the 1790s, but her education enabled her to read Fletcher's *Checks to Antinomianism*. This provided her with 'those clear views of Christian life, that she retained to the end of her life.' John Hannah, a Lincoln atttorney, had been prepared for the conversion he was to experience among the Methodists by the instruction 'in the principles of religion' given by his parents who were both devout Anglicans.[18]

Upbringings of this kind also inculcated a concern with moral questions that were often the basis for a search for the assurance of personal salvation through evangelical conversion. Catherine Hubbard, who was born at North Scarle in 1768, was brought up by parents who were 'in low circumstances in life, and members of the Established Church', but 'paid ... attention to their morals'. Adolescent lapses from the values learnt in the parental home are frequently referred to in Methodist biographies to point up changes brought about by eventual conversion. George Shadford said that his 'propensity to sin' increased with his 'flow of animal spirits' and his fondness for 'wrestling, running, leaping, football, dancing, and such like sports' grew. During the time that William Robinson served his apprenticeship as a wheelwright at Kelstern in the late 1740s and early 1750s he was 'as careless about the salvation of his soul as though he had not one to be saved or lost'. Charles Richardson, on the other hand, was reckoned to have been providentially directed and controlled when he was hired as a farm servant at Horncastle Statute Fair in 1811. It was then that he entered the employment and household, and so came under the influence of Mr William Riggall, a Wesleyan circuit steward. There might also be an element of rebellion in becoming a Methodist. The father of Mary Andrews of Hogsthorpe was a 'strict churchman' who saw Methodists as the false prophets spoken of in Scripture. Nevertheless, the search to fulfil the values and address concerns that had been imparted through education and upbringing lay behind the conversion of many early Methodists.[19]

Meeting houses and chapels

As well as those Methodists who remained close to the Church of England, the report of 1800 also identified local societies whose members rarely went to church and had begun to administer the Sacrament at their own meetings. The increasing numbers of Lincolnshire societies that petitioned the Methodist conference to hold the Lord's Supper in their own meeting houses marked the beginning of a new phase in the development of Methodism in the county. These moves arose out of the individual circumstances of local societies, working within the context of parish communities. There were no general characteristics that distinguished places where this course of action was adopted. Joseph Benson argued that preaching was held in church hours only in 'extensive' parishes, where the minister was notoriously wicked, taught 'dangerous' doctrines, or in large towns. Even there the celebration of Holy Communion by the Methodists did not clash with that in the parish church. In 1800 societies in parishes as different as South Kelsey, Grimsby, Grainthorpe, and North Somercotes asked for permission to celebrate the Sacrament, although by 1802, when places such as Barton-upon-Humber, Brigg and Sleaford were also granted permission to hold the service, market towns were well represented among the places petitioning Conference. Boston joined them in 1803. Whatever the particular local context, as more meeting houses were built and used by Methodists who had less direct experience of the Church of England than an earlier generation, the sense of separate Methodist identity increased.[20]

The building and maintenance of chapels involved local societies in considerable expense. Those at Aubourn and Navenby on the Lincoln circuit were provided by leading local Methodists, but care was needed to ensure that these buildings were legally secured to the connexion as a whole. A new chapel built at Market Rasen in 1800 was registered for worship as the property of Samuel Fox, but although three men financed one opened at Skillington in 1802 it was 'settled upon trustees, at the time of its erection, in the usual way of security to the society'. The willingness and ability of societies and their members to take on the responsibility for chapels was seen as enhancing their standing in their local communities as they moved from house-based worship to a more public position in local life. In 1801 the chapel at Lincoln was said to have become 'regularly occupied by persons of greater respectability ... than had formerly been the case so that in the minds of some persons ... the tide of public feeling appeared to be turning in favour of ... the Wesleyan cause'. Yet while there were already some 40 chapels and preaching rooms that were used solely for worship in Lincolnshire by the end of the 18th century there were another 210 societies that did not have this advantage. By 1851 the situation was reversed. Just short of 90 per cent of the 462 Wesleyan places of worship in the county were, in effect, chapels, and classified as separate buildings given up to worship (Fig. 23). Only 47, such as the dwelling house in Swallow where a congregation of fourteen or fifteen people assembled, remained from the period when Wesleyan Methodism had largely depended on meetings in private houses or premises that were temporarily set aside for worship. The transition from a religious life with a predominantly domestic base to one based in chapels and meeting houses represented a profound shift in many aspects of Methodist life.[21]

The social composition of Methodism

The use of private houses for religious meetings meant that women were able to extend the influence that they exercised in domestic matters into religious life. The proportion of women who were involved in Lincolnshire Methodism remained high, although the type of influence that they exerted changed towards the end of the 18th century. Dinah Simpson, who died at Epworth in 1805 where she had belonged to the local society for over forty years, had led a class composed of single women. In 1769 the Grimsby society had a class of 20 members made up exclusively of women and there was another at Louth with 16 members. By 1784 55 per cent of membership of the 31 societies in the Grimsby circuit were women, and although the percentage had decreased by 4 per cent by 1790 and was 47 per cent by 1792, the proportion of women in other places remained higher. It was 53 per cent in the 27 societies of the Spalding circuit in 1823 and had increased to 59 per cent by 1837. By then the place of women within Methodism had changed as the number of married couples in local societies increased. In 1784 39 per cent of class members in the Grimsby circuit were married couples and the proportion rose to 49 per cent by 1790. The number of male members who were married grew at the expense of the unmarried, although the proportion of unmarried women in the Grimsby circuit societies remained constant at 9 per cent of membership and there was no increase in the number of married women who were members without their husbands. Sixty-eight per cent of the Spalding circuit members in 1823 were married, although not all to each other. These changes ultimately strengthened the importance of the household and family in Methodist life leaving local societies less apparently welcoming to those whose place in the local community was less secure. As patterns of authority changed so did the roles of the sexes and in 1788 the Grimsby circuit minister William Fish saw the ideal Methodist minister's wife as 'able to preach by the fireside and in the class, or by a sick bed'. Her husband occupied the pulpit.[22]

A substantial proportion of the new and married male Methodist members were farmers. Their numbers grew from 9 per cent of membership in 1784 to 14 per cent by 1792 and they quickly became dominant in small village societies. The appellation 'farmer' covers a variety of circumstances in Lincolnshire, but comparisons between farmers from different areas are less important than the position that their occupation gave them within their own local communities. '[I]nfluential' farmers possessed the authority to lead the mobs that attacked Methodist preachers in south Lincolnshire parishes, but those of them who became Methodists began, as established figures in their communities, and as heads of households, with their wives and families also in membership, to provide leadership to local Methodism. A 'number of farmers' were 'led to espouse the cause' in Skillington. Their 'steady attachment to the interests of [M]ethodism distinguished their character for a succession of years' and made the society 'one of the best and most influential in the circuit'. Tradesmen and craftsmen were another important group in Methodist life, particularly as town membership grew and became more varied, although craftsmen such as weavers, who comprised 6 per cent of the Grimsby circuit membership in 1784, became less important within village societies. By 1790 the proportion of tradesmen in local Methodism had more than doubled and 2.5 per cent of members were shopkeepers, a sixfold increase over the position in 1784. Shoemakers, who were 2 per cent of its membership in 1784, increased to 4 per cent in the same period. These increases were at the expense of other groups. Labourers had made up 14 per cent of the members in eastern Lincolnshire in 1784, but the proportion had dropped to 11 per cent by 1790. The most remarkable change in the period was, however, among female members.[23]

There were 168 married and unmarried females said to be employed as spinsters recorded as members in the Grimsby circuit in 1784. They had almost totally disappeared from its records by 1790. While this may be due in part to differing record keeping practices, the fact that they ceased to be recognized as a group is indicative of the changes which were taking place within Methodism as it moved from the predominantly domestic base in which these female workers played an important part. This was associated with broader changes in patterns of female employment in the county, especially in the Marsh where many of the societies in the Grimsby circuit were located. The need for domestically based female hand spinners lessened as the local wool industry declined in the face of opposition from arable farmers and landlords concerned to control the local labour supply.

It was a change that impinged on the ministry that women were able to exercise within local Methodism.[24]

John Wesley had attempted to 'put a final stop to the preaching of women' in the Grimsby circuit in 1780, but at this date they still had a place in cottage meetings giving scope for the 'ardent spirit' of women such as Ann Carr, a revivalist preacher from Market Rasen. The minister Zachariah Taft, who gave Ann her first society ticket in the late 1790s, was married to another female preacher. Like her, Carr had quickly graduated from class leader to preacher. As an independent woman – '[s]ome thought her too obtrusive, talkative, and zealous' – it became difficult for her to find a place within the hardening structures of Wesleyan Methodism, particularly after Market Rasen became the head of a circuit rather than a distant appendage of Grimsby. After leaving the county and a period in which she was involved with the early Primitive Methodists, she became a roving evangelist among the textile workers of the Leeds area. Many of these women were migrants from the countryside whose work was supplanting that of the disappearing spinsters of rural Lincolnshire. Preaching among them, Carr found the freedom for her distinctive religious voice that was being denied her in the changing Methodist societies of Lincolnshire.[25]

Growth and consolidation

The revival that began among the Methodists at Epworth during Christmastide 1781 was rooted in prayer meetings held in houses, but it spread into the local linen manufactories and their workforce of children and young women. It was marked by its demonstrative fervour as people experienced visionary dreams and fell to the floor crying for mercy and 'a larger manifestation of the love of God'. The Epworth revival was noteworthy for its scale and its initial impact among a well defined group of people. Many of the other conversions that brought people into Methodism were on a less large and dramatic scale, although their significance for the individuals involved remained considerable. Thomas Edman, who was awakened during a 'reviving time' at the Horncastle circuit Quarterly Meeting in 1786, went on to become a full-time travelling preacher. Cycles of revival brought extraordinary growth, but needed to be consolidated into society membership. In Cleethorpes the scattered farmhouse and cottage meetings of the earliest phase of Methodist life coalesced into a group of 15 or 16 members that continued at this level into the late 1770s. A revival pushed membership to a height of 42 by the early 1780s. This declined over the next ten years and was 26 in 1791. Another revival took membership to 54 in 1796, to fall back again to 37 by 1800.[26]

Spread across the county as a whole these patterns of growth and consolidation produced a relatively steady increase in Methodist membership throughout the 18th century. Slower progress in the late 1790s coincided with the constraints that came from the transition into the more ordered environment of chapel-based religion. There was a loss of 69 members in the county by 1800, and national membership also faltered in the same period, but at 1.97 per cent of population, the level of Methodist membership in Lincolnshire was more than twice as high as that in Britain as a whole. While it is possible to seek an explanation for general patterns of Methodist growth by considering the fluctuating material circumstances of converts, their decisions were ultimately located in their personal experiences and concerns. Changes in the sorts of people who became converts reflected the ways in which Methodism was developing and the expectations that they had of it. The demands of a more institutionalized religious life left less room for the idiosyncratically personal approach of preachers such as Ann Carr, while the general relationship between membership growth and increases in the level of real wages that became apparent from the late 1790s is evidence of the way that Methodism was becoming an attractive outlet for religious aspirations of those with time and resources to devote to it.[27]

Despite the fears that were aroused by itinerant preachers – a 'wandering tribe of fanatical leaders, mostly taken from the lowest and most illiterate class of society' – Methodism was becoming an increasingly conservative body whose leaders were concerned to gain the 'respect' that they were reported as achieving on the Lincoln circuit by the early 19th century. Their status was seen as being enhanced as societies moved into chapel buildings, so that even revival became a more structured phenomenon when it was confined within their walls. There was a 'very gracious spiritual awakening and conviction of sin' in Aubourn that began at Christmas 1827 and continued for several months, but it took place among the hearers who had filled the village chapel after its enlargement rather than people unattached to chapel life. Other revivals at Bassingham, Branston, and Heighington were taken as signs that the chapels in these places answered the purposes for which they were built. They were also the bases from which the emerging elite of male farmers, tradesmen and craftsmen controlled Wesleyan affairs. William Mawer had battled against '[re]proach and persecution' during his early days as a local preacher in the Lincoln circuit. His later life was marked by the esteem that he had acquired through service to Methodist institutions as a 'trustee for almost all the Chapels built in this neighbourhood, for the period of twenty years' as well as being society and circuit steward, and treasurer of the missionary and other societies.[28]

Eight of the 13 trustees for the new Wesleyan chapel at Barton-upon-Humber in 1798 were farmers. They served with two carpenters, a shopkeeper, a tailor, and a miller. Over the next forty years chapel affairs in the Isle of Axholme also came to be dominated by farmers who comprised

88 out of a total of 156 trustees: the largest single occupational group. The next largest group of trustees was 21 craftsmen, while there were nine tradesmen and nine labourers. They were the leaders who set the tone of Methodism. Chapel congregations were more broadly based. The early 19th century register for the Lincoln circuit recorded the baptisms of children from 26 families that were sufficiently committed to Methodism no longer to want to go to the established church for the rite. It shows that at this stage of Methodist development its leaders were less inclined to separate totally from the Church of England than these more modest members of local communities. While the baptismal registers included three families of farmers, there were also the children of two labourers, two framework knitters, with a weaver, a brush manufacturer, a cordwainer, a tailor, a bookseller, a carpenter, a stocking maker, a basket maker, a shoe maker, a mason, and a leather cutter. There was, however, also a brewer and a surgeon.[29]

Spalding circuit covered an area in which small farmers were an important part of the local agrarian economy, but there were nearly twice as many labourers as the 42 farmers among the parents who brought their children to Spalding chapel for baptism between 1823 and 1837. The number of craftsman exceeded that of farmers by one, while there were

Fig. 24   New Bolingbroke Wesleyan Methodist chapel. Built in 1825 it gave the Wesleyan Methodists a visible presence in this new fenland community. The building was arranged to provide space for the preaching that was a central part of Methodist chapel life.

also eight fathers who were tradesmen. In areas with a larger number of town-based members the proportion of Wesleyan Methodist employed in retail trades was greater so that, with skilled workers, they made between 45 and 47 per cent of the parents whose children were baptized in Lincolnshire in the first four decades of the 19th century. In the county as a whole around 40 per cent of the parents having children baptized in Wesleyan chapels were unskilled workers, the majority of whom were labourers. Yet while these figures are significant, the large number of people in similar occupations who remained outside Methodism is a reminder that its general impact among these social groups remained limited.[30]

Despite the varied social composition of the people who chose Methodist baptism for their children, there was still a sense that 'instead of the Gospel being, as at the first, principally preached to the poor' its net had begun to be spread to 'enclose the rich'. It was even said that there had been a 'solicitous angling for large fishes'. The increasingly complex institutions of Methodism not only needed prosperous supporters, but provided the newly prosperous with a field for service in which they gained the recognition through office that might still be denied them in more socially conservative communities. As the number of circuits grew, more ministers were also needed to serve on them. Their increased status in a highly developed organization meant that their personal expectations also grew. When John A. Beech became a probationary minister on the Horncastle circuit in 1810, Wesleyan ministers did not 'usually come from a humbler rank in life than did the Apostles and Evangelists of the Saviour'. While 'not many mighty' were called, neither could they 'properly be said to be gathered from the offscourings of society'. By 1820 the Grantham circuit accounts not only included payments for the houses and the stipends of ministers, but a provision for domestic service which, at two guineas a quarter, was nearly a tenth of total circuit expenditure.[31]

Ministers began to gain esteem as much for their administrative abilities as their spiritual leadership. Robert Day was presented with a 'handsome silver cup' when he left Boston circuit after three years in 1833. His 'judicious and indefatigable exertions to promote the welfare of the societies under his care' had led to the removal of both the circuit debt and that at Boston chapel. Despite the relatively short time individual ministers stayed in circuits, cooperation between them and lay officers was strengthened as they visited the homes of leading laymen. Here they received gifts as well as hospitality, particularly on their visits to country chapels. It was claimed in 1838 that even the pastoral visits of ministers were influenced by their 'almost intuitive perception of the strict necessity of making frequent calls in certain directions while ... a large part of the flock may be neglected with impunity'.[32]

*Fig. 25   Boston Centenary Wesleyan chapel, showing the arrangement of seats.
Those that were in the most desirable positions commanded the highest rents. The
income from them was used to heat, light, and maintain the building.*

The maintenance of the institutions of Methodism figured large among the preoccupations of both ministers and lay officers, and there was a danger that mission would become subordinated to it. The greater value that was accorded to the contributions of the prosperous not only made itself felt in the general social life associated with chapels, but was demonstrated in arrangements for worship. The special collections and subscriptions that accompanied the opening of new chapels were used to reduce the debts incurred in building the new premises. Over £18 was collected on two successive Sundays when special sermons were preached to mark the opening of the chapel at Humberston in 1835. Thirty pounds had been raised by private subscription, but in the end responsibility for these debts lay with local congregations who also met the running costs of chapels including heating, lighting, and maintenance. A regular income came from renting chapel seats to worshippers. In large town chapels such as Centenary in Boston, opened in 1840 and built at a cost of nearly £10,000, it was possible to offer a variety of seats. The highest rent at Horncastle chapel in 1818 was the three shillings a half year charged for the front row of the gallery. In the body of the chapel front row seats were two shillings a half year reducing to a shilling – the lowest pew rent in the building – for the back rows. A range of people was able to afford rented pews in the more modest village chapel at Horsington in 1840, but while ten of the twenty farmers and six of the 13 craftsmen in the parish rented pews, only six of the 32 labourers' families had seats there.[33]

William Bailey Gilbert of New Leake, who died in 1876, was the third generation of his family be a Methodist member. Wesleyan members were coming increasingly from within the groups that had already had some sort of association with the connexion. Gilbert's conversion had come after he had attended a sermon at Alford. Summertime open-air preaching undertaken in the villages of the Grantham circuit in 1817 was seen as an innovative revival of a 'primitive and apostolic practice'. People who attended worship without entering into full membership, and whose children attended Sunday schools, were a further potential source of new members. They were also a considerable addition to the influence of Methodism, and their numbers were an important indicator of the place that Methodism occupied within local communities. Adult adherents were often sufficiently regular in their attendance at worship to rent pews and the people who did this consistently outnumbered members. Fifty-nine people rented 90 seats in the chapel at Fenton in 1851, although there were only 30 members in the local society. In the 1830s it was reckoned that Wesleyan congregations were three times the number of members, and this was still the situation in the fifteen chapels of the Wainfleet circuit in 1851 where membership equalled 32 per cent of the congregations at the best-attended services. In other areas the percentage was higher, although less markedly so in some. It was 35 per cent in Sleaford circuit, and 37 per cent at Epworth, but rose to 43 per cent in Barton, 45 per cent in Coningsby, and 47 per cent in Grimsby. The small numbers in many village societies meant that the movements of only a few people caused official membership figures to fluctuate widely and there were considerable variations in the ratio of members to adherents at this level. This may have been a factor in the low ratio of 4 to 1 members to adherents in the congregations of the two Lincolnshire chapels in the Stamford circuit, although it was one of the areas where Wesleyan Methodism was less well developed.[34]

REVIVALISM AND WESLEYAN REFORM

Primitive Methodism originated as an 'offshoot' from Wesleyan Methodism. Its early leaders moved beyond the conservatism and rigidities that had developed in the parent body in their quest for a more vigorous approach to evangelism, attracting new converts and adherents from outside existing Methodist organizations. This distinguished them from the Reformers in the 1850s whose members came out of the parent body and established new organizations in fulfilment of their ideals. Despite the appeal which the leaders of the Reform 'secession' made to general constitutional principles, their grass roots support was built up from a sense of unease at the apparent insensitivity of ministers and officers to the spiritual and social needs of local societies and their adherents that had developed in the first half of the 19th century. By the 1850s the rhetoric of what were to most local members relatively abstract constitutional issues provided the vehicle for the articulation of their more mundane, but nonetheless keenly experienced concerns. In the politics of a situation where personality as well as persuasiveness was often crucial in determining local outcomes, individual ministers and laymen played a pivotal role.[35]

The Ranter revivalists

Primitive Methodists came into Lincolnshire from Derbyshire and Nottinghamshire in 1817 and 1818, after spreading eastwards from Staffordshire and Cheshire. Its leaders, Hugh Bourne and William Clowes, had been expelled from Wesleyan Methodism for revivalist activities that had taken them outside its formal structures and discipline. Thomas Cooper's account of Primitive Methodist activities in Gainsborough encapsulates the impression created by Primitive preachers, whose style earned them the soubriquet of Ranters. They entered the town in late 1818 'singing aloud as they walked along the street, in their way to the market-place – "Turn to the Lord and seek salvation!"' In the relative freedom of the town it was possible to follow up open-air preaching with meetings in houses. A society was formed and a building acquired for use as a small chapel. At Grantham the Primitives were able to find some protection for their open-air preaching because of the divisions that existed among the authorities in the town, although this was not before the preacher John Wedgwood had been imprisoned. Like the early Methodists of the 18th century, the Primitive Methodists also faced opposition when their preachers first entered villages. Accounts of their persecution are, like those of the early Wesleyans, often formulaic: the 'heralds of the coming day' are pitched against 'benighted villagers'. The crowds that John Hallsworth faced in the Lincoln area in 1818 were said to have expressed their opposition to his activities and their adherence to the *status quo* through engaging in traditional pastimes. As well as the eggs, stones, and dirt that were thrown, it was said that 'Cocks were fighting; – bells were ringing; – men were drinking and smoking and holding up their hands and hallooing'. Primitive Methodist preachers were objects of suspicion for the way they attracted 'farmers' servants, day-labourers, and village mechanics' so that 'constables wishing to ingratiate themselves with the upper classes, laid information against these poor preachers as disturbers of the peace'. As their preachers ranged across the area in their search for souls, 'being designedly met by people from neighbouring parishes', parading the streets 'with turbulence and uproar' and openly denouncing the clergy, they were, in the eyes of a clergyman from the Spalding area, an 'organized banditti of strolling Methodists, vociferating Ranters, and all that impious train of *et caeteras [sic]*'.[36]

All-day Primitive Methodist gatherings for preaching and prayer were named camp meetings after the North American frontier gatherings, accounts of which had inspired Bourne and Clowes. They incurred the condemnation of Wesleyan leaders, fearful that assemblies of large numbers of people combined with what appeared to be uncontrolled revivalism would affect the standing of Methodism in the eyes of the civil authorities. Reports of the first camp meetings to be held in Lincolnshire did not express fears of unrest, but they were sufficiently popularly tumultuous occasions to attract people away from their local communities and the constraints that might be imposed on their behaviour in them. Worried commentators attempted to discredit the meetings. Their large numbers were a cause for comment, while the proceedings were said to have occasioned derision if not consternation among 'the rational part of the auditors'. One at Caistor in 1819 was said to have been attended by between three and four thousand people, while there were 1,600 at a camp meeting at Waltham in August 1821. Another held to the north of Lincoln in May 1819 – a time when farm servants moved to new hirings and were free from the restraints of employment – attracted 'farmers' labourers with a large proportion of women and children'. The Caistor meeting was described as 'an ill spent sabbath' and the 'tendency to confusion rather than order' that was said to be engendered by the Primitives led commentators to make specious comparisons between them and the Ranters of the 17th century. They wound themselves up '[t]o such a pitch of frenzy ... that their gesture and actions assimilate nearer to the orgies of the Heathen, than to the dignified deportment and calm devoutness of the Christian worshipper'.[37]

People like Samuel Sharp, a thatcher from the village of Messingham, found a revivalistic fervour among the Primitives that they felt was absent from the increasingly decorous and institutionalized religious life of the Wesleyan Methodist chapels. Sharp had been a Wesleyan but, after a lapse of three years, joined the Primitives in 1819 together with 'some of the elders among the Wesleyans who had seen Primitive Methodism in the days of Wesley' and 'knew it again when they saw it in the days of Clowes and Bourne'. The preachers John Harrison and Sarah Healand were accused by a Wesleyan local preacher in Caistor of creating divisions in Methodism. Harrison's response that they wanted 'none of his sheep, but those which were upon the mountains, which had no shepherd ... the outcasts of society' was an accurate assessment of the place that the Primitives came to occupy within Lincolnshire Methodism. They were able to build on informal revivalistic networks that had developed on the fringes of official Methodism. John Oxtoby, a former East Riding agricultural labourer and freelance preacher who had been in a number of villages in the Grimsby and Louth area, was among the first to welcome William Clowes to Hull in January 1819. Later that year Clowes began to preach in north Lincolnshire, accompanied by John Harrison. Although Harrison was an officially designated Primitive Methodist travelling preacher he was in contact with the female revivalist Ann Carr, while Sarah Healand with whom he had visited Caistor was another female in the same tradition. These women preachers were still able to find the place which they had lost with the Wesleyans among the large number of cottage meetings that characterized the early development of Primitive Methodism. This type of meeting remained important until relatively late. In 1851 a quarter of their congregations still met in houses, so that even after full-time female preachers largely disappeared as the Primitives moved away from their Ranter past, women like Elizabeth Moore of Welby, near Grantham, were able to exercise distinctive ministries within the context of their domestic lives. In spite of the problems of holding her home together and bringing up three children during a widowhood of more than forty years, she continued to bear public witness from her house almost up to her death at the age of 80 in 1869. Although so enfeebled that she had to sit, she still managed to address 'a few words of piety to the people'.[38]

    John Oxtoby became a full-time preacher with the Primitives in 1821. His preaching was said to be 'often crude' and 'his pronunciation and attitude' was 'uncouth' since he had 'no wish to add to his strong faith, ceaseless prayer, and deep piety, those mental stores which embellish the man, expand and refine the minds of the Christian and give increasing qualification and sweetness to the zealous and powerful preacher'. It was a time when 'the work to which the early Primitive Methodist preachers were called in the order of Providence did not require much learning, and little or no polish or refinement'. There was little difference in this respect between full-time and local preachers. John Bell of Sturton by Stow, a farm servant, was converted in 1818 and only served as a local preacher for six months before he began to travel full time on the Boston circuit in July 1820. As late as 1848 it was still being said that the sort of education that made a man unfit to speak to the most illiterate congregations was unsuitable for the Primitive Methodist ministry, although by then full-time preachers were being described as ministers and using the title 'Rev.' The work of Primitive Methodist preachers among the 'agricultural poor' was based on a shared set of values and attitudes. While there was less difference between the Primitives and the Wesleyans in the support that they attracted from among labourers than might at first seem to be the case, the Primitives were distinctive in the extent to which they provided an ambience with which rural workers could identify in a number of ways and at a variety of levels.[39]

*Fig. 26   Primitive Methodist Places of Worship, 1851. The Primitive Methodists
were, after the Wesleyans (see Fig. 23), the second largest nonconformist
denomination in 1851, but they had far fewer chapels and meeting places. A much
higher proportion of them were not set solely aside for religious worship. Like the
Wesleyans they were dependent on local circumstances in parishes in order to build
places of worship, but their generally less prosperous members and adherents were
not able to support chapels in all the villages where Wesleyan activity indicated that
conditions were favourable for this. Their greater success in opening chapels in
places in the north of the county was related to strong and relatively independent
village communities with large numbers of agricultural labourers and small
farmers, tradesmen and craftsmen. This was also the case in the fens of south
Lincolnshire.*

Source: Rel. Wor.; 1851 Census Ret.

The revivalistic fervour that characterized the early development of Primitive Methodist activity in the county was compared to 'the ostrich dropping its eggs ... scattering good that seldom or never comes to perfection'. While many converts were made, preachers had 'paid very little attention to forming classes, and to introducing rule and order'. In 1825 and 1826 no membership figures were published. Places where a presence had been established as early as 1818 and 1819 were lost and it was necessary to carry out missionary work in them again. In others, such as Timberland, there was greater continuity and from 1820 Samuel Toynbee was 'for more than thirty years ... a bright ornament to the little church meeting in his house'. As increased emphasis began to be placed on the creation of secure and better disciplined local organizations, places where worship had been established without any concern for its long-term viability were abandoned. Of the ten meetings in the Kesteven division of the county in 1829 only three – Fulbeck, Martin, and Rippingale – still existed in 1851, although the number of Primitive places of worship in the area had increased to thirty-one. This increased stability was associated with chapel building and, as was the case with the Wesleyans, it was seen to be indicative of the organizational maturity of the local congregations that supported it.[40]

Fig. 27   Little Hale chapel, 1837. This early Primitive Methodist chapel, on a small plot off the street, was the only place of worship in a township where divided landownership made it possible to obtain the land on which it was built.

There was a total of 221 Primitive Methodist chapels and meeting places in Lincolnshire by 1851, although the Primitives remained far less chapel orientated than the Wesleyans (Figs. 23 and 26). Whereas nearly 90 per cent of the places used for Wesleyan worship in 1851 were purpose built a total of 57, or just over a quarter, of those used by the Primitives met in premises that were not set aside solely for worship. The Wesleyans, with almost three times as many members and with just over twice the number of people at their best-attended services far outstripped the Primitives in the amount of accommodation that they provided, with a total of 78,862 sittings compared with 25,168 in Primitive Methodist chapels and other meetings. Primitive Methodist buildings were also smaller. While the average capacity of Wesleyan premises was nearly 170, that for places used by the Primitives was just under 114. Primitive Methodist chapels, like those belonging to the Wesleyans, were financed through seat rents, which provided the largest source of local income in many places. Smaller buildings were less expensive and needed a less high level of income, but in some areas such as Caistor and Brigg the proportion of rented seats in Primitive Methodist chapels was as high as 73 per cent. Nearly 87 per cent of the accommodation at Kirton in Lindsey chapel, built in 1819, was taken up with rented seats. The proportion was lower in other places. In the Holbeach district where Primitive Methodist chapels were often the only convenient place of worship for the scattered population of the fenland parishes, and so attracted congregations less committed to the connexion as such, the proportion of free seats was nearly 47 per cent.[41]

Like the Wesleyans, the Primitives were able to achieve an established position in local life through their chapels, but the spirit that had characterized Ranter evangelism was still strong enough to break through the walls of the new buildings that were built with increasing frequency from the 1830s. There was said to be 'a scene seldom witnessed' in the city at the opening services of the Mint Lane premises at Lincoln in 1819. In the evening 'the cries and groans of the infatuated followers of the sect' led to 'a tumult' to defy all description. The opening of the new chapel at Donington in 1834 was reported as marking a transition in the local development of Primitive Methodism, with the title Primitive Methodist used on its date stone said to have been assumed in place of the more generally used 'Ranter'. The services at the opening of the chapel at Gosberton Clough in April 1835 were said to have been 'a powerful time', while the conversions which marked the opening services of Martin chapel near Timberland in July 1837 were a sign that 'the spirit of the Lord accompanied the word of his grace', as they spilled out of the building and into the village and neighbourhood. Nonetheless, settings other than chapels continued to be used by the Primitives, and older styles of worship continued to be maintained into the second half of the 19th century.

*Fig. 28   Heckington Fen Primitive Methodist chapel. Primitive Methodist
meetings were first held here in thatched farm buildings adjoinging a cottage.
They were destroyed by fire, rebuilt in 1855 and again in 1873.*

Open-air evangelism was one of them, but when camp meetings were held
at Claypole, Fulbeck, and Rauceby in the summer of 1835 they were
followed by love feasts in the chapels. In August 1842 the Donington
Primitives retained enough of their Ranter characteristics to shock an
Anglican sympathizer with their 'prayers, singing, shouting and preaching'
at a camp meeting held outside the village.[42]

Primitive Methodist leadership

The local leadership of Primitive Methodism was close to the communities
of Lincolnshire. The influence that lay officers exercised through the
connexion's constitution also meant that it was responsive to local
influences. These officers were predominantly male, but while some 24 per
cent of Primitive trustees were farmers in the period 1800 to 1870 they
were a far less dominant influence than among the Wesleyans, where they
constituted 43 per cent of local trusts. Primitive trusts also had a large
number of working-class men on them, mostly labourers but including a
small number of partially skilled workers such as gardeners and braziers.
The chapel opened at Lutton in 1834 had nine trustees of whom six were
labourers. Three of them used a mark to witness the trust deed as did a
carpenter, a blacksmith, and a cordwainer. Overall, a third of Primitive

Methodist trustees were partially skilled manual workers, and while the growth in the number of chapels in towns and larger communities meant that there was some increase in the proportion of craftsmen and tradesmen at the expense of labourers, this was a sign of the continuing responsiveness of Primitive Methodism to new conditions. There were 20 trustees for the chapel that was built on Cleethorpe Road in Grimsby in 1861. They comprised two fishing-smack owners, a painter, mariner, shoemaker, sawyer, pilot, roper, baker, fish merchant, three fishermen, a cabinet maker, plumber, two builders, a joiner, and one labourer. Their occupations reflected the developing economy of the town from which they came.[43]

In the same year that the chapel on Cleethorpe Road, Grimsby, was built, the Primitive Methodists of the south Lincolnshire village of Wilsford also opened a more modest building. Potential leaders were far thinner on the ground in this small rural society. Nonetheless, the Wilsford trust, which was made up of four labourers and two grocers, still retained a

Fig. 29 Mill Road Primitive Methodist chapel, Cleethorpes. Opened in 1876 it was the third Primitive chapel to be built in central Cleethorpes. Essentially a suburban chapel, trustees included people who were beginning to move into the new houses that were being built in the town.

Fig. 30   Ewerby Primitive Methodist chapel. With a style adapted for the estate village of Ewerby, where the Primitve Methodists only obtained land on which to build in 1879, the chapel is remarkable for its bell cote.

substantial local component, and there were four Wilsford men included on it. These strong local links became less evident on some trusts as the influence of circuits increased at the expense of local societies, but into the second half of the 19th century their local base distinguished the Primitives from the Wesleyans, although this did not mean that they were necessarily more successful in establishing a presence in the communities of Lincolnshire. Their 462 places of worship meant that the Wesleyan Methodists were present in a majority of Lincolnshire parishes (Fig. 23), but the Primitives were to be found in only 221 (Fig. 26). While there were few places where the Primitives were the only branch of Methodism, there was also a number of parishes which might have been expected to provide 'growing space' for them but where they were either absolutely or relatively unsuccessful. There was a crowded house meeting and converts were being made in the large parish of Ruskington in 1821. Here lack of landlord control gave considerable freedom for the development of religious dissent, but a Primitive Methodist class that was established there had ceased to exist by 1829. In other parishes that also seemed ripe for the Primitives, they failed to develop as extensively as the size of the population would have seemed to warrant. In Middle Rasen, with a population of 948 in 1851, and divided landownership, the best-attended service at the Primitive Methodist chapel attracted a congregation of only 18, while there were 160 people at the Wesleyan service held at the same time. Attendances at Primitive Methodist services were often proportionately larger in smaller places. Brattleby had a population of 169 in 1851 and about a hundred Primitive Methodists assembled for Sunday worship there, while about fifty attended week-night activities. These high levels of attendance were achieved within the context of a house meeting, and demonstrated the continuing strength of those aspects of Ranter revivalism which, with its narrow and intense focus on the needs of individual souls, was able to function most effectively at a local level untrammelled by more complex organizations.[44]

The origins of Reform

The development of what was described as a 'full consciousness of church life' among the Primitive Methodists was largely achieved without major difficulties, despite complaints that the growth of 'officialism' and the administration of complex rules led to quarrels at meetings. These were said to damage the spiritual lives of individuals and hinder approaches to 'the outcasts of society'. On the other hand, the tighter organization and more centralized institutions of Wesleyan Methodism emphasized the pastoral and constitutional authority of full-time ministers and engendered considerable tensions. They were exacerbated by differences about the nature and direction of evangelism, while the temperance movement, which had quickly found a place in the life of the Primitives, was another cause of friction among the Wesleyans.[45]

Alexander Kilham's antipathy to the Church of England had some basis in his experiences as a Wesleyan travelling preacher on the Horncastle and Gainsborough circuits between 1785 and 1787, but his movement for the constitutional reform of Methodism, which had led to the establishment of the Methodist New Connexion, had met with only a limited response in his native county. The New Connexion, led by Kilham until his death in 1798, had places of worship in Boston and north-west Lincolnshire in 1851 with a total of 852 people at its best-attended services on the evening of Sunday 30 March. Members of another of the schismatic branches of Methodism, the Wesleyan Methodist Association, whose origins also lay in disputes about the constitution of Methodism, had sold their chapel in Watergate, Louth, in 1846, but the following that they had attracted was a reminder of the continuing debates that brought secessions from Wesleyan Methodism.[46]

There had been discontent in the early 1840s with the Wesleyan ministers of Louth over their claims to control the admission of members, while in Boston the pseudonymous 'Hater of Priestcraft', the surgeon William Small, had been expelled from the Wesleyans in 1841 on suspicion of writing letters critical of the ministers. Another William Small, also involved in Radical politics and teetotalism, was associated with the town's Methodist New Connexion chapel, and played a prominent part in the clashes over church rate that divided Boston into the 1850s. The Grantham Wesleyan society had also been reported in 1842 to have been uneasy with the claims of their superintendent minister: 'an incessant stickler for the supremacy of the sacerdotal office, and for oligarchical power'. Church rate disputes in Louth had pushed the town's Wesleyans towards a political Liberalism that sat uneasily with the Toryism of its ministers. James Booth Sharpley, a Wesleyan Methodist officer and member for over thirty years, who was to play a leading part in the formation of the Free Methodist Church in Louth, was a Liberal. In Lincoln the leadership of Free Methodism was also closely identified with political Liberalism. Charles Akrill became honorary secretary of the Lincoln Liberal Association and was 'an advanced man' in literature and Biblical science as well as in social questions and politics.[47]

By the 1850s the tensions within Wesleyan Methodism could no longer be contained and from its beginnings as a 'paper war', albeit one that was characterized by the 'caustic and abusive' as well as the highly personalized tone of its debates, the movement for Methodist Reform brought division to Lincolnshire Wesleyan Methodism. The second of the *Fly Sheets*, published anonymously between 1844 and 1848, were in the hands of the ministers of Louth circuit by at least 1846 when William Bacon wrote to Jabez Bunting deploring their 'vile and calumnious'

*Fig. 31   Market Rasen Wesleyan Methodist chapel, 1863. This impressively
dominant building reflects the importance of the town of Market Rasen
at the head of a circuit.*

contents. They were a savage attack on the hierarchy of ministers,
dominated by the 'central and colossal figure' of Dr Bunting. It was alleged
to have subverted Wesleyan Methodism through its London based-
dominance of affairs. Samuel Dunn, William Griffith, and James Everett,
the ministers who were expelled by the Wesleyan Methodist conference in
1849 – Everett as the putative author of the *Fly Sheets*, with Griffith and
Dunn as his supporters – visited Boston, Lincoln, Louth, and Spalding in
1849 and 1850. Griffith's Sunday sermons in the Lincoln Corn Exchange
were said to have attracted 'very large congregations of the lower orders of
society'. These meetings, with the newspaper propaganda and
pamphleteering that accompanied them, were aimed at the constitutional
reform of Methodism and not the creation of a new division of it. There had
already been discussion in the Louth circuit of the possibility of stopping
supplies – withholding contributions – in an attempt to control the
Buntingite hierarchy and when Dunn, Everett, and Griffith visited the town
it was at the invitation of fifty officers from the circuit and local lay
dignitaries. Some of the prominent officers in Louth were said to be
opposed to Methodism 'as it is', although not identified with the expelled

ministers. In July 1850 a meeting of the circuit officers memorialized the Conference requesting reform. There was also considerable sympathy for the Reformers in Gainsborough, but it was reported at the beginning of 1850 that most of the members there were unwilling to take any action which would be seen as divisive.[48]

Men like J. B. Sharpley of Louth became prominent on the national scene, but the concerns of the people who worshipped in local chapels were more immediate. The differences between people and ministers had been exacerbated by the fact that ministers who spent only two or three years in a circuit were able to exercise their considerable powers in contexts which they had little time to understand. The problem was aggravated by the way in which their ministerial work was often seen to be carried out at the expense of smaller country societies. The superintendent of the Louth circuit had expressed concern in 1836 that its size meant that, like his predecessors, he had not found it practicable to extend 'any thing more than an indirect and defective pastoral influence' to nine 'country places' for which he and his colleagues were responsible. They were only able to preach once a quarter in six others. Another six places 'of considerable methodistical importance' had no Sunday preaching from the ministers, while there was only Sunday, but no week-night, preaching by them in another five where there were 'good chapels'. In the Grantham circuit three full-time ministers and 46 local preachers led the services in 31 places of worship in the period June to October 1847. The pulpit at the town chapel in Finkin Street was occupied each Sunday morning and evening by a full-time minister, although the only Sunday preaching at Manthorpe, Londonthorpe, Easton, and Honington, which were not far distant from the town, was by local preachers. Great Gonerby was also close to Grantham, but even in this more important local centre of Methodism a minister appeared on Sundays only four times a year when he presided over the quarterly collection. The week-night meetings of the society were better served and one of the circuit ministers attended them on a fortnightly basis. In places such as these, what was perceived as neglect fostered independent attitudes. In Louth local preachers were favoured over Conference ministers at the new chapel that was opened at the Riverhead in 1849.[49]

The varied local outcomes of the Reform agitation depended initially on the responses of individual circuit ministers. Despite the existence of a Reform party in Grimsby, which organized a meeting in the Baltic warehouse, the circuit remained in the long term unaffected by the movement, although it rejected a proposal to invite a minister to the circuit who was said to be a 'violent' supporter of Conference. Attempts to institute Reform meetings in the Coningsby circuit were countered by references to 'the kindness' of their minister; but when William Bacon moved from the Louth to the Lincoln circuit, he adopted a confrontational policy in which retention of the control of circuits was regarded as paramount even though the expulsion of dissidents resulted in a loss of members. When he wrote in September 1850 to seek advice as to how to deal with the 'disaffected' preachers, class leaders, and over five hundred members who had stopped their financial contributions, he was urged by Dr John Beetham, the President of Conference, to abandon conciliation, a policy that only enabled 'the Agitators' to strengthen their positions and to proceed with 'measures equal to the emergency'. In March 1851 Bacon referred to the the loss of four hundred members as being ultimately beneficial to the circuit.[50]

In Louth the preachers were alleged to have attempted to 'silence all discussion, and "cut off" all who dared speak freely' on the issues raised by the expulsion of Everett, Dunn, and Griffith so that 'individuals who had long lived in the affection of their brethren, as consistent members and officers of society were marked for summary expulsion'. There were twenty-five delegates from Lincolnshire circuits at a Reform meeting held in London in March 1850 with Lincoln, Louth, and Spalding particularly well represented. The three delegates from Grantham were tried and expelled by the Wesleyan authorities and began to preach in the town's Primitive Methodist chapel, but a theatre was soon fitted up as a place of worship and opened by William Griffith in August 1850. The Lincoln Reformers had begun to send delegates to the movement's national conference by 1852, but in Louth, despite expulsions that included the three delegates to the London meeting, the campaign for Reform was still being conducted from within the circuit. Alternative sets of preaching plans were issued in November 1852, and it was not until December 1853 that the Louth Free Methodist Church was established. Its formation followed the departure of two leading local members, J. B. Sharpley and Joseph Larder, from Wesleyan Methodism in reaction to the withdrawal of membership tickets from a hundred people. They had remained Wesleyans, with other officers of Reforming sympathies, despite attempts by the superintendent minister to isolate them. He feared that the circuit would be 'carried off by an organized opposition, conducted by persons who are at present officers and members'.[51]

The Free Methodist and Reform churches

For seven years between 1850 and 1856 Reform delegates met annually at the same time and place as the Wesleyan Conference until they united with the Wesleyan Methodist Association to form the United Methodist Free Churches in 1857. By then the expulsion from Wesleyan Methodism of the people who were to make up the Lincolnshire Reform churches had already taken place. The growth of the Reform movement can be measured from its impact on Wesleyan membership. The effect of the drop from 22,629 in

1850 to a low point of 15,626 in 1854 was felt at different times in different circuits. The impact was greatest at Grantham where a membership of 1,056 declined to 448 between 1850 and 1851, while Spalding circuit lost over 65 per cent of its members in the two year period between 1850 and 1852. In Louth where the greatest losses came between 1852 and 1853, they were just under half the total membership. As these members left or were expelled from Wesleyan Methodism they either attempted to continue to worship in existing chapel premises or moved to new ones. The effect on people who attended chapel without seeking full membership is more difficult to gauge, although the loss of local leaders was demoralizing for congregations.[52]

There were 14 Reform places of worship in Lincolnshire by 1851 and their best-attended service on the evening of Sunday 30 March attracted a total of 2,115 people at a time when the Wesleyans had lost a total of 2,684 members. These figures are almost certainly underestimates since there are no returns for services in the Epworth, Spalding, and Market Rasen circuits where Wesleyan members had been lost to the Reformers by 1851. The converted theatre, where 600 were said to have attended the evening service arranged by the Grantham Reformers, and the Corn Exchange at Lincoln, where there were 560 worshippers on the evening of Sunday 30 March 1851, were fitting venues for a religious body that was shaped in large public meetings concerned with constitutional issues, but the group who described themselves as the Wesleyan Reform Methodists of Thurlby Green had to crowd into temporary premises. They had left the village's Wesleyan Methodist chapel only a quarter full and noted that the place where they met for worship in 1851 had been 'opened for divine worship in consequence of the arbitrary, unjust and expelling acts of the Wesleyan ministers of the Bourn circuit'. Such local developments in the Reform movement often took place in an atmosphere of contentious bitterness as groups that could not retain the legal title to chapels settled on the Wesleyan Conference were forced to leave buildings with which they had long associations. At Fiskerton in December 1850 the Lincoln minister nailed up the windows and locked the doors of the chapel in order to ensure that it remained in the possession of the Wesleyans. It had opened again by 1851, although attended by fewer people than the hired room used by the Reformers.[53]

The influence of the circuit on local chapel affairs fed the grievances of local Reformers. Local Wesleyan chapel trusts had frequently included groups of outside trustees, often men who were important in circuit affairs, and who acted for a number of chapels in an area. When new Reform trusts were established they were a better reflection of local chapel communities. While farmers continued to be important as office holders in rural Reform churches, they comprised only 16 per cent of trustees in the Louth circuit compared with 48 per cent among the Wesleyans, while the proportion of shopkeepers more than doubled to 32 per cent. Businessmen were prominent among the leaders of Free Methodism in Spalding and their accession to office in the Reform movement matched their advancement in local civic affairs. Major Shadford combined service to Free Methodism with local office as chairman of the improvement commissioners and school board, vice chairmanship of the board of guardians, and eventually

Fig. 32   Market Rasen Free Methodist chapel, built in 1861, a short distance from the Wesleyan chapel, was testimony to the aspirations of the town's Wesleyan Reformers. While they were a source of great pride and enhanced the standing of the local congregations that built them, the provision and maintenance of such buildings imposed heavy financial burdens on local congregations.

an aldermanship of Holland County Council. William North of Market
Rasen, a leather merchant and currier in town for 45 years, was said at his
death in 1883 to have been elected to almost every public office of trust and
responsibility in the town. At time of disruption he was a Wesleyan class
leader, but the Methodist Free Churches opened up new opportunities for
him to exercise responsibility in church affairs. His fellow townsmen who
served with him on the trust of the Market Rasen United Methodist Free
Church from 1860 included a maltster, and tailor and draper, as well as a
coal agent. Their assumption of responsibility in church affairs was, like
the Congregationalists of Brigg, paralleled by their advancement in civic
life. Several of his fellow church members were elected with North to the
local board when it was created in 1878, although town-based businessmen
did not reign supreme on Reform trusts. The number of their trustees with
partially skilled occupations approached that of the Primitive Methodists.
These diverse groups were held together by a constitution that gave lay
people a considerable influence in church affairs and so met the grievances
that had fuelled their secession. The Reformers were, however, more than a
collection of eccelsiastical democrats. They were also distinguished by
their commitment to revivalism and a strong interest in temperance affairs.
These provided, particularly in the case of revivalism, a positive basis for
their participation in the lives of the local communities of Lincolnshire.[54]

    Although revivalism had moved to forms and methods more appropriate
to settled communities than the North American frontier religion that had
inspired the early Primitive Methodists, the conservative and chapel-bound
Wesleyan leadership remained distrustful of it. The Irish-born American
Methodist revivalist James Caughey employed these newer approaches
among the British Methodist congregations where he preached for five
years until he was, in another assertion of the authority of the ministers in
Conference, excluded by the Wesleyans in 1846. His populist campaigns,
conducted at the invitation of local people, pushed aside official
arrangements for worship. Meetings at the Lincoln Wesleyan chapel in
June 1846 were reported to have turned it into 'a place of purveyance for
asylums and brothels' as the educated classes ignored his prayer meetings,
leaving women and children as the 'victims' of the excitement engendered
by his revival techniques. While 'respectable' Wesleyans were said to
'shudder at the desecration this impudent American ranter' cast over their
services, loads of 'stupid-looking rustics' were transported to his meetings.
Special packet boats were used to bring people into Boston during
Caughey's visit to the town and on the Sunday official preaching plans
were cast aside as Methodist chapels in the area closed. The Lincoln
society was, however, keen to publicize the benefits of his visit as local
membership began to increase after a period of decline.[55]

    After he was refused the use of Wesleyan Methodist chapels Caughey found an outlet in those belonging to the New Connexion and Wesleyan Methodist Association. They were more sympathetic to the exercise of lay power and local opinion, while he was also welcomed by the more revival conscious Primitives. The action of the Wesleyan Conference had called into question its commitment, and that of its ministers, to vigorous evangelistic effort through revivalism. William Brown, who was associated with the Wesleyan Methodist Association chapel in Louth, referred to the need to let men such as Caughey 'whom God has given an extraordinary call to revive his work ... freely to preach the Gospel in any circuit that might call for their help'. Caughey was in Louth in 1859 when many were 'delighted with the gracious visitation' that attended his labours, although 'others were much annoyed'. When he returned to Britain between 1860 and 1862 the revivalistic spirit of the Reform churches continued to provide a basis for Caughey's work. Similarly, the American female revivalist Phoebe Palmer was supported by the Free Methodists of Louth, including J. B. Sharpley, with whom she stayed when conducting revival services in the town. A commitment to revivalism was also evident in the embryonic Spalding United Methodist Free Churches circuit. William Booth, the founder of the Salvation Army, had his vocation confirmed when he served as a minister on it between 1852 and 1854. Although enjoined by his fiancée to guard against '*mere animal excitement*', the revivalistic ethos of the circuit matched the 'passion for soul-saving' which he exercised among its fenland congregations. American revivalists, including Caughey, were Booth's exemplars, while another aspect of their work was invoked in the camp meetings that were held in the Sleaford Wesleyan Reform circuit from the 1850s. There was also a place for enthusiastic spontaneity in its more formal round of worship. At the Paper Mills chapel anniversary in 1875, 'while the brethren were addressing the meeting, one sister could hold out no longer, but broke out in praising God for what He had done'.[56]

Temperance and teetotalism

Temperance, like revivalism, raised issues of authority within Wesleyan Methodism. Its conference effectively withheld official support for temperance and teetotal organizations in declarations on the question in 1841 and chapels were closed to their meetings. While it was divided about temperance, Wesleyanism was even more seriously split over total abstinence from alcoholic drinks. Discord over the issue was reported from south Lincolnshire in the early 1840s and when Wesleyan Methodists in Lincoln joined the city's Primitives in a celebration of the Lord's Supper at the Temperance Hall the elements included the 'fruit of the vine uncorrupted' in 1842. Early the next year the Lincoln circuit ministers were reported to have expelled from the circuit plan a local preacher who had

been accepted for the full-time ministry for his refusal of alcoholic
Communion wine. In 1844 divisions in Barrow on Humber led the teetotal
Wesleyans to build their own chapel.[57]

The growth of the teetotal movement began to outstrip that of the more
moderate British and Foreign Temperance Society in Lincolnshire. Its
radical stance linked it to the political elements of the agitation for
Methodist Reform, while in so far as it appealed to a working-class
constituency it was in touch with social groups that revivalists sought to
reach. The Temperance Society at Louth was using revivalistic methods as
early as 1845, when its annual festival included a camp meeting. The wide
constituency of the temperance movement meant that there was not an
exclusive association between it and the development of the Reform
churches, but it was an important element in shaping their identity. There
was a climate of radical teetotalism in the Louth area associated with the
Primitive minister and teetotal advocate John Stamp, while a total
abstinence union had been established among the Louth Wesleyans by

*Fig. 33   Heckington Wesleyan Reform chapel 1852. A Wesleyan Reform chapel
was built quickly in Heckington, a village where, like other places on the Sleaford
Wesleyan Reform circuit, there was a considerable temperance interest.*

1849. The Sleaford Reform circuit was strongly involved in temperance advocacy. In Ruskington the development of the temperance society and Band of Hope had been part of the process through which the Reformers established themselves in the village in the 1850s and the Temperance Hall had been used for their services. The Temperance Hall in Navenby was said to belong to the Wesleyan Reformers, while Heckington, another village where the Wesleyan Reformers were established early, was a strong temperance centre. Teetotalism had not, however, become fully embedded in the Spalding circuit in William Booth's time and leading laymen were keen to offer alcoholic beverages to sustain him on his journeys across the winter-bound fens.[58]

Notes to Chapter V

1   W. L. Doughty, *John Wesley in Lincolnshire*, London, 1938, pp. 23–4; *Reas. Enthus.*, p. 113; *Wes. J*, 8, pp. 78–9.

2   *Wesley*, 17, p. 421, 19, pp. 273, 349–50, 21, p. 221, 22, pp. 148–50, 23, p. 138 ; *Wes. J.*, 8, p. 79; *Reas. Enthus.*, pp. 57, 272.

3   *Wesley*, 22, pp. 240, 421; *Wes. J*, 7, p. 414, 8, pp. 77–9; M. Edwards, 'John Wesley', A. R. George, 'The People called Methodists – 4. The Means of Grace', and J. Walsh, 'Methodism at the End of the Eighteenth Century' in *Hist. Meth. Ch.*, I, , pp. 54–5, 264–5, 286–7; *Wes. Min.*, I, p. 236; PRO, RG31/3, Registers of Meeting Houses; W. Myles, *A Chronological History of the People Called Methodists, of the Connexion of the Late Rev. John Wesley; From their Rise in the Year 1729, to Their Last Conference in 1802*, 3rd ed. 1813, pp. 322, 329; Baker, 'Beginnings', pp. 8, 10, 12, 13–16; 18th C. Chap., pp. 13, 15.

4   *Wesley*, 19, p. 275, 20, p. 232, 21, p. 221–2, 23, pp. 176, 213, 215; *Grims. Meth.*, pp. 16–17, 25–39; Edwards, 'Wesley', pp. 57–8; *Wes. J.*, 7, p. 410; *Georg. Linc.*, p. 70; T.R. Leach, 'The Preaching Squire – Robert Carr Brackenbury (1752–1818)', *LH*, 2, 11 (1964), pp. 21–2, 28; *Gran. Wes. Meth.*, p. 288.

5   *Reas. Enthus.*, p. 238; F. Baker, 'The People Called Methodists. 3. Polity', *Hist. Meth. Ch.*, I, p. 231; *Grims. Meth.*, pp. 54–5; *Wes. Min.*, I, pp. 56, 91, 389 , II, p. 96, III, pp. 218, 1900, pp. 533–5; *Linc. Meth.*, pp. 49–50; *Gran. Wes. Meth.*, pp. 171, 231, 258, 287.

6   W. Leary, *Methodism in the Town of Boston*, Boston, 1972, p. 8; *MNCMin.*, 1839, p. 7; *PMMin.*, I, pp. 2, 10, III, p. 6, V, p. 10, 1896, p. 15, 1900, p. 14.

7   *Wesleyan Delegate Takings: or short sketches of personal or intellectual character as exhibited in the Wesleyan delegate meeting, held in Albion Street Chapel, London, 12, 13, 14 and 15 March 1850*, Manchester, 1850, pp. 178–9, 182, 184, 186, 189; J. T. Wilkinson, 'The Rise of Other Methodist Traditions', in *Hist. Meth. Ch.*, II, pp. 316–17; *Wes. Assoc. Min.*, 1837, p. 35, 1838, p. 36, 1846, p. 10; *UMFC Min.*, 1857, pp. 77, 78, 1859, pp. 89, 90, 1861, pp. 82–5, 1862, p. 86, 1869, p. 93, 1880, p. 42, 1900, p. 67; *WRUM*, 1, 8, p. 106; *CW* (1881), p. 148.

8 *MM*, XXV (October 1802), p. 466, I (3rd ser.) (June 1822), p. 412, XL (XVI new ser.) (August 1819), pp. 598–9; Spec. 4.

9 Soc. Struct. 18thC. Meth., Appendix 3, p. 49; Spec. 4.

10 Spec. 4.

11 Spec. 4; *MM*, XXIII (April 1800), p. 149, (June 1819), p. 405.

12 D. Hempton, *The Religion of the People: Methodism and Popular Religion c.1750–1900*, London, 1996, p. 161; Diss. Certs., p. 173; Baker, 'Beginnings', p. 5.

13 *Hornc. Meth.*, p. 80; *Grims. Meth.*, pp. 107, 110–11.

14 *Gran. Wes. Meth.*, pp. 132–3, 145.

15 *Lives,* 1, pp. 248–9; *Linc. Meth.*, pp. 31–2.

16 *Report,* pp. 8–9, 11–12, 15–16; J. Walsh, 'Religious Societies: Methodist and Evangelical 1738–1800', in *Voluntary Religion*, ed. W. J. Sheils and D. Wood, SCH, 23, Oxford, 1986, pp. 284–5; *Gran. Wes. Meth.*, pp. 143–8; *Linc. Meth.*, pp. 60–61, 100.

17 *Diss.*, I, pp. 422–4; P. Muskett, 'Elementary Education to 1800' in *Atlas*, pp. 76–7.

18 *MM*, XXVI (May 1803), pp. 193, 196, XLIV (XVIII new ser.) (September 1821), p. 674; *Lives*, VI, pp. 137, 138–40.

19 *MM*, XXXVII (XI new ser.) (July 1814), p. 481, XXXVIII (XII new ser.), (November 1815), p. 844; *Lives*, VI, p. 140; *Peas. Prea.*, pp. 12–14.

20 *Wes. Min.*, II, pp. 57, 140, 186; *Vindic.*, p. 9.

21 *Linc. Meth.*, pp. 58, 60; PRO, RG 31/3, Lincoln Diocese 1740–1852, 505; 18th C. Chap., p. 14; Baker, 'Beginnings', p. 11; W. Leary, 'A Survey of Lincolnshire Methodism in the Eighteenth Century', *JLMHS*, vol. 1, 9 (Autumn 1967), p. 12; Relig. Wor., p. ccxi; 1851 Tab. Ret., fols. 69–181; *1851 Census Ret.*, p. 219.

22 D. M. Valenze, *Prophetic Sons and Daughters: female preaching and popular religion in industrial England*, Princeton, New Jersey, 1985, pp. 25–7; *MM*, XXVIII (July 1805), p. 332; Soc. Struct. 18th C. Meth., p. 23, Appendix 1, pp. 1–31, Appendix 2, pp. 1–14, Appendix 3, pp. 1–6; SHARO 326/1/1, Grimsby and Horncastle Circuit Records, 1769–1782; SGS, Meth. 10; *Wesley*, 23, p. 138; L. F. Church, *Early Methodist People*, London, 1948, p. 231.

23 Soc. Struct. 18th C. Meth., pp. 7–12, 18, 21–2; C. D. Field, 'The Social Structure of English Methodism, eighteenth–twentieth centuries', *British Journal of Sociology*, vol. 28, no. 2 (June 1977), p. 202; *Gran. Wes. Meth.*, pp. 132, 184.

24 J. A. Perkins, *Sheep Farming in Eighteenth and Early Nineteenth Century Lincolnshire*, Sleaford, 1977, pp. 26–7; L. F. Church, *More About the Early Methodist People*, 1949, p. 140.

25 Valenze, *Prophetic Sons and Daughters*, pp. 57–8, 188–95, 204; Z. Taft, *Biographical Sketches of the Lives and Public Ministry of Various Holy Women*, II, Leeds, 1828, 1982 repr., pp. 288–9.

26 T. Saxton, 'An Account of the Late Work of God at Epworth', *The Arminian Magazine* [later *MM*], VII (January and February 1784), pp. 45–50, 103–6; 'The Experience of Thomas Edman, Preacher of the Gospel', *MM*, XXIII (April 1800), pp. 50–51; *Clee. Meth.*, pp. 38–9.

27 R. Currie, A. Gilbert and L. Horsley, *Churches and Churchgoers: patterns of church growth in the British Isles since 1700*, Oxford, 1977, pp. 65, 139–40; *Diss.*,

II, pp. 66–73.

28 W. R. Ward, *Religion and Society in England, 1790–1850*, London, 1972, pp. 50–51; *Report*, pp. 6, 9, 12; *Recollect.*, pp. 27–8.; *Linc. Meth.*, pp. 98–9, 114, 120–21, 127–9.

29 B. A. H. Barley, 'Methodist Beginnings in Barton-upon-Humber Circuit', *Proceedings of the Wesley Historical Society*, VIII (1912), p. 132; Ep. Cir. Trusts; PRO, RG4, 1644, Lincoln Wesleyan Methodist Baptismal Register, 1810–1839.

30 SGS, Meth. 1; *Diss.*, II, p. 745.

31 *Linc. Meth. Recoll.*, pp. 82–3; J. H. Beech, *The Good Soldier. Outlines of the Life, Labours, and Character of the Rev. Hugh Beech, Wesleyan Minister*, London, 1856, pp. 31–2; B. J. Biggs, *Our Colsterworth Heritage: two centuries in the life and times of the Methodist people*, Colsterworth, 1996, p. 14.

32 *LRSM*, 23 August 1833; *Rel. & Rur. Soc.*, pp. 186, 200–201.

33 *LRSM*, 31 July 1835; W. Leary, *Methodism in the Town of Boston*, Boston, 1972, p. 31; *Hornc. Meth.*, p. 52; *Rel. & Rur. Soc.*, p. 198.

34 *Gran. Wes. Meth.*, pp. 130, 368; *WMM*, III (6th ser.) (1879), p. 480; *1851 Census Ret.*, p. lii.

35 R. Currie, *Methodism Divided: a study in the sociology of ecumenicalism*, London, 1968, pp. 55–76.

36 *Orig. & Hist.* I, pp. 77, 79–82, 88, 99, 101, 189; *Biog. Sket.*, pp. 188, 477; [Thomas Cooper], *The Life of Thomas Cooper Written by Himself*, London, 1877, p. 37; *Hist. PM*, p. 73; *Gran. Wes. Meth.*, pp. 370–7; R. Heath, *The English Via Dolorosa or Glimpses of the History of the Agricultural Labourer*, London, 1884, p. 63; *PMM*, 2, p. 45; *LRSM*, 20 August 1819; *Christian Remembrancer*, 3 (March 1821), pp. 136–8.

37 *LRSM*, 28 May, 20 August 1819, 16 June 1820, 17 August 1821.

38 W. Sanderson and W. Harland, *Trophies of Grace or the Power of Religion Manifested*, Hull, 1839, pp. 16–17; *Oxtoby*, pp. 14–15, 21, 25; *Prim. Meth. Conn.*, pp. 105–6; *Orig. & Hist.*, I, p. 36; *Hist. PM*, pp. 85, 87, 88; *Biog. Sket.*, pp. 303, 323, 370, 371; *PMM*, 3 (March 1821), pp. 57–8 (June 1821), p. 131, 8 (new ser.) (May 1870), p. 300; 1851 Tab. Ret., fols. 69–181.

39 H. Leigh, *'Praying Johnny'; or, the Life and Labours of John Oxtoby, Primitive Methodist Minister*, 6th ed. London, 1867, pp. 80–82; *Oxtoby*, pp. 41, 43, 49; *PMM*, III (new ser.) (May 1833), p. 161; J. Gair, 'Rev. John Dickenson' in *Heroic Men: the death roll of the Primitive Methodist ministry, being sketches of those ministers who have died between the conferences of 1888–9*, London [1889], pp. 133–5; Ch. in Lincs., p. 269; *Rel. & Rur. Soc.*, p. 195.

40 *LRSM*, 7 June 1839; *Biog. Sket.*, p. 429; *Hist. PM*, p. 250; *Orig. & Hist.*, I, p. 434; LA, Parts of Kesteven, Clerk of the Peace's Papers, A Return of the Number of Places not of the Church of England, June 1829.

41 R. W. Ambler, 'Religious Life in Kesteven – A Return of the Number of Places of Worship not of the Church of England, 1829', *LHA*, vol. 20 (1985), p. 63; Rel. Wor., p. ccxi, 82, 84; *Relig. & Rur. Soc.*, pp. 222, 250; 1851 Tab. Ret., fols. 164, 171; *1851 Census Ret.*, p. 231.

42 *LRSM*, 5 June 1835, 19 August 1842; *PMM*, V (new ser.) (October 1835), p. 393, VII (new ser.) (December 1837), pp. 472–3.

43 Soc. Comp., pp. 144–5, 149, 151; PRO, C54/11219/15, C54/17168/4, C54
    /15682/1.

44 PRO, C54/15701/13; Relig. Wor., p. ccxi; *Relig. & Rur. Soc.*, p. 238–9; *1851
    Census Ret.*, pp. 119, 225; *Dir. Lincs.*, p. 770; *PMM*, 2, June 1821, p. 131.

45 *Orig. & Hist.*, II, pp. 357–8; An Old Fashioned Methodist [George Walker],
    Methodist Ritualism, or a Few Thoughts on the Methodism of To-day, [London,
    1885], pp. 39–40.

46 Wilkinson, 'Rise of Other Methodist Traditions' in *Hist. Meth. Ch.*,II, p. 281; T. D.
    Crothers, 'Historical Sketch of the New Connexion', in *The Centenary of the New
    Connexion 1797–1897*, ed. G. Packer, London [1897], p. 74; Rel. Wor., p. ccxi;
    LRSM, 17 July 1846, 14 August 1846.

47 J. F. Smyth, *A Vindication of the Conduct of the Wesleyan Methodist Preachers
    Composing the Lincoln District in Reference to the Examination of Some Young
    Men, Candidates for the Ministry, at their Annual Meeting, held in Boston, May,
    1841*, Boston, 1841, p.13; *BLLSH.*, 30 April 1839; *LRSM*, 18 June 1841, 1 April
    1842, 31 July 1846, 8 June 1849, 23 November 1849, 11 January 1850, 22 February
    1850, 12 July 1850; Currie, *Methodism Divided*, p. 49, 74; N. R. Wright, 'The
    Builders of Boston Centenary Wesleyan Methodist Chapel, 1839/40', in
    *Lincolnshire People and Places: essays in memory of Terence R. Leach
    (1937–1994)*, ed. C. R. Sturman, Lincoln, 1996, p. 150; P.P. 1845 XLI (428)
    Abstract of Returns Relating to Church Rates, 1832, p. 136; D. A. Gowland,
    *Methodist Secessions. The Origins of Free Methodism in Three Lancashire Towns:
    Manchester, Rochdale, Liverpool*, Manchester, 1979, pp. 16–17; *Lincs. Pol.*, pp.
    58–60; *The United Methodist Free Churches Magazine*, XV (November, 1872), p.
    740; *The Methodist Monthly. A Magazine of the Methodist Free Churches*, VII (new
    ser.) (August 1898), p. 206.

48 *Lincs. Meth.*, p.80; Meth. Arch., MAM PLP/ 4/ 70/ 11, 12; B. Gregory, *Side Lights
    on the Conflicts of Methodism during the Second Quarter of the Nineteenth Century,
    1827–1852*, London, 1899, p. 495; *BSLH*, 27 November 1849, 25 December 1849.

49 *1851 Census Ret.*, pp. 79, 106–7; *Earl. Vict. Meth.*, pp. 154–5; LA, Methodist
    Preaching Plans, Grantham Circuit Wesleyan Preaching Plan 6 June–17 October
    1847; *LRSM*, 23 February 1849, 3 August 1849.

50 Grimsby Central Library, Skelton Collection 1851/11v.; *LRSM*, 12 April 1850;
    Lincs. Meth., p. 81; Meth. Arch., MAW 36.9, MAM PLP/ 4/ 70/ 14.

51 *The Regulations of the Louth Free Methodist Church with Introductory
    Observations*, Louth, 1854, pp. 2, 3; *LRSM*, 19 July 1850, 9 August 1850, 27 August
    1852, 26 November 1852; *Wesleyan Delegate Takings: or short sketches of
    personal and intellectual character, as exhibited in the Wesleyan Delegate Meeting,
    held in Albion Street Chapel, London, 12, 13, 14 and 15 March 1850*, Manchester
    1850, pp. 178, 179, 182, 184, 186, 189; Louth Free Meth., p. 411.

52 G. Eayrs, 'The United Methodist Church and the Wesleyan Reform Union' in *A
    New Hist.of Meth.*, I, ed. W. J. Townsend, H. B. Workman, and G. Eayrs, London,
    1909, pp. 534–7; *Proceedings of the Twenty-Second Annual Assembly of the
    Wesleyan Methodist Association, and of the Representatives Belonging to the
    Methodist Reform Circuits, 29 July–10 August 1857*, p. 7.

53 Rel. Wor., p. ccxi; W. Leary, *The Ecclesiastical Census for Methodist Chapels in
    Lincolnshire 1851*, [Lincoln, 1970] p. 3; *1851 Census Ret.*, pp. 14, 79, 103, 106–7;

LRSM, 6 December 1850.

54 Louth Free Meth., p. 8; *Spalding*, pp. 144, 150; *The United Methodist Free Churches Magazine*, XXVII (new ser., I) (August 1884), pp. 526–7; PRO C54/ 16548/ 19; Soc. Comp., pp. 152–3.

55 *Prim. Meth. Conn.*, p. 60; R. Carwardine, *Trans-atlantic revivalism: popular evangelicalism in Britain and America, 1790–1865*, pp. 104–7, 111, 128–31; *LRSM*, 19 June 1846, 26 June 1846, 30 October 1846, 3 July 1846; *BSLH*, 16 June 1846, 30 June 1846.

56 Carwardine, *Trans-atlantic revivalism*, pp. 131–3, 175; W. Brown, *Fly Sheets for the People; containing some Popular Information for the Members and Lay Officials of the Wesleyan Methodist Societies; very much needed at the Present Time; on the Past and Present Disturbed Condition of the Connexion; with a Statement of the Causes; and Hints Suggestive of the Duties of the Members of the Wesleyan Church at the Present Crisis; in a Dialogue between John Ask'em and William Tell'em*, Louth, 1849, p. 13; Dr and Mrs Palmer, *Four Years in the Old World*, New York, 10t^h edit. 1866, p. 692; *Spalding*, p. 149; *Booth*, pp. 174-5; *SFP*, 4 May 1852; *WRUM*, 8 (August 1861), pp. 95–6; *CW*, 15 (1875), p. 40; P. W. Robinson, 'Sleaford Circuit and the Wesleyan Reformers', *JLMHS*, 5, 1 (Spring 1997), pp. 11–12.

57 Gowland, *Methodist Secessions*, p. 157; Currie, *Methodism Divided*, p. 70; *LRSM*, 8 July 1842, 1 December 1843, 17 May 1844.

58 L. Billington, 'Popular Religion and Social Reform: a study of revivalism and teetotalism, 1830–50', *Journal of Religious History*, 10 (1978–79), pp. 265-93; *Orig. & Hist.* I, pp. 452, 454–5; *LRSM*, 5 September 1845, 3 August 1849; *CW*, XXXII (1891), p. 248; Ward, *Religion and Society*, pp. 289–90; *SG*, 9 April 1859; *Booth*, pp. 160, 164–5.

CHAPTER VI

RENEWAL AND REFORM

A Church Renewed? The Church of England 1830–1900

LEVELS OF ATTENDANCE

There were 51,789 men, women and children at the services of the Church of England in Lincolnshire on the morning of Sunday 30 March 1851 when the Census of Religious Worship was taken. In the afternoon congregations totalled 46,723, while in the evening, when fewer churches were open, 13,178 attended them. These figures take no account of individuals who were there more than once but, taking the total number of people who were at only the best-attended service on the Sunday of the Census, the Church of England can be seen to have attracted between 12 and 13 per cent of the total population of the county. This was not out of line with Archdeacon Stonehouse's calculation, made in 1846, that a population of 1,000 would be expected to yield a congregation of 150, while extra children would come in through a Sunday school.[1]

The overall figures for attendance at religious worship in Lincolnshire did not include the people who were at the 74 churches for which no returns were made, nor did they take account of any people who only attended worship occasionally and were missing on Census Sunday. The Census figures were given an added margin of uncertainty by the inclusion of children where Sunday scholars were said to be in church at the same time as the adult congregation. Some allowance can be made for the people who attended other services, or only attended church occasionally, by assuming that a third of the people who were at the two least well-attended services did not attend any other and adding their numbers to those for the services that were best attended. If this is applied to attendances in Lincolnshire it shows that 17.6 per cent or, making some allowance for places for which there are no details of attendances, up to 20 per cent of the population of the county. worshipped in the Church of England on Sunday 30 March 1851. These figures were little different from the average for England and Wales as a whole, but they subsumed a variety of practice.[2]

There were differences between patterns of church attendance in various parts of Lincolnshire and at parish level. In general terms the Church of England's greatest strength lay in the south-west of the county in the

Bourne, Grantham, and Stamford districts, but it also achieved a high share of the church and chapel attendances around Spilsby, especially for morning service, as well as in the Lincoln area. One of the highest local levels of church attendance was at the Anglican chapel of Wilsthorpe. The small township had a population of 66 and lay within the parish of Greatford, but separate services were provided from those that were held at the parish church. On the afternoon of Census Sunday 40 members of the general congregation and 6 Sunday scholars were said to have attended Wilsthorpe chapel. This was just short of 70 per cent of the total population of the township. The village of Tothill in the Louth registration district was slightly smaller than Wilsthorpe, with a population of 59 and was a separate parish, but here the size of its population was inversely related to attendance at its parish church. Its rector did not make a return for the Census of Religious Worship, but the figures for attendances at its church were obtained by the census enumerator. It had a congregation of three, one of the lowest proportions of population to worshippers of any parish in Lincolnshire.[3]

The Church of England was the only place of worship in both Wilsthorpe and Tothill, but attendance levels also varied where there were alternatives to the church. While there were places where the Church of England was poorly attended compared with nonconformist places of worship, it attracted comparatively high levels of attendance in others. At South Kelsey a rounded set of returns for both the village's church and Wesleyan chapel on 30 March can be taken as generally indicative of levels of levels of religious observance in the parish. The total attendance at the church, including Sunday scholars, was 120, or nearly 46 per cent of the population of the parish, at a time when a service was also being held at the village's Wesleyan Methodist chapel. On the other hand, in the village of Ruskington, which had a population of 1,027, attendance at the parish church was eclipsed by that at the Wesleyan Methodist chapel. While there were 30 people at the morning church service and 45 in the afternoon, the chapel was almost filled to capacity with 121 Sunday scholars in the morning and a general congregation of 200 in the afternoon, together with the 121 Sunday scholars attending for a second time.[4]

Although Tothill was remarkable for the small proportion of its inhabitants who attended religious worship, the size of a place was usually an important influence on attendance. A much higher percentage of the population tended to go to church in small parishes than in large and in south Lindsey villages with less than 200 people attendances were as high as 34.5 per cent of the population on the afternoon of Census Sunday. In larger places with a population over 600 they dropped to as low as 7.4 per cent at morning services. There was also a tendency for villages that were under strong landlord control to have higher church attendances, while the freedom of others provided an opportunity for nonconformity to develop. This was complicated by a number of factors. South Kelsey had a resident landowner to take an interest in church affairs, but this had not prevented the Methodists from gaining a substantial following in the village. Larger villages such as Ruskington tended to be free of landlord control, so that low attendance at their parish churches can either be linked to their size, social structure, or both.[5]

Nor were all landlords anxious to favour the church or to allow the parson too great a voice in parish affairs. This meant that the religious complexion of these more closely controlled parishes was not as uniformly Anglican as might at first appear likely. In Great Limber, at the heart of the Brocklesby estate, there was a Methodist chapel competing with the parish church for the allegiance of the Earl of Yarborough's tenants. The squire of Blankney sought a complaisant rector and the living had been given to his brother-in-law who was described in 1857 as 'a nice quiet fellow' who suited him very well. Although Revesby was effectively controlled by the Stanhope family who lived at the Abbey, relations between the squire and parson of the parish had deteriorated into open conflict. Nonetheless, attendances at worship did not slip below at least the average for the county. Just under 15 per cent of the population of the parish were present at the best-attended service at the church on Census Sunday. These examples are all aspects of the complex situation that was revealed by the 1851 Census of Religious Worship. Above all, it demonstrated the influence that the variety of local contexts in which the parish communities of Lincolnshire conducted their affairs had on their religious lives.[6]

CLERICAL RESIDENCE AND ITS CONSEQUENCES

The Religious Census was taken at a time of change within the Church of England when new standards of clerical diligence were beginning to provide more opportunity and, through more assiduous standards of pastoral care, the incentives for increased attendance at the services of the Church of England. It was said in 1849 that, despite adequate church accommodation, the people of Lincolnshire were 'in no respect superior in ... the knowledge and practice of religion and morality to persons in the same rank in the manufacturing districts'. The 'lax notions of ministerial office' that had been widely accepted in the 18th century continued as a function of widespread non residence. Contacts between clergymen and people remained at a low level, while arrangements for worship and the administration of the sacraments were said to be especially discouraging to the poor. Three hundred and seventy-two of the 588 parishes on which there was information had only one service, and services were said to be 'irregular' in another 12. This left 204 churches where there were two services each Sunday. The situation began to change as the amount of pluralism and non residence that had restricted the ministrations clergymen were able to offer began to diminish. While either the incumbent or the curate was resident in 59.6 per cent of glebe houses in 1832, the proportion had increased to 71.5 per cent by 1844, and to just over 80 per cent by 1853. Although a number of parishes remained that had no suitable housing for their incumbents, there was an increase in the number of places where clergymen resided without using the glebe house. Nearly 14 per cent of the 559 parishes in Lincolnshire for which information is available were served in this way in 1844. Just over 63 per cent of Lincolnshire parishes had been without a resident clergyman in 1832, a situation that had not changed a great deal from that at the end of the 18th century, but the proportion had dropped to just short of 47 per cent by 1844 and just over 38 per cent by 1853. The bishop had noted in 1852 that 409 incumbents from 593 benefices in the county were either resident in their parishes or performed services in person.[7]

The gaps left by non-resident incumbents continued to be filled by stipendiary curates and, as measures were taken to improve their payment and to restrict the number of curacies that they held, more of them became resident in the parishes for which they were responsible. There were 270 stipendiary curates in Lincolnshire in 1832 and 179 in 1853. The proportion of parishes in which they were used declined from 49.1 per cent in 1832 to 32.9 per cent by 1853. Whereas 51 per cent of curates were resident in at least one of the parishes for which they were responsible in 1832, and 63 per cent of them lived in the parsonage, just over 66 per cent were resident by 1853, although the proportion living in the glebe house declined to 42 per cent. The changing role of curates in church life was also apparent in the increase in the number of assistant curates who, instead of acting as a substitute for a non-resident clergyman, worked under an incumbent who was in direct charge of the affairs of his parish either through residence, or close proximity to it. There were 61 assistant curates in 1844 and 54 in 1853. Although the essentially short term nature of their appointments meant that their numbers fluctuated, assistant curates were another manifestation of the increasingly close involvement of clergymen in the lives of their parishes.[8]

These changes took place within a framework for church reform provided by the work of the Ecclesiastical Commission, created in 1835. The Bishop of Lincoln, John Kaye, was a member of it. He had been appointed to the diocese in 1827, but it was not until the work and influence of the Commission began to manifest itself in legislation, particularly the Pluralities Act of 1838, that Kaye acquired the authority of statute for his efforts to reduce the extent of non residence and to ensure that parishes had two services each Sunday. Until then he depended on the influence of his office and earlier legislation. The assistance that was available for work on glebe houses under Gilbert's Act of 1776 was a further encouragement to incumbents to take personal responsibility for their parishes. George Case, Rector of the north Lincolnshire parish of Withcall, yet resident in 1828 at Twyford, near Winchester, was one of the first clergymen who found himself under pressure from Kaye. He lived 'in close vicinity' to the parish of St Michael in Winchester which he had served for 'upwards of 17 years', never being absent from 'the sacred trust reposed in me, but at very short intervals'. Despite Case's claims that he had 'ever observed the same form of notification to Bishops Tomline and Pelham', Kaye returned the papers relating to his non residence at Withcall on the grounds of their 'informality'. Such efforts to secure residence were inevitably piecemeal in their effect and frequently involved compromise as they ran up against entrenched interests. Kaye acceded to an arrangement that enabled the curate of Grainthorpe to retain also the curacy of Yarburgh for two and a half years until the absentee Rector's son could be ordained and serve the parish. He achieved more direct success in increasing the stipend of the curate of Bassingham to £100 in 1831, despite the plea of its aged rector that his twenty-five year's absence in the 'discharge of college engagements' in Oxford had meant that the value of the living had been diminished.[9]

After the area of the diocese of Lincoln had been reduced to the counties of Lincolnshire and Nottinghamshire, Kaye was able to develop a closer contact with its affairs. Change also came as an older generation of clergymen were replaced by men more attuned to the new demands that were being made of them. It was inevitably a gradual process dependent on the passage of time. The power the bishop possessed to appoint clergymen sympathetic to his reforming views was limited by the relatively small proportion of patronage that he had at his personal disposal – 5.6 per cent of the livings in the county – although the increasing tendency of lay patrons, who controlled nearly 49 per cent of advowsons, to involve the bishop in appointments was another indication of a changing understanding of the role of the parish clergy. Patrons' ideas did not always chime with those of the bishop, although when the Earl of Yarborough proposed offering a living to his father's godson in 1849 he sought Kaye's opinion of him.[10]

In 1834 Kaye reckoned that £200 was the minimum level of income needed by a parish clergyman, while 'the possessor of a living even of £500 a year, with a family and without any private sources of income, if he administers as he ought to the temporal wants of his parishioners, has little or nothing to spare'. It was an ideal that was far from being achieved in Lincolnshire. Increases in income as a result of agricultural improvement had tended to enhance livings that already had a high value and the mean value of benefices in the county which stood at £285 in 1830 was inflated by a small number of rich livings, such as Washingborough at £1,637 a year. Between 21 and 22 per cent of them were worth £100 and under, and another 26.5 per cent between £101 and £200, although the temporal circumstances of clergymen began to improve generally when the rent they received for their glebe land and the value of their tithe income rose as agriculture prospered in the middle years of the 19th century. The Governors of Queen Anne's Bounty and the Ecclesiastical Commissioners continued to augment poor livings and by 1872 nearly half in Lincolnshire were worth more than £300.[11]

An increase in the number of men that were being ordained meant that livings could be filled more easily. By the 1820s the number of ordinands was double what it had been in the middle years of the 18th century. This upward trend was to continue until 1886. By 1853 nearly 74 per cent of the clergymen who had been instituted to their livings after 1838 were resident. As they moved into their parishes they brought with them changed perceptions of their role for which they had begun to be prepared in new ways. Bishop Kaye, a Cambridge man, had a strong preference for graduates, especially from his own university. They were urged to attend Divinity lectures while they were there, and from 1843 Kaye insisted that they had passed the University's Voluntary Theological Examination. Kaye's ordination examinations were rigorous and included lengthy vivas with the bishop. This was continued by his successor and in 1858 Jackson's preparation and examination of ordinands occupied three days. Nonetheless Jackson mistrusted theological colleges and feared that they would create a clerical caste. It was not until 1874 that the diocese of Lincoln had its own institution to train both graduates and non-graduates for ordination. The first intake of Lincoln Theological College, known initially as the *Scholae Cancellarii*, who studied there from January 1874 until August 1875, included six men who had graduated from Oxford and Cambridge and five who had been Nonconformist ministers or local preachers. Yet despite changes in attitudes towards the clerical office, perceptions of the significance of ordination changed slowly and the actual rite was often not regarded highly. At Michaelmas 1839 it was reported as being performed after the congregation for morning service had left the cathedral. Charles Anderson said that after an ordination in 1853 the men involved were to be found 'smoking with clays and drinking gin and water in the public room of an inn'.[12]

As a new generation of resident clergymen moved into rebuilt glebe houses they were faced not only with the need to respond to changing official expectations of their roles, but to relate these to the complex scenarios created by social change and the growth of nonconformity in many of their parishes. Although the pace at which this took place varied from place to place, a new set of relationships developed in local communities as clergymen came to be increasingly involved in their parishes as religious functionaries rather than as officers of the establishment. Some parish communities remained content with the more detached type of relationship with their clergy that had characterized church life when levels of non residence were higher. It was reported in 1847 that for 'many years' the sick of Skillington 'had not been duly visited, the school attended, or any attention (except the most casual) given to the parishioners (save the Sunday duty)'. Part of the church was 'in very bad repair', but the parishioners still 'clung' to the non-resident curate. This was because of his 'easiness of disposition, his never troubling them'. Since he 'never gave offence to any by interference and was personally agreeable to others, his inattention to parish duties was overlooked'. The strong group of Methodist farmers in the village feared that 'a more active clergyman ... would interfere with the dominion which they try to exercise'.[13]

The Rector of Branston was able to maintain sufficient control over the four hundred inhabitants of his parish for them to remain content to defer to the arrangements that he made for them. He owned the adowson, and his position was described in 1827 as 'hereditary'. There was only one Sunday service, although he was resident, but he also held the neighbouring parish of Potterhanworth, where he was said to be likewise rector and patron. His control of the 'considerable' parish charities meant that he retained the allegiance of the poor, while the churchwarden was the tenant of his glebe land. The 'generality of farmers' at Branston chose not to interfere in parish affairs. In other places new expectations of the 'character of a clergyman' were being evoked, and with increased frequency. Sir Charles Anderson assured Samuel Wilberforce when he invited him to Lea in 1828 that a parson 'may fire off his gun here without getting into disrepute with his parishioners', but in 1829 the Vicar of Anwick was accused of being seen 'almost daily with his gun, when he ought to be studying his Bible, following the hounds instead of the divine precepts of his Master, visiting races, ball-rooms, plays and fairs, and neglecting the chambers of the afflicted, disconsolate and dying'. In 1844 the churchwardens and parishioners of Covenham St Mary 'thought themselves ill used in not having a clergyman to reside among them' while 'A Farmer' writing from Thorpe on the Hill noted 'it isn't just a gentleman's riding over once a week that will do us much good'.[14]

Services

Once clergymen were resident they were enjoined to undertake two Sunday services. Kaye's first visitation charge adopted a robust approach that left little room for the man who was 'satisfied with himself' merely because his parishioners were 'satisfied with him'. The Consolidated Act of 1817 was invoked against resident clergymen who were 'so insensible' to the obligations they had contracted that 'from a mere regard to [their] own ease or convenience' they deprived their parishioners 'of the opportunity of paying their devotions in the temple of God twice on the Lord's day'. By 1858 nearly 76 per cent of the 174 parishes on which there is information about the frequency of services had two services on Sundays. The majority of them were in the morning and afternoon, but as resident clergymen began to initiate new patterns of worship in their parishes they came up against the ingrained preferences of parish communities such as those that had sustained the status quo at Skillington.[15]

However much it may have been seen as enhancing opportunities for worship, the introduction of two Sunday services did little to change the patterns of attendance of the many individuals for whom it was sufficient to attend church once on a Sunday, nor did the greater choice of times of service stimulate the indifferent. After the perpetual curate of Cowbit began to hold an evening service in 1829 'the aggregate of the congregations scarcely exceeded the single one' and generally speaking there was 'a deficiency of at least one third' in the congregations at each of the two services. He held out little hope of ending the 'deep rooted antipathy' that existed towards the church and of carrying out the bishop's wishes for more frequent services. '[M]any' people in the parish had not been in a place of worship 'more than a dozen times in as many years'. Even in the smaller and more closely controlled parish of South Ormsby, Francis Massingberd found in 1833 that after the introduction of two services each Sunday, very few came twice to church, so 'a very good congregation' had been 'divided into two rather scanty ones'.[16]

In 1842 Richard Bradley thought that a more regular pattern of services at Ruskington would make it easier for his servants to attend church. He feared that for lack of any other opportunity they 'may be led to the Meeting-houses'. This was said to be the case at Lutton in 1832 where, for lack of services at the parish church, people were left free to attend Ranter services. J. R. West, the vicar of Wrawby, and within whose parish a substantial part of the town of Brigg was situated, noted in the 1840s that while people went to both church and chapel they seemed to think it 'quite immaterial' whether they went 'to one chapel or another'. The people of Lincolnshire were not as eclectic in their worshipping habits as West implied, but as two services were held in more and more places clergymen became conscious that they were in competition for their congregations with the Methodists in the afternoon, and particularly in the evening. At Humberston Joseph Gedge's first attempts to hold an evening service in the church during the summer months 'were looked on as opposition'. The balance of the local community was changing by early 1833 and his position in the village was becoming more secure. The principal farmer by then was the brother of a clergyman, while some Methodist farmers had left and been replaced by 'as many churchmen'. The situation at Thornton le Moor in 1838 was less propitious, and the churchwarden had informed the incumbent that the unanimous opinion of all the inhabitants, whom he had seen the night before at the Methodist meeting, was that one Sunday service 'performed at regular hours' was sufficient for them. Nonconformists opposed to an increase in the number of church services were also able to make their influence felt in towns. Church attendances at Market Rasen were said to have been built up at the expense of the dissenters in 1833, but unsympathetic rate payers left the clergyman to pay for the heat and light for evening services.[17]

The Rector of Swaby noted in 1851 how 'In most churches the practice has been to have the one service in the church alternately morning and afternoon, and the service (or preaching as it is at the chapels) is regulated accordingly'. At Welton le Wold the rector also suggested that arrangements at the Wesleyan chapel took account of those at the parish church, while an even greater degree of reciprocity was said to exist at Kelstern where the steward of the Wesleyan Methodist chapel noted that 'The service alternate(s) 2 and 6, 2 one Sunday, 6 the next, etc. No service in church hours, the congregation attends the church also'. These arrangements were confined to the Wesleyan Methodists and Church of England. The Primitive Methodists of Welton le Wold held services in both the afternoon, when there was also one in church, and in the evening when the Wesleyans worshipped.[18]

As the number of places where two services were held in the parish church increased, those where there were reciprocal arrangements between church and chapel diminished, although influential members of the parish community were still often able to secure their continuance, or even to ensure that church services were arranged so as not to affect chapel attendance. Joseph Grimes, the churchwarden at Aubourn said in 1858 that he was a Wesleyan who attended the chapel 'regular'. In 1871 the Wesleyan chapel at Spridlington was still rarely open at the same time as the parish church. Its congregations left it early enough to attend morning worship at the church, while 'a united family of Church and Dissent' met in the Wesleyan chapel following the afternoon service at the church. Even after the collective manifestations of mutual respect that were demonstrated in arrangements for services became less common, individual Wesleyans continued to demonstrate it, so that movement between the Church of England and Wesleyan chapels remained an important feature of religious life in Lincolnshire to the end of the 19th century. John Rushby of Toynton St Peter was a staunch Wesleyan, but was reported in 1875 to have been 'not unfrequently a worshipper at his parish church'. After the Wesleyan local preacher and office holder, Henry Lunn, moved from Horncastle to West Ashby in 1876 he occasionally occupied the pew in the parish church assigned to his house and 'communicated from time to time'.[19]

RITES AND CUSTOMS

Even though an increase in the number of services provided by the Church of England did not necessarily bring a corresponding growth in attendances, the recourse that the people of Lincolnshire had to the church for the rites of baptism, marriage, and burial were indicative of the extent to which these observances had become embedded in their consciousnesses as a valid expression of their needs and aspirations at turning points in their lives. The Dissenting Marriages Act of 1836 allowed nonconformist chapels to be used for the solemnization of marriages, and the provision made for civil marriage from 1837 widened the choice of ceremonies that were available. Only 33 chapels had been licensed in the whole of Lincolnshire by 1842. Twenty of them were Independent, Congregational, or Baptist and another nine Roman Catholic. Civil marriage was used relatively little. The establishment of a national system for the registration of births under the Civil Registration Act of 1836 had little direct impact on church life, although reactions to the measure were indicative of the differences that existed between popular understandings of baptism and the official teachings of the church. The authority that clergymen exercised over churchyards remained a matter of contention until the Burials Act of 1880, although the actual registration of deaths was not something that impinged directly on parish life.[20]

Marriage

By 1850 about 3 per cent of the 2,708 of marriages in Lincolnshire were performed by civil ceremony, making it one of the areas with the lowest proportion of civil marriages in England and Wales. The more frequent use that began to be made of nonconformist chapels had a greater impact on the number of church weddings, although by 1871 just over 74 per cent of the 787 marriage ceremonies in the most rural areas of south Lindsey were still performed in parish churches. The doubts and misgivings that surrounded a civil ceremony were evident in the case of the couple who contracted a civil marriage but underwent a second full ceremony in Cowbit church in 1847. Civil marriage could be imposed by Boards of Guardians as a condition of relief and was used in cases where an illegitimate birth was imminent, but the Revd T. B. Wright of Wrangle regarded a woman from the parish, married 'through the intervention of the Board of Guardians of the Poor at Boston', as 'being de facto excommunicated'. The need to resort to the local workhouse for a civil marriage ceremony meant that it was hardly an attractive proposition, although considerably cheaper than church. When the Rector of Horsington complained in 1856 of the expense incurred by a couple who were asked to pay the same fee for the publication of the banns in the groom's parish of Bardney as they would have done had the marriage been solemnized there, it was said that the custom had doubled the price of church marriages to £1 2s 0d compared with seven shillings 'at the Union' and in dissenting chapels.[21]

Archdeacon Bonney expressed concern at the levity occasioned by weddings, but despite the great popular significance of marriage ceremonies parish clergymen were largely able to maintain control over the way that they were conducted. The party of old ladies that had assembled by custom in the nave of Horsington church to pelt bridal parties with hassocks had been disbanded by a 'scandalized' rector as early as the 1780s. The belief, from Barnoldby le Beck, that the first of a couple who knelt to be blessed at their wedding would die first was one of a very limited number of folk beliefs or practices that were associated with the conduct of the ceremony, and even this did not impinge on it publicly. Other unofficial practices and usages took place outside the church. Cake was thrown over brides and grooms in Crowle and its neighbourhood, but it was on their return from church, while in the village of Helpringham marriages were given public acclamation when the bride and bridegroom walked around the village after the wedding day tea. Parish communities were more concerned with the bases on which marriages were established, and their subsequent development, rather than the ceremony by which they were made. In this context the publication of the banns of marriage attracted much attention, although manifestations of public interest were relatively restrained. The parish clerk at Claxby, near Market Rasen, adopted the local custom of the area and said 'God speed them well'. Nonetheless, about half the farmers and all of the gentry, clergy, and their children in south Lindsey avoided even this level of intrusion into their personal affairs and were married by licence, so that in 1850 between 18 and 19 per cent of church marriages were arranged in this way.[22]

Baptism

The extent to which Lincolnshire people continued to have their children baptized in the Church of England was a measure of the importance of the ceremony to them, although their perceptions of it often represented a view of the Church that, in the words of Bishop Wordsworth, saw it as 'a department of State, and not a divine institution'. Twenty-two public baptisms of both adults and children from the Fen side and Norlands cum Littlemoor parts of the parish took place in Sibsey parish church on a Sunday afternoon in late January 1838. They were said to be in consequence of a report that punishment by fine or imprisonment would be inflicted under the new Registration Acts on all parents or guardians omitting to have their children baptized before the first of February. While clergymen sought to emphasize the spiritual importance of baptism, sections of the laity were also concerned with its social significance. The Prayer Book rubric stated that it should be administered 'upon Sundays, and other Holy-days, when the most number of people come together', but this was ignored in a large number of places in Lincolnshire. The rite for private baptism, which provided for cases where there was 'great cause and necessity', was used in ways that suited the personal circumstances of parents. In 1822 the churchwarden at Langton by Wragby sent a girl with his infant son to the clergyman for private baptism. When it was refused the child was 'dispatched to another parish' so that its father could hold a celebratory feast. As late as 1850 the Revd W. Winston reported to the bishop that nothing, apart from funerals, had given him so much trouble in the Toynton parishes as baptisms: 'The clergyman, they thought, was bound privately to baptize a child, whether well or ill, when required to do so'. In scattered fenland communities it was less easy to arrange prompt public baptisms as laid down in the prayer book. At Whaplode infants were said in 1845 to be brought to the clergyman's house 'generally on or about the third day'. Here he was to some extent in control of a situation in which he acquiesced, since in a parish where 'a vast number of infants die' private baptisms were an attempt to ensure them the burial service that the Prayer Book denied the unbaptized.[23]

A private ceremony also meant that nonconformist parents were able to have their children baptized without godparents, who were only required when a child was brought to church for public certification of the private ceremony, usually referred to as christening. It was also said that at Ranby in 1832 private baptisms were conducted in church to enable dissenters to 'get their children entered in the register'. When, in what was not a unique occurrence in Lincolnshire, a woman at Croxton presented three children for christening in 1840 who had been baptized by 'a methodist preacher', John Morgan felt that he was obliged to refuse the ceremony. The woman was 'poor'. Parishioners with greater influence were able to adopt a more independent attitude. In the period between 1825 and 1850 the majority of children were almost certainly baptized privately on weekdays in six south Lindsey parishes where a resident clergyman was available, although most of the labourers' children were baptized on Sundays when the ceremony was more likely to be public. Public baptism as required by the Prayer Book rubric was practised in 129 out of 207 churches in south Lindsey by 1873, but in 26 of them baptisms were still being performed after the main service was over, usually in the afternoon, and in another 25 instances they were not being held at the recommended time. These transgressions against the spirit of the Prayer Book rubrics were a measure of the extent to which members of the parish community remained able to impose their own terms in church affairs.[24]

The performance of the other rite associated with birth, the Thanksgiving of Women after Child-birth – 'Churching', as it was commonly known from its alternative title in the Book of Common Prayer – also led to contention between clergymen and their parishioners. Popular perceptions of the significance of the ceremony came up against the attempts of clergymen to ensure that it was conducted in ways that deferred to their authority in church affairs. It was, according to J. H. Overton, who went to Legbourne in 1860, looked upon with 'an almost superstitious regard'. The strength of these feelings arose from the close association of the ceremony with notions of purification. The verb 'cleansed' was being employed in connection with it at Cadney as late as 1897. Although there was no specific provision in the prayer book for it to be performed publicly some clergymen attempted to enforce this. There was a measure of prudery, if not feelings of indelicacy, in the objections voiced at churches in the Spalding area to attempts 'on those interesting occasions when Her Majesty's subjects are increased' to seat women who were to be churched in a special and separate pew. They were said to be 'subjected to the scrutiny of all present'. Overton was forced to move the timing of churchings in order to achieve public baptisms. If he had not made this concession women who had not been churched would not have walked down the church aisle for the baptism of their children.[25]

Burial

The provision for the civil registration of deaths excited little controversy. The problems that arose over churchyards were considerably greater. Although they were the only place for burial in the majority of Lincolnshire parishes, the new generation of clergymen who sought to assert the distinctive position of the Church of England in parish life was less disposed to see churchyards as the property of the whole community irrespective of religious allegiance. The control that the Church exercised over burials signified its official place in the life of the local community. Bishop Wordsworth saw the various proposals that culminated in the Burials Law Amendment Act of 1880 as part of 'the tide which is setting in very strongly against the Church of England as the Church of the nation'. In adopting this position he ignored the largely unrecorded occasions when the claims of the church had been foregone by individual clergymen in the interests of communal harmony. The burial of a dissenter without any service in Billinghay churchyard in the late 1820s was an example of the type of negative accommodation that could be reached when clergymen were not inclined to assert their position.[26]

The 1880 Act allowed non-Anglican ministers to conduct burials according to their own rites provided this did not constitute an affront to the

*Fig. 34   Old Clee. Gravestone of a friendly society member. The obsequies
for members of friendly societies could bring conflict over the use of
the churchyard. Gravestones at Clee commemorate members of the
order of Oddfellows from the parish.*

CEMETERY CHAPEL, BOSTON.

*Fig. 35   Boston cemetery chapel. As town churchyards became full,
cemeteries funded by rate began to be provided, giving nonconformists the
freedom to conduct their own burial rites, but separate chapels were
built for the Church of England and for other denominations.
There were two exactly similar buildings at Boston in 1855.*

Christian religion or give offence to members or ministers of any denomination. These definitions of the type of ceremony that was permitted took no account of other customs surrounding burial that were equally strongly held and maintained. Indeed other supererogatory proceedings at funerals constituted a greater challenge to clergymen, especially in so far as they were part of a highly developed popular sense of the need to mark the occasion in a full and proper manner. Hymn singing was associated particularly with Methodist funerals and could give rise to friction, although Edward Steere was willing for them to sing over the grave of one of their members at Skegness. The Methodists at Beckingham, who had been said to 'sing the corpse' to the churchyard gate, began to ask in 1844 if they could in some cases also sing at the grave. The same year John P. Parkinson of Ravendale expressed his concern at the 'extempore speeches and unauthorised singing' that had occurred at the conclusion of a funeral service. The Elsham Primitive Methodists were more openly confrontational and, according to the curate Henry White, had adopted 'a determined plan' to sing hymns in the church instead of accompanying the officiating clergyman to the grave.[27]

Attendance at Claypole parish church on Sunday 30 March was said to have been affected by the funeral of the member of a friendly society that had taken place immediately after the afternoon service. Many of these societies were nominally loyal to the Church of England and their annual feasts usually included a special church service, but the expression of their fraternal values and the desire to provide a seemly set of obsequies led them to seek to supplement the church's burial rites with their own funeral observances. These were as great a test of the ability of clergymen to maintain control over an important rite of passage as the proceedings at Methodist funerals. The Oddfellows of Pinchbeck were content to read the oration that their rules required after the officiating clergyman had left the graveside. According to the Revd W. Wayet, who wrote to the bishop about it in 1839, this had been permitted in many places. There was nothing 'objectionable' in it. Wayet was advised that the bishop would not seek to prevent the oration taking place provided that it was made after the clergyman had left, but it should be stopped should there be any 'disorderly' conduct. The funeral address used by the Foresters at Kirton in Lindsey in 1840 proclaimed their 'deference to our superiors in church and state'. They were content to deliver it outside the churchyard wall until the bishop gave his opinion on its use, but in 1849 Kaye backed Edward Moore in his refusal to allow additional material to the burial service to be read in the churchyard at Weston.[28]

The continuing closeness of many Wesleyans to the Church of England meant that they were more inclined to accept the burial arrangements provided by the church, although confrontations occurred where the attitude of clergymen was excessively rigid. In 1865 the Louth Wesleyan ministers joined some sixty office holders in a petition to the bishop from the circuit's Quarterly Meeting against the way the Revd S. H. Wynn of Burgh on Bain had truncated the funeral service of one of his Wesleyan parishioners and refused to admit her body into the church. The issue was made more acute by the fact that the woman had been baptized by Wynn and had been 'an occasional attendant on the services of the Church of England'.[29]

A more frequent cause of contention was in cases where parish clergymen questioned the validity of baptisms performed by nonconformist ministers and sought to deny a full funeral to the people they

Fig. 36   Brigg cemetery entrance lodge. The town had no churchyard of its own and a cemetery was opened in 1857. The boards responsible for the management of these new burial grounds provided an arena for parish politics in places such as Brigg.

had baptized. This was usually done by reading the burial service in the churchyard. In 1836 Octavus Luard of Blyborough refused to take the corpse of a child baptized at the Primitive Methodist chapel into church, but held the service at the grave side. In early 1843 the curate of Sutton St Edmund was reported for not only omitting the part of the burial service normally read in church, but for keeping his hat on during the funeral of the infant son of a Methodist. When Edward Moore refused in 1849 to read the burial service at Weston for a child he claimed was unbaptized, but which had in fact been baptized in a nonconformist chapel, he was reminded by the bishop that as it had been baptized with water in the name of the Trinity it should have had the burial service read over it.[30]

Confirmation

The divergence between older popular attitudes towards the rites of passage, and the attempts by newly resident clergymen to assert their control over the manner in which the church and its surroundings were used, also extended to confirmation. The rite had a continuing appeal to large numbers of young people, but frequently not in ways or for reasons that accorded with the ideals of the clergy. Kaye wished to ensure that young people who were to be confirmed were instructed and prepared. It was reported that the 'appearance, conduct, and demeanour' of the large numbers that attended the confirmation and visitation at Grantham in 1834 demonstrated how well this had been done. Yet when John Mackinnon, the Rector of Bloxholm and Vicar of Digby, acting on the bishop's instructions, had refused in 1843 to give a ticket to allow a young woman who had not been 'examined or instructed' by him to be confirmed, her father was able to obtain one from another clergyman. The predecessor of Sidney Neucatre at South Kyme had been in the habit of issuing tickets for confirmation 'as a matter of course' on the Sunday before the service was to be held. Neucatre explained that the dearth of candidates from the parish in 1840 was because he was concerned to ensure that they were prepared for the rite. Other clergymen were more interested in maintaining the numbers presented to the bishop and so responded to general pressure by issuing confirmation tickets. It was alleged that in the Boston area in the 1840s 'a-shilling a-head and a holiday was the lure held out to tempt the lads and lassies to kneel reverently before the Bishop'.[31]

There was a total of 10,238 people confirmed in Lincolnshire in 1840. The large numbers of young people who gathered for the rite meant that until the second half of the 19th century it continued to be an occasion of carnival, often far removed from its spiritual purpose. Kaye managed proceedings at confirmations by separating males from females in church, by arranging for access to it to be restricted, and for quiet to be maintained in churchyards during the service. While there was enough control over the actual conduct of the service for 'roughs' from the village of Ruskington to be turned out of Sleaford church at a confirmation in 1858, the arrangements for the female candidates from the village to be driven to the service in a seemly manner were negated by their drunken driver. He fell into a ditch from the shafts of the waggon in which they were being conveyed. The smaller and more frequent confirmation services that began to be held in village as well as town churches, meant that the problems associated with the large crowds who had gathered for confirmations in the past abated and the rite came to be administered more on the clergy's own terms. In 1864 Jackson noted that while candidates were fewer in number they were better behaved, although confirmation was becoming less appealing to young men. Jackson confirmed 4,701 people in 1865, of whom 60 per cent were female. It has been estimated that by 1873 30 per cent of the males and 52 per cent of the females from the 15 to 19 age group were confirmed in some parts of the county. In 1874 the vicar of Grantham gave a course of week-night lectures for confirmation candidates as well as holding classes for females, but it was less easy to marshal young domestic and farm servants for this type of structured educational experience.[32]

WORSHIP AND ITS CONTEXT

The efforts that clergymen made to control and define the terms on which the rites of passage were made available were part of a more general increase in their influence over the conduct of worship. This was associated with a greater consciousness on their part of the distinctive nature of their calling and of the status that it conferred on them. The issues that surrounded the conduct of weekly Sunday worship and the setting in which it was conducted were complicated by questions of control over the interior of churches. Elected churchwardens exercised their responsibilities on behalf of parish rate payers, while the maintenance of chancels belonged to rectors. Disagreements became formalized in disputes over church rates. Where changes to church interiors were associated with the restoration of the building, the norms and values that informed the work also provided grounds for discord.

In the parish church at Ruskington 'sanctity of devotion' was said to be 'a thing unknown' until the arrival of a new clergyman in the middle of the 19th century. The 'lawless behaviour' that 'reigned paramount' was associated with the influence exerted by a gallery 'filled with rabble' and a 'choir' of 'hautboys, clarionets, violins, flutes, bassoons &c.' which imposed its own musical agenda on the worship of a church where the parish clerk gave out notices of auction sales during service and retreated to the public house in sermon time. Under the new regime 'the old hands with their musical instruments' were dispersed and a 'vocal choir' was installed in the clerk's pew. It was a move that was repeated up and down the county

*Fig. 37   St Peter's church, Markby.   An unrestored interior in which pulpit
and reading desk dominate a church filled with family pews.*

as old-style choirs were dispersed, often supplanted in their galleries at the
west end of the church by harmoniums or organs. A new organ was
installed at Denton in 1843 with the stamp of the authority of Sir William
Welby who met most of the costs, while later in the same year General
Birch Reynardson paid for one at Holywell. The subscription list for the
patent harmonium installed in Threckingham church in 1847 was said to be
headed by nobles and gentlemen.[33]

There were fewer subscribers to support the introduction of new styles
of worship in the differently ordered parish of Tydd St Mary where the new
organ was the gift of the curate's daughter. The wives and daughters of
clergymen, farmers, and landowners, as well as village schoolmistresses,
tended to have the skills needed to play the new instruments so that the new
musical arrangements for worship were associated with a relatively small
group in the parish. Barrel organs served until suitably trained organists
were available, although that at Raithby near Louth was part of the fittings
of the church which was rebuilt in 1839. Some parish clerks were able to
retain a place in worship by operating them, but keyboard instruments were
a greater challenge, and their introduction provided a further opportunity
for clergymen to extend their control over worship through the
appointment of organists who shared their ideals and were amenable to
their direction.[34]

*Fig. 38   St Mary and St Gabriel's church, Binbrook. Built in 1869 to designs
by the local architect James Fowler of Louth to replace the two decayed churches
that had served the village, work on the new parish church was heavily
dependent on contributions from outside the parish.*

The reform of the musical life of the parish church was an issue on
which the people who had the means to join the subscription lists for new
organs could unite with the parish clergy, but deeper emotions were stirred
when the physical reordering of the church extended beyond the removal of
a gallery of rustic instrumentalists to affect the general arrangements by
which the parish community was organized for worship. Although the
politics of church seating was another issue through which the parish
community continued to identify with the church, the abolition of
appropriated sittings, which comprised some 57 per cent of seats in
Lincolnshire in 1851, meant that there was less scope for interference by
lay people in the arrangement of church interiors. Most of them were not
actually rented out for the use of individuals or families but were
'appropriated, either by custom or the authority of the church officers, to
particular persons'. In many places seats were associated with the
ownership or occupancy of a particular house or property, although when
the Rector sought to increase the proportion of appropriated seats in the
church at Wainfleet in 1842 he noted that 'the poor as well as the rich like to
have a place which they can consider as their own'. At villages such as
South Carlton the arrangement of seats reflected the local social hierarchy
with Lord Monson at its head in his chancel pew. In less structured

communities the tensions generated by the appropriation of church seats reflected the preoccupations of local society as the space of the parish church became the arena for more general issues of property, status, power, and ownership. These were often heightened by the control that churchwardens exercised over the allocation of pews. A man and his wife who objected to the way that seats were apportioned by the churchwardens at Anwick were ejected from the church by police on Trinity Sunday 1864 and fined £5 by the magistrates' court for their 'indecent and disorderly conduct'. In 1861 the Rector of Caythorpe had found it necessary to present the churchwardens to the archdeacon's court for removing the local surgeon from a seat one of them wished to claim for himself.[35]

In such a climate moves to repew a church could develop into a major issue. Like the installation of organs, the authoritative support of a munificent and sympathetic benefactor could ensure that repewing was carried through without objections, otherwise voluntary fund raising prevented a struggle over the issue with rate payers in the parish vestry meeting. The cost of providing open seats at Whaplode church in 1850 was met by voluntary contributions. The voluntary nature of a subscription of £3,500 to repew and restore Boston parish church in 1851 was pointed up by the fact that it was one of a number of schemes competing for the attention of the population of the town and appeared alongside efforts by the Wesleyans and Independents to pay off chapel debts. In most Lincolnshire towns, and in a number of villages, the church's claims for financial support became increasingly contested. Although for all the heat that the issue generated, rates in support of the church continued to be levied in a majority of Lincolnshire parishes. All the costs of services and the repair and maintenance of the church – £52 over a period of seven years – were met from a rate in the small village of Healing in the 1850s, and this was also the case with the ordinary church expenditure in larger places such as Grantham. Nonetheless there were disputes at some time or other in most Lincolnshire market towns from the 1830s until compulsory church rates were abolished in 1868. Dissenters took the lead in opposing church rates. The continuing attachment of many Wesleyan Methodists to the church meant that they were less likely to oppose them, although some of the leading supporters of the large town chapels were prominent in local campaigns. A majority of the Wesleyans who voted in a poll at Horncastle in 1836 were among the successful opponents of a rate. Even smaller communities, where there were few nonconformists apart from the Methodists, became embroiled in church rate disputes and the Wesleyans of Tealby were said to have been foremost in defeating a proposed rate there in 1837. In the Gainsborough church rate contests of the late 1830s and early 1840s the town divided on party political lines. Churchmen did not lose all the polls that were forced on them. A contest at Gedney in 1840 led to a decisive vote of 111 to 44 in favour of a rate. Despite past divisions in Spalding, a 2½d rate was carried the same year without any opposition.[36]

Church restoration

When a church rate was set for Sleaford in 1838 a distinction was made between what were deemed to be necessary repairs and more substantial work on the church fabric. This was described as ornamental and was to be covered by a separate subscription, as was the case with much church refurbishment and restoration in 19th century Lincolnshire. Seven hundred pounds were raised by subscription to meet a large proportion of the costs of a new church at Amcotts in the 1850s and to provide a more seemly setting for worship by replacing what was 'a very poor building covered with thatch'. In cases like this churches were rebuilt not only to meet the need for additional church accommodation, as had happened with the more utilitarian Georgian buildings provided in the newly drained fens in the early 19th century, but in response to new ideals of what was the proper architectural setting for Christian worship. The 'architectural beauty' and 'congregational convenience' of the new church built in the Early English style at Stainby in the 1860s was compared with the 'non descript' style of

Fig. 39   All Saints' parish church, Wold Newton, 1862, said by contemporaries to be a 'very successful' rebuilding of the old church. It embodied many of the ideals that inspired the Gothic revival of the 19th century.

its Georgian predecessor of 1805. It demonstrated the ideals that informed the transformation of the fabric and furnishings of many of the parish churches of Lincolnshire in the 19th century. Paid for by the rector, it was one of some 370 pieces of work carried out on Lincolnshire churches with the authority of a faculty in the period between 1840 and 1900, although there were others that were not officially authorized. There was an average of just over six restorations and rebuildings a year by faculty in the 60-year period from 1840, but the pace of the work increased markedly in the 1860s. The number of faculties that were granted reached a high point of 21 in 1868, with other peaks in activity in 1874, when there were 16, and in 1878 with 14. These not only included 44 rebuildings, but 294 restorations, including separate work on chancels not usually paid for from parish funds, and another 25 refurbishments that dealt specifically with seating arrangements.[37]

Sir Charles Anderson was busy 'Gothicizing' part of Lea church in 1829, although according to Archdeacon Stonehouse it was 'not quite in the style which a skilful Ecclesiastical Architect would admire'. New standards in church architecture were given a more coherent initial expression through the Cambridge Camden Society, formally established in 1839 for 'the study of Ecclesiastical Architecture and Antiquities'. It had only eleven members in Lincolnshire by 1847, six of whom were clergymen, but the Society's influence had already been felt when it commented in characteristic manner in 1844 on the dilapidated and neglected state of churches in the Spilsby area. Many were 'brick rooms in the pagan style rebuilt in the last century'. It was the establishment in the same year of what became the Lincoln Diocesan Architectural Society, probably through the interest of a member of the Camden Society from Louth, that provided a more widely influential critical coherence to the work of church restoration in the county. In its early days the Architectural Society cultivated an exclusively Anglican and clerical character, refusing election to a local Wesleyan minister. With local grandees and noblemen for its patrons, and clergymen making up the bulk of its membership, the organization and proceedings of the Society largely epitomized the manner in which church restoration was effected in Lincolnshire. The protracted struggles between the parish vestry and incumbent over the restoration of Stow church, described by the local newspaper as being between a 'parish of hard-struggling farmers and a clergyman pledged to the fashionable study of archaeology', illustrated in an extreme form the issues that were raised by church restoration and the tensions they could generate within parish communities.[38]

At the lunch that followed the reopening of Donington church in 1868 the bishop said that there could be 'no church restoration without a good deal of that self denial which consisted in giving up old prejudices', but church restoration involved a commitment that extended beyond a change of attitudes. The work at Donington had cost a total of £2,300 raised by public subscription. Like the work at Sleaford and Amcotts, restorations on this scale were heavily dependent on the generosity of individuals, although major repairs, if not full-scale restorations, were carried out at Frodingham in 1841 and at Winteringham in 1847 with loans that spread the cost to local rate payers. The extent to which the funds for church work generally came from outside local parish communities, or from a relatively narrow part of them, increased the sense in which the work was seen as an innovation imposed from the outside. In parishes under landlord control the expectation that change would come from above was greater than in more loosely structured towns and villages. The Rector of Winteringham had considerable problems in securing the agreement of the churchwardens, 'both men of immoral character' who considered 'a place of worship in less respect than their own pig sties'. It was said at Springthorpe that without the support of the largest landowner in the parish there would be 'very great difficulty' in having the church restored.[39]

The fund to build a new church at Binbrook was headed by two of the main landowners who contributed £1,000 each, while others from the neighbourhood gave smaller amounts. There was also £100 or £50 from three of the leading farmers, but neither of the principal landowners was resident and the project was bitterly contested by a hostile vestry. The grants available from the Incorporated Church Building Society to supplement subscription lists for restoration were small. The Society made a grant of £185 towards increased accommodation when the nave of Kirton in Lindsey church was restored in 1860 at a total cost of £1,500, but a quarter of the donations towards the work came from the area of the vicar's previous parish in Hertfordshire.[40]

Members of the Cambridge Camden Society were forbidden from entering into theological debate, but their concern with the 'symbolical and material expression' of the church's beliefs led them towards the study of liturgy and an interest in ritual. Kaye felt able to give the Lincoln Architectural Society his cautious support, but he withdrew from the Camden Society because of what were seen as its Romanizing tendencies. In Sir Charles Anderson's opinion a well-restored church was enough in itself to excite devotion. The oversimplified associations that were made between innovations in worship and the Oxford Movement obscured with prejudice the more widely based origins and widespread adoption of changes in the conduct as well as the context of worship in Lincolnshire parish churches, some of which were relatively modest. While clergymen were often relatively eclectic in these matters they were constrained in the introduction of new patterns of worship by their churchmanship and, in some rural parishes, by the resources available to them. At Gainsborough in 1848 the Evangelically inclined vicar, C. S. Bird, resisted attempts to push him towards introducing 'the Cathedral Service' with 'intoning &c.'. Bird had been prepared to go as far as introducing two hymns into the services, despite the mistrust of congregational hymn singing that still existed in the 1840s; but the development of the musical side of parochial worship meant that choirs became integrated into worship. Male voices were easier to find in market towns where the introduction of robed choirs was another element in moves towards a more elaborately distinctive style of church worship. A choir was begun at Grantham in 1868, and the same year some eighty or ninety seat-holders in Boston parish church initiated attempts to induce the vicar and churchwardens to robe the choir there. This was the year that the church lost the privilege of compulsory church rates, and both these developments can be seen as an assertion of its position by emphasizing the distinctiveness of its worship.[41]

ANGLICAN PARISH LIFE AND RURAL DECLINE, c. 1870–1900

Although the structures of church life in Lincolnshire remained strong at the end of the 19th century, with resident clergymen supplying regular and indeed enhanced opportunities for worship, the influence of the church on the hearts and minds of the people of the county was more problematic. In so far as this can be measured in terms of formal religious practice, and in the absence of the firmer, if elusive bench marks provided by the Census of Religious Worship half a century earlier, there would appear to have been no general increase in the numbers who attended worship, although more distinctive criteria of churchmanship had developed that were based on an increased emphasis on the significance of Holy Communion. These changes were personified by Bishop Edward King whose reaction to the Lincolnshire returns made at the first visitation after his arrival in the diocese in 1885 – 'Dissent! Dissent! Dissent!' – expressed not only his overwhelming sense of the strength of nonconformity in the county, but the extent to which the Protestant culture represented by the chapels was deeply embedded in the county. The position of the Church of England was also sapped as agricultural depression reduced the incomes of country clergymen, affecting their morale and their ability to maintain their place in parish life. They became increasingly defensive as they worked to find a continuing and valid role for the church amidst a general ambience of decline generated by falling village populations. The establishment of elected parish councils in 1894 not only finally separated the sacred and the secular functions of the parish, but increased the marginalisation of clergymen in rural parish life. Those that were able to maintain their position in the local community did so because of individual and personal circumstances and qualities.[42]

The Church of England's problems were not confined to rural areas. A count of church attendances at Lincoln in January 1873 confirmed the predominance of nonconformity in the city, while similar exercises at Spalding and Gainsborough in 1881 and 1887 also showed the comparative weakness of the Church of England. Although the gap between the total attendances at church and nonconformist chapels in Spalding and Gainsborough was considerably less than at Lincoln, both were, in terms of church attendance, nonconformist towns. At Brigg nonconformist attendances were nearly twice those at the town's church in 1886. Yet in terms of the provision that it made for worship the position of the Church of England was as strong as it had ever been since the late 17th century. By 1900 all except a few small parishes had a clergyman living in them and 484 had at least two Sunday services, usually Morning and Evening Prayer, although there was a group where the evening service was still performed in the afternoon. There were also 121 parishes where there was still only one Sunday service. They were usually small and the low value of their livings meant that they were among the relatively few held in plurality. A number of larger places had daily services, and there was also evidence of innovation in patterns of worship through the introduction of services for children. These tended to be on Sunday afternoons and in towns such as Bourne, but they were also held in the large village of Binbrook. There was a monthly children's Eucharist at Stickney.[43]

The augmentation of what had become an established pattern of morning and evening prayer by increasingly frequent celebrations of Holy Communion from the middle of the 19th century meant that by 1900 the Sacrament was held at least weekly in 252 parish churches, fortnightly or twice a month in 139, and monthly in 184. Variations might occur in the few places where clergymen still held more than one living, but there was only a handful of places where the quarterly Sacraments continued. These included the small parishes of Bag Enderby and Somersby, although the continuance of quarterly communions was not related to parish size. Some larger places such as Toynton St Peter and All Saints had a similar level of provision. Yet, despite its increasing availability Holy Communion became less an inclusive if infrequent mark of association with the official religious life of the parish, and more a measure of the specifically Anglican religious identity of the generally lower numbers who regularly partook of it. While a high proportion of the population of the county continued to be formally identified with the Church of England through baptism, large numbers of them did not go on to qualify themselves to receive communion through confirmation nor, when confirmed, even become regular communicants.[44]

The bifurcation in church life between regular communicants in the Church of England and those who were less strongly associated with it through baptism was seen at Harmston at Easter 1890 when there were 25 communicants at the choral celebration of Holy Communion that was held at 8.30 a.m, in the morning and 10 at another communion service at 12 noon. The services of Matins and Evensong with sermons were very much more popular and attracted congregations of 80 and 150 respectively from a village population of some 320 people. In the archdeaconry of Lincoln, an area that covered the southern half of the county and included about half its population, 4,462 infants, or some 75 per cent of the children under a year old, were baptized in 1900. The 2,179 people from the area who took the next step towards full association with the church by being confirmed represented only between 2 and 3 per cent of the population under 15 years of age. The differences in participation levels between men and women that had existed from at least the middle of the century continued, and 55 per cent of the confirmation candidates were young women.[45]

There were said to be 22,756 communicants in the archdeaconry of Lincoln in 1900–1901, just under 9 per cent of its population, although the number that communicated regularly cannot be known. The Vicar of Billinghay identified the various levels of commitment to the church that had developed in his strongly nonconformist parish by 1900. There were 70 potential communicants out of a population of 2,023. Their attitude to the Holy Communion was similar to that revealed by the Easter attendances at Harmston, so that while an average of 10 people attended communion at Billinghay, there were some 50 people at other church services. In the more deferential Kesteven village of Aswarby an average of nearly half the total number of communicants in the parish attended fortnightly communion services. The situation was similarly varied in the developing towns of the county. There were said to be about 500 communicants from a total population of 16,268 in the new parish of St John the Evangelist, New Clee. An average of 30 took the sacrament at each celebration of it. The parish had been created in 1879 to serve Grimsby's growing fishing community. It had a more unstable population – an estimated 1,329 men were not included in its census returns in 1901 because they were away from home on the North Sea fishery – than the other developing towns of Lincolnshire such as Gainsborough. Yet, despite provision of new churches to serve these places and the development of new modes of pastoral care, untrammelled by the old structures of rural parish life and the mentalities they engendered, the number of communicants was not markedly better, even in the most efficiently run town parishes, than they were in the villages from which many of their parishioners had come. In the new parish of Holy Trinity Gainsborough the proportion of Easter communicants reached just over ten per cent of the population of the parish as a result of the pastoral diligence of its vicar, but only about a fifth of them made their communion Sunday by Sunday.[46]

In country parishes clergymen blamed increased mobility and rural depopulation for their failure to bring forward more candidates for confirmation. The Rector of Algarkirk said in 1900 that 'The "Rural Exodus" takes them away so early', but more long-standing problems continued, including the opposition of nonconformists to confirmation. Young men were subjected to peer group pressure. It was noted at Blyborough that, although dissenters continued to use the church for baptism, marriage, and burial they were not prepared to become more closely identified with it through confirmation. A pressure 'little short of persecution' was brought to bear on the young to prevent them from becoming candidates and it was reported that 'A young labourer on a farm who is preparing for confirmation becomes the butt of his mates and older labourers'. In many country parishes confirmation continued to be identified with the stage in their lives when young people left home and so were able to leave behind whatever church associations had marked their childhood. Many country incumbents were able to persuade the small numbers of young people that were confirmed to make their first communion, but others noted the failure of some to make even this minimal acknowledgment of their new status within the Church of England. Only one of the boys confirmed at Aubourn in 1900 became a regular communicant, although three made their communion occasionally. Most of the rest had been lost to the church when they became farm servants and left the village.[47]

The increased importance that was attached to Holy Communion was associated, although not exclusively, with the growth of Ritualism, itself a statement of the distinctive claims of the church. The list of 31 churches in the *Tourist's Church Guide*, published from 1874, included places where there was at least a weekly celebration of Holy Communion, where vestments and altar lights were used, and where the eastward facing position was adopted during the prayer of consecration at the Eucharist. It covered about half the clergymen in the county who can be said to have been in varying degree Ritualist. By 1881 56 churches from the county were included in the *Guide*. At the end of the century the militantly Protestant Church Association − the body that lay behind the prosecution of Bishop King for what were alleged to be illegal ritual practices during a celebration of Holy Communion at the Lincoln church of St Peter at Arches in 1887 − identified 288 clergymen serving in the county who were said, through their practices and the groups and societies to which they were affiliated, to be 'helping the Romeward movement in the National Church'. These figures were said by moderate sympathizers with the aims of the Association to be 'grossly indiscriminate and inflated'.[48]

Despite the efforts of Ritualist clergymen to make worship more attractive, as well as those of their colleagues who adopted some of their

Fig. 40 St Andrew's church, Grimsby, was consecrated in 1870 for one of the new parishes created to serve the growing towns of Lincolnshire. It provided church accommodation for over 1,000 people.

*Fig. 41   St Martin's church, Owston Ferry. Although not finally completed
until the early 20th century, the furnishings of this church embodied the ideals
of the Ritualist movement within the Church of England.*

practices without necessarily embracing strongly Ritualistic positions, all
of them had to face the continuing and pervasive Protestantism of the
people of Lincolnshire. In some places this manifested itself in open
opposition to Ritualistic practices. Its occurrence, often in parishes where
the clergyman had been presented to the living by collegiate clerical
bodies, was another indication of the extent to which parish clergymen
were moving away from the mainstream of the lives of the communities
that they served. Nonconformist chapels continued to be identified as a
source of authentic religious experience. A clergyman from north
Lincolnshire wrote in 1865 of a woman in his parish who considered her
father and mother-in-law to be 'religious' because their attendances at
church were supplemented by worship at their local chapel. Edward Steere
was told by one of his Skegness parishioners that they went to church in the
morning to please him, but to chapel at night to save their souls.[49]

The importance of personal experience in Methodist religious life meant
that its worship was seen to be imbued with a warmth less easily cultivated
in the formalized observances of the Church of England. It was a need that
innovations in worship, no matter how aesthetically attractive, appeared
largely to fail to meet. The range of institutions and activities associated
with chapel life also supplied a wider social context for worship than was
provided in most parishes, particularly in the countryside. In Beelsby the
church managed to maintain a hold over religious observance down to

1900, so that few people except the aged were said to neglect to attend it, but nearly all of them also went to the Methodist meeting that was held in the village. In 1901 the Vicar of Addlethorpe said that no one attended any part of worship 'unless some secondary object is present'. While the children of Ashby cum Fenby attended the parish church with their Wesleyan Sunday school teachers for catechism on every thirteenth Sunday, they were said to remain loyal to the Methodists because of the books and trips to the seaside that were given by them.[50]

Some clergymen, particularly those of Evangelical persuasion, cooperated with nonconformists, although the extent of this is difficult to quantify. It varied in its nature and intensity. Field Flowers of Tealby went as far as speaking at Wesleyan missionary meetings and joining Methodists at British and Foreign Bible Society meetings. Identification with nonconformist causes often implied an acceptance of the means that they employed in their work, but the range of social as well as religious activities that sustained the associational life of nonconformists, even in small villages, was never matched by the Church of England, although attempts to develop this side of church life were far from being confined to Evangelical clergymen. The life of the town parish of Holy Trinity Gainsborough was enriched by an exceptional range of church-based institutions that involved its largely working-class parishioners. In the very different circumstances of what was essentially the decaying market town of Caistor in 1900, the Confraternity of the Blessed Sacrament, the Guild of All Souls, and the Guild of St Peter and St Paul all strengthened the religious life of this High Church parish. A Bell Ringers' Guild and Girls' Friendly Society were less devotionally orientated.[51]

In larger village parishes such as Metheringham, bodies like the Church of England Working Men's Society provided links with national bodies and wider horizons to church life, as well as worship and social activities. A special service for the local branch of the society held in November 1889 was followed by a knife and fork tea, but many such activities retained the paternalistic ethos that was implicit in the Society's title. Parishioners in Metheringham were invited to send their newspapers and books for the use of members of the men's Bible class after they had finished their studies. The lectures on Canada and on Buddhism and Burma that were held in connection with the local annual meetings of the Society for the Propagation of the Gospel at Waddington and Navenby in 1890 contributed to the social life of the villages by providing entertainment as well as information on church concerns. Other similar events arranged by incumbents had more general, if to some extent educationally improving, aims. The lecture on the Beginnings of Christianity in Britain that was held at Coleby in 1888 gave a historical context to the church's activities. Lectures of this kind, together with the antiquarian material that found its way into parish magazines, can be seen as an attempt, however informal, to strengthen the position of the church through an appeal to local historical sentiment. In April 1888 a quarter of the four pages of the Barrow on Humber monthly church magazine was given over to historical notes. Lectures held in the winter months at Metheringham in 1890, of which the first was on Norway and illustrated by magic lantern, lacked any specifically religious, let alone denominational, content but it did have the benefit of conferring on the incumbent, as its organizer, a role as a leader of the public social life of the parish.[52]

CHURCH EDUCATION AND THE DEVELOPMENT OF RELIGIOUS
UNDERSTANDING

The Girls' Friendly Society, Band of Hope, Men's Guild, and parish Reading Room that had been established at Kirmington by 1900 were an almost unique example of this range of church provision in a Lincolnshire rural parish. Less than one per cent of the population of south Lincolnshire were members of village reading rooms, while the few parish guilds that existed were predominantly feminine, attracting a total of 2,696 members of whom 2,000 were women or girls. This was between 1 and 2 per cent of the female population of the area. Only a handful of people – 326 – were associated with church institutes, while the small number of church temperance societies were made up largely of young people and had 1,854 juvenile and 857 adult members. Where the Church of England made its greatest impact was not through these relatively new agencies of parish work, often developed in an urban context, but through the continuing strength of its parish schools. Ninety schools associated with the National Society for Promoting the Education of the Poor in the Principles of the Established Church had been established in Lincolnshire by 1851 with a total of 7,813 boys and girls in them. There were also another 160 schools connected to the church with 8,764 pupils, compared with only 37 nonconformist day schools. Some 35 per cent of the children aged between 5 and 10 years in the county were being educated in church day-schools in 1851. There was almost certainly an overlap between the children who attended them and the 432 Sunday schools that were an extension of the church's commitment to education. They had 25,296 pupils in 1851, but were more geographically widely spread than the day schools.[53]

In terms of their impact on the religious lives of the individuals that passed through them, the establishment and upkeep of church schools was arguably the most significant aspect of the reconfiguration of the parish life of the Church of England that took place in the course of the 19th century. They had become sufficiently well established to be in a position to maintain a significant influence when elementary education became

*Fig. 42   East Ravendale. The church school and the church just visible
to the right, built together in 1857, demonstrate the importance that was
attached to the maintenance of a close relationship between the
Church of England and education.*

compulsory from 1870. Church schools were founded and maintained in
the generally paternalistic spirit that had animated most of the other
changes that had taken place in church life in Lincolnshire in the 19th
century, although some clergymen bemoaned the indifference of landlords
to education. When the establishment of a district church board for
education was mooted at Brigg in 1840, Weever Walter lamented the lack
of interest from either the Duke of St Albans or Mr Corbett, neither of
whom would attend its inaugural meeting. Nonetheless, the financial
support given by the gentry was an essential element in the provision of
church education in many places. Landlords contributed to schools built in
parishes on their estates: Lord Aveland met the cost of erecting that at
Langtoft in 1859. The gentry were also among the larger subscribers to the
diocesan board of education that was established in 1839 and which
provided grants towards school building and improvement from 1843.
Gentry patronage was not always enough to match local needs, while there
might be active opposition to the establishment of church schools in
parishes where nonconformity was strong. That which the curate of
Toynton St Peter met in his efforts to establish a National School in the
1840s was part of a general pattern of conflict between church and dissent

in the parish. His insistence that the day-school children attend the church Sunday school was said to deprive the Wesleyans of 'the fruits of their labours' in a parish where they had for a long time been 'the only labourers in the field of Sabbath school instruction'.[54]

Whatever interest they were able to arouse among the gentry, the parish clergy remained at the forefront of local educational provision and were heavily involved in meeting the costs of both establishing and maintaining schools in their parishes. The level of support given by local communities varied from place to place, again depending on local circumstances. Parents also contributed through school fees. Although there was some reluctance in the 1840s and 1850s to accept inspection, government grants were another source of income. The 'principal farmers' at Great Carlton contributed between £2 and 10s a year towards the parish school, but their counterparts gave no help at Scampton. Differences such as these meant that the level of 'school pence' parents were asked to pay varied. It was the only form of subscription that was received towards school costs at Waddingham in 1855.[55]

Although the 1870 education act exposed deficiencies in the coverage of the county by voluntary schools, it also stimulated further efforts to erect more church schools and stave off the creation of elected school boards with their more limited undenominational religious instruction. Places like the fenland district of St Luke's Holbeach Hurn were provided with a church school for the first time, while in the demanding circumstances of the expanding Lincoln parish of St Andrew a series of church school buildings, erected at a cost of £6,481, provided accommodation for the thousand children who attended the boys', girls', and infants' schools by 1900. Despite the schools' urban location, the Swan family of Sausthorpe, who owned land in the area, were generous in their patronage of them. In strongly dissenting communities like Brigg efforts to stave off the creation of a school board by expanding provision at the National school were defeated, but the clergy of Stamford contrived to dominate a committee set up to deal with education in the town. A decision to build church schools at Friskney rather than establish a board was carried by vote. The question as to whether to establish a board was taken to a poll at North Kelsey where the proposal of the dissenters, who had dominated a meeting called to discuss school provision, was defeated. At Crowle it was the vicar who moved that a school board be established.[56]

In parishes where the church's position was less secure the establishment of a school board could become the occasion for a test of denominational strength. School board elections gave the parish's Methodists the opportunity to assert their position at North Somercotes, where the churchmen were defeated by Wesleyan, Primitive, and Free Methodist candidates. In another of the variety of scenarios that developed over education in the 1870s, the Wesleyan Methodists of Gainsborough joined church people in a poll on the establishment of a school board, as they had done over the church rate, to defeat the town's Independents, Unitarians, Primitive and Free Methodists. Although the rejection of the proposal to establish a board in Spalding was seen as a victory for the church, it was said that the real cause was not religious feeling but the dread of the rate a board would levy. Although the people of Ruskington did not usually demonstrate a strong attachment to the church, it was decided at a parish meeting in 1870, and with the support of some of the village's leading dissenters, to raise £100 by voluntary subscription to extend the church school rather than pay the threepenny rate. It was a fear that Bishop King, a strong advocate of church schools, and displaying an insight into Lincolnshire mentalities that went beyond purely spiritual dimensions, did not hesitate to play on. When he opened the new school buildings in St Andrew's parish, Lincoln in 1883 he cited the high rates levied by school boards in some Lincolnshire parishes.[57]

For whatever reason, the commitment to church schools in Lincolnshire remained such that a large proportion of children continued to be educated in them up to the end of the 19th century and beyond. Although not all the 424 parish day schools that existed in 1900 were formally attached to the National Society, the majority were clearly linked to the church through the active participation of the clergy in religious instruction, while the wives and daughters of clergymen were also reported to play an important role in church education, especially in Sunday schools. Some 50 per cent of school-age children were in church schools in the archdeaconry of Lincoln in 1900. Even where there was no specific school provision by the church some clergymen were able to exert their personal influence over village schools. The day school at South Ferriby was associated with the nonconformist British and Foreign Schools Society in 1900, but said to be managed by the Rector. The vicar of Corby was chairman of the local school board, while in a few places such as Bassingham, where the church school had been given up and its buildings leased to a board, strong links were maintained with the church. Clergymen still even gave religious instruction in a few former church schools that had been taken over by boards.[58]

The instruction of the poor of the county in 'suitable learning, works of industry, and the principles of the Christian Religion according to the Established Church' had been set out as the central purpose of education provided by the Church of England at the meeting that established the National Society on a county basis in 1811. Concern that the schools inculcate the social discipline which would ensure the survival of the established order in church and state was another strong motif in the rhetoric of the supporters of church schools, while the need to render the poor 'honest, obedient, courteous, industrious, submissive and orderly' was said to be one of the objects of the early Sunday schools that supplemented, and in places were a substitute for, church day schools. They continued to be an important part of the church's provision until the end of the 19th century. There were said to be 460 in Lincolnshire in 1900 and the 10 Sunday schools with 1,095 children on their books that operated in the parish of Boston were a measure of their continuing influence. The emphasis placed on instruction in the church liturgy and the catechism that gave both day and Sunday schools their distinctive church tone also continued to the end of the 19th century. It was explicitly mentioned in visitation returns, such as that for Surfleet, in 1900. In some places text books based on the catechism were employed, and the rules of Bardney school from the 1850s prohibited the use of any religious publications that had 'not been sanctioned by the Trustees, or by the Lord Bishop of the Diocese'.[59]

Regular church attendance was a further element in the experience of children who attended church schools. Some of the children at Bardney were selected to sing the hymns and psalms, as well as repeat the responses, at Sunday worship in the parish church in the mid 1850s, while all had to learn the catechism and collects for each Sunday by heart. Yet the levels of commitment to church worship of Lincolnshire children in later life showed that the specifically and distinctively church-orientated content of the teaching they had received had little hold over them once they had moved away from the influence of the schools. Nonetheless the reports of schools inspectors demonstrate that, although standards of instruction were not always of the highest order and were impaired by the demands that agricultural work made on children in rural areas, more general religious knowledge was an important element in the body of material that was imparted in church schools.[60]

The knowledge of the catechism that was shown by the children of Binbrook National school at an inspection in 1876 was 'not so good in proportion' as that of Scripture in which they were reported to have passed 'a very good examination ... showing by their answers accurate knowledge of, and considerable interest in, the subjects in which they have been instructed'. Failure to master the catechism may well have been a rejection of rote learning, but it can also be seen as part of a process through which the people of Lincolnshire shaped their own religious sentiments by a process of internalized discrimination between the various elements in the religious education that was available to them. It was an approach to religion that matched their eclecticism in worship in those parishes where they were able to exercise the choice. In so far as it was Biblically based their church school education contributed to the development of a mentality that was congruent with the general Protestant cultural ambience

him the work of the police would have been made more difficult.[65]

The Irish labourers who gathered at Stamford in 1845 were said to have been allowed to hear Mass in the priest's house. It was a condition of their admittance to the church at Lincoln that, although it was accepted that their clothes were ragged, they should wear clean shirts. Yet despite these concerns, seating arrangements in Lincolnshire Catholic churches did not seem to have been generally highly segregated, although they reflected the social composition of local Catholic communities. There were only twelve free seats out of a total of 144 sittings in the estate chapel at Hainton, while a distinction was made between the free space in the older town chapel at Market Rasen and the 117 sittings set aside for its permanent congregation. The churches in Boston, Grimsby, Gainsborough and, in the 1870s and 1880s, at Spalding, Skegness, and Sleaford were built in response to changes in the distribution of the Catholic population of Lincolnshire. Although there had been Catholics in Boston in the 18th century, the first chapel in the town, after a period when they were served by priests from Lincoln, was provided by the Jesuit Father Addis in 1827. This was in response to the growth of the Catholic population as navvies, who had originally come to work on fen drainage, had settled in Boston's 'Irishtown'. The new Catholic community of Grimsby had been served on a weekday by a priest from Louth until Father Phelan was sent there in 1850. His congregation was largely Irish and new to a place where there had only been twelve men and seven women of Irish birth in 1841. The newcomers were a far more heterogeneous group than was implied by their shared Irishness. Nor was this necessarily a guarantee of either Catholic orthodoxy or habitual religious practice. They included various types of workmen who had come to Grimsby by a number of routes to work on the new dock works. There was an inner core of married couples who provided lodgings for at least some of the large numbers of single young men who were employed there. In so far as the household was important in this context they may have had an influence on levels of religious practice.[66]

The rounded attendance figures given in the Catholic return for Grimsby for the 1851 Census of Religious Worship make it difficult to draw firm conclusions about levels of devotion among the transient workers of the town. The provision that was made for them, like that for other more permanent groups of Irish emigrants, marked the beginning of a lasting Catholic presence there. This was first established in a building described as the Ropery, away from the old town centre and near the docks where most of the town's Irish workers lived. Hired premises were also used in Gainsborough, and in 1848 it was reported that a priest from Brigg said Mass in a room up the yard of the Marquis of Granby inn. Later a room in Silver Street was used. By the time that most of the new Catholic churches of Lincolnshire were built the congregational initiatives that had provided

Catholic chapels from the latter part of the 18th century had largely died out. There had, in any case, been no direct experience of them in the county, since they had been developed mainly in the towns of north-west England.[67]

J. B. Naghten, the priest at Gainsborough, referring to the extreme poverty of his flock, expressed the hope that 'some of the rich and charitable Catholics of England' would be inspired to help to 'raise a temple to the Lord of Hosts in this very important town'. Although their control over Catholic life diminished because of the growth of town congregations in which the influence of the parish priests was strong, the patronage of local Catholic gentry remained important in local church building. T. A. Young of Kingerby, who also contributed to the churches in Crowle, Market Rasen, and Grimsby, responded to the pleas for help from Gainsborough. He also provided the church, school, and presbytery of the church of the Immaculate Conception and St Norbert in Spalding consecrated in 1876. St Mary's church built in Grimsby in the late 1870s benefited from the Heneage interest in the town.[68]

There was both a boarding and day school connected with the Catholic church at Spalding by 1878. The numbers in them were said to be 'very small' but the provision of schools was an early priority in many local Catholic parishes. They reinforced the religious identity of their children by providing a separate education for them. There was a Sunday school at Stamford attended by 20 children that taught reading and writing in 1842, while a simple one-room school was built at Boston in the middle of the century. New schools were built in Market Rasen in 1850 and another was begun in Stamford in 1869. Sleaford's first Roman Catholic church building was a combined school and chapel opened in June 1882.[69]

There is little direct evidence of the extent to which the children from these schools went on to practice their religion locally. There were 304 Catholics in Boston and Skirbeck in 1878 and 167 of them fulfilled their Easter duties of confession and holy communion. A total of 241 people attended Gainsborough Roman Catholic church on 27 March 1887. Fifty-five of them were at the early morning service, 89 later in the morning and 97 in the evening. There were considerably fewer than this when the local paper took a similar census the next year, although these 97 attendants had increased to 131 by 1889, when there were 65 in the morning and 66 in the evening. A total of 175 people attended the Catholic church at Brigg on 28 November 1886, when the evening congregation of 77 was said to be below average. It is difficult to translate these figures into numbers of individual adherents, although it has been argued that attendance at evening devotions was a more fully voluntary religious act than the more formal identification with the church that was represented by going to Sunday morning Mass. In 1873, 173 out of a total of 372 attendances at

Fig. 45   St Hugh's Roman Catholic church, Lincoln. Built in 1893,
the church expressed the new confidence of the Roman Catholic church
in the second half of the 19th century in a style that emphasized its continuity
with the Catholic past of the Middle Ages.

Lincoln were at the evening services. The balance of attendances in the city swung even more strongly towards evening worship just after the end of the century when, on 14 March 1903, a total of 471 people worshipped at St Hugh's church: 159 in the morning and 312 in in the evening. While the morning Mass had a congregation that was evenly balanced between men and women, there were nearly twice as many many women as men in the evening.[70]

Vespers began to be held as an evening service at Gainsborough in 1849. They had been part of an earlier, undemonstrative and distinctively English pattern of Catholic devotion, but their performance as evening prayers in English had been prohibited from 1838. Their introduction at Gainsborough in this new form was an aspect of a process through which the devotional life of Catholic parishes was enriched as new churches were opened and, like the parish churches of the Church of England, priests settled to serve them. Gas lighting made it possible to offer evening services at Market Rasen from 1848, and by 1875 the Sunday devotions there included Compline, the Rosary, and Benediction as well as Catechism. Like ritual innovations in the Church of England, this richer liturgical life was an assertion of the distinctiveness of the church's position and what was seen as its new place in English religious life in the second half of the 19th century. The more elaborate patterns of devotion and the diversification of the organizations associated with local Catholic churches that supported it were not in themselves evidence that they were necessarily widely supported by their potential constituency. The mere existence of confraternities such as that associated with the Blessed Sacrament at Market Rasen or the Sacred Heart at Stamford in 1875 is not in itself proof of their strength.[71]

There are some references to converts being made at Spalding, but they were hardly numerous and the church that was built there was large for its congregation. There were 64 worshippers at morning service and 69 in the evening in December 1881, but they were in accommodation designed to take 200 people. The conversion of the Elwes family in 1874 contributed to the sustention of the Catholic church in Brigg. In a development that recalled the seigneurialism of an earlier period, a new church was opened in the old coach house of their Brigg Manor House, but its dedication to the Immaculate Heart of Mary was redolent of the new patterns of devotion that were changing the identity of the Roman Catholic church in England. Certainly the priests in the town appeared to maintain a far more independent position than had been enjoyed by the household chaplains of an earlier period, although it was still probably easier to influence the behaviour of the Irish field labourers of the Ancholme valley than it was to build up the religious commitment of town workers. The Congregation of the Most Holy Redeemer was one of the missionary orders introduced from the Continent in the 19th century. The 'floridly Italianate' doctrinal and devotional sympathies of its priests meant that they were firmly associated with the newer patterns of practice and observance of the second half of the 19th century; but after they had laboured on a mission to Grimsby in 1890, a thousand of the town's two thousand Catholics were left so totally unimpressed that they were deemed to have lapsed altogether.[72]

Notes to Chapter VI

1 Rel. Wor., pp. clxxi, ccxi; *Stow Ch. Res.*, pp. 5–6.

2 *Diss.*, II, pp. 671–4.

3 R. W. Ambler, ' Attendance at Religious Worship' in *Atlas*, pp. 104–5; *Diss.*, II, pp. 704–5; *1851 Census Ret.*, pp. 6, 178.

4 *Census. Ret.*, pp. 59, 217–18.

5 *Rel. & Rur. Soc.*, pp. 38–9, 154–5; *Dir. Lincs.*, p. 476.

6 *Census. Ret.*, pp. 146, 214–15; Wilb. MSS, bundle d. 28; *Dir. Lincs.*, pp. 785–6; Kaye Corr. /4/131.

7 R. Gregory, *A Plea in Behalf of Small Parishes with Particular Reference to the County of Lincoln,* London, 1849, pp. 5, 6, 12, 13, 36; Bish., Cler. & Peop., p. 380; *Works*, p. 420.

8 Bish., Cler. & Peop., pp. 380, 381, 382, 383.

9 *19th C. Ch.*, pp. 153–4; Bish., Cler. & Peop., pp. 3, 74, 75; Kaye Corr., /4/27/5, /4/44/5; *9 Charges*, pp. 15–16, 19.

10 Bish., Cler. & Peop., pp. 323, 326–7, 421; Kaye Corr. /4/62/11.

11 *9 Charges*, pp. 105–6; Bish., Cler. & Peop., p. 420; *Rel. & Rur. Soc.*, p. 113.

12 *19th C. Ch.*, pp. 107, 110–11, 112–13, 116, 121–2, 209; Bish., Cler. & Peop., pp. 137–8, 395; *Ch. in Age of Neglig.*, p. 136; *A History of Lincoln Theological College, 1874–1974*, Lincoln, 1974, pp. 5–7; Letters, p. 66; *LRSM*, 27 September 1839; Wilb. MSS, VIII, d. 27.

13 Kaye Corr. /4/73/8.

14 Kaye Corr. /4/32/3, /4/33/3, /4/43/3, /4/51/3; Wilb. MSS, I, d.24.

15 *9 Charges*, pp. 14, 18–19, 21; *Works*, pp. 55–6; Art. of Enq.

16 Kaye Corr. /4/33/6, 4/84/3; *19th C. Ch.*, pp. 77–9, 143.

17 Kaye Corr. /4/1/3, 4/51/1, 4/87/3, 4/90/10.

18 *1851 Census Ret.*, pp. 172, 185–6, 189.

19 Art. of Enq.; *Rel. & Rur. Soc.*, p. 214; H. S. Lunn, *Chapters from My Life*, London, 1918, pp. 6–7.

20 O. Anderson, 'The Incidence of Civil Marriage in Victorian England and Wales', *P&P*, 69 (1975), p. 50; Parl. P. 1842, XIX, [423] Fourth Annual Report of the Registrar-General of Births, Deaths and Marriages in England, p. 15.

21 Parl. P., 1852 XVIII [1520] Births, Deaths and Marriages (England): Thirteenth
    Annual Report of the Registrar-General of Births, Deaths and Marriages, in
    England, p. 4; Anderson, 'Civil Marriage', pp. 55–6; 19th C. Ch., p. 102; Kaye Corr.
    /4/57/1.

22 H. K. Bonney, *A Charge Delivered at the Spring Visitation of the Archdeacon of
    Lincoln, in May, 1854*, London, 1854, p. 8; E. H. Rudkin, *Lincolnshire Folklore*,
    Gainsborough 1936, repr. Wakefield, 1973, p. 50; *Examples*, pp. 231, 232–3; *Rel. &
    Rur. Soc.*, p. 136; Thirteenth Annual Report of the Registrar General, p. 4.

23 *Words.*, pp. 270–71; *LRSM*, 2ᵗ February 1838; *DSN*, 1 February 1822; Kaye Corr.
    /4/54/1, /4/70.

24 Kaye Corr. /4/68/5/6, 4/89/3; *Rel. & Rur. Soc.*, pp. 128–9; *19th C. Ch.*, p. 89.

25 *The Peacock Lincolnshire Word Books 1884–1920*, compiled by M. and M. Peacock
    with E. A. Peacock *et al.*, ed. E. Elder, Scunthorpe, 1997, p. 87; *Examples*, p. 228;
    19th C. Ch., p. 90; *SFP*, 15 February 1848.

26 *Words.*, pp. 266–7; Kaye Corr. /4/1/8.

27 *19th C. Ch.*, p. 104; Kaye Corr. /4/1/8, 4/8/1, 4/114/6, 4/115/10; Letters, p. 70.

28 *1851 Census Ret.*, p. 90; Kaye Corr. /4/67/7, /4/77/3, /4/79/4.

29 Kaye Corr. 4/39/1, 4/67/7.

30 Kaye Corr. /4/7/5, /4/67/7; *LRSM*, 20 January 1843.

31 *LRSM*, 22 July 1834, 8 September 1843; Kaye Corr. /4/64/7, 4/79/6; *19th C. Ch.,* pp.
    26–7.

32 *Rel. & Rur. Soc.*, pp. 131–5; *19th C. Ch.*, pp. 92, 95; *SG*, 13 March 1858; P. J. Jagger,
    *Clouded Witness: initiation in the Church of England in the mid-Victorian Period,
    1780–1875*, Allison Park, PA, 1982, p. 156; *GJ*, 22 August 1874.

33 R. W. Ambler. 'A Nineteenth Century Village Annalist: Thomas Ogden of
    Ruskington', *LHA*, 5 (1970), pp. 78–9; *LRSM*, 18 August 1843, 8 December 1843,
    26 November 1847.

34 *LRSM*, 28 December 1849; Pevsner 2, pp. 605–6; *Rel. & Rur. Soc.*, pp. 147–9.

35 Kaye Corr. /4/61/4; Rel. Wor., p. cxxxv; *Rel. & Rur. Soc.*, pp. 109–10; *LRSM*, 10
    May 1861, 3 and 24 June 1864 .

36 *LRSM*, 21 April 1837, 17 August 1838, 24 May 1839, 13 November 1840, 22
    February 1850, 28 March 1851; Parl. P. 1854 XX, Commons Papers, Session 1,
    Return from Each Parish within Several Archdeaconries of England and Wales,
    setting forth the Gross Amount Expended During the Last Seven Years for Church
    Purposes; *Lincs. Pol.*, pp. 60–61.

37 LRSM, 16 February 1838; *Stow Visitat.*, p. 31; Pevsner 2, p. 65; *GJ., 12 August
    1865; LA, Faculty Papers, Fac 11–14, 1861–1900.*

38 Wilb. MSS, d. 24; *Stow Visitat.*, p. 7; Sir Francis Hill, 'Early Days of a Society',
    LHA, no. 1 (1966), p. 58; T. R. Leach, 'Edward Trollope and the Lincoln Diocesan
    Architectural Society', in C. Sturman (ed.), *Some Historians of Lincolnshire*,
    Lincoln, 1992, pp. 18–19; *LRSM*, 30 August 1844; *Stow Ch. Res.*, p. xix.

39 *LRSM*, 19 June 1868; *Stow Visitat.*, p. 45; Kaye Corr. /4/3/6; *Rel. & Rur. Soc.*, p.
    111.

40 L. A. E. Dejardin, *The Church in Kirton in Lindsey*, Kirton in Lindsey, 1992, pp. 18–19; C. Rawding (ed.) *Binbrook in the 19th Century*, Binbrook, 1989, pp. 53–57; *19th C. Ch.*, pp. 64–5.

41 Hill, 'Early Days', p. 58; J. F. White, *The Cambridge Movement: the ecclesiologists and the Gothic Revival*, pp. 19, 35, 37, 44, 67–8, 146, 225; Wilb. MSS, d 28; Kaye Corr. /4/26; *19th C. Ch.*, p. 104; *Rel. & Rur. Soc.*, pp. 148–9; *GJ, 17 October 1868; LRSM*, 30 October 1868.

42 *King*, p. 21; J.A. Newton, *Search for a Saint: Edward King*, London, 1977, p. 78.

43 *Vict. Linc.*, pp. 253–4, 312; *The Lincolnshire Chronicle*, 2 December 1881; *GN*, 2 April 1887; *LRSM*, 3 December 1886; Furth. Vis. Ret.

44 Ch. Work Stats.

45 *The South Cliff Parish Magazine*, May, 1890; Furth. Vis. Ret.

46 Ch. Work Stats.; Furth.Vis. Ret.; I. Beckwith, 'Religion in a Working Men's Parish 1843–1893', *LHA*, 5 (1970), p. 36.

47 Furth. Vis. Ret.

48 G. W. Herring, 'Tractarianism to Ritualism: a study of some aspects of Tractarianism outside Oxford from the time of Newman's conversion in 1845, until the First Ritual Commission in 1867', 2 vols., unpublished University of Oxford D.Phil. thesis, 1984, vol. 2, *passim*; *Tour. Ch. Guide*, 1874 and 1881; *The Ritualistic Clergy List being a Guide for Patrons*, London, 1902; G. I. T. Machin, 'The Last Victorian Anti-Ritualist Campaign, 1895–1906', *Victorian Studies*, 25, 3 (Autumn 1981), pp. 283.

49 *LRSM*, 12 April 1867, 21 and 28 June 1867; Ch. in Lincs., pp. 263–4; *Rel. & Rur. Soc.*, p. 157.

50 Furth. Vis. Ret.

51 *Rel. & Rur. Soc.*, pp. 168–9; Beckwith, 'Religion in a Working Men's Parish', pp. 33–7; Furth. Vis. Ret.; Ch. Work Stats.

52 *South Cliff Parish Magazine*, November, 1889, November, 1890; *The Barrow Monthly Monitor*, no. 117, April 1888.

53 Tab. Sch., pp. cxlviii, clxxvii.

54 Kaye Corr. /4/43/11, 4/70; *LRSM*, 30 September 1859; *Hist. Sch.* 3, p. 32.

55 *Hist. Sch.* 3, pp. 34, 49–50, 88, 91; Furth. Vis. Ret.; Ch. Work Stats.

56 [J. E. Truman], *Church of St Andrew, Lincoln: a record of its growth and development 1870 to 1910*, [Lincoln] 1910, p. 8; *LRSM*, 21 October 1870, 28 October 1870, 9 December 1870, 6 January 1871, 29 September 1871; *Vict. Linc.*, p. 274; *King*, p. 26.

57 *LRSM*, 13 January 1871, 17 and 24 February 1871; *SG*, 17 December 1870; *Vict. Linc.*, p. 274; *King*, p. 26.

58 Furth. Vis. Ret.; Ch. Work Stats.

59 *Hist. Sch.*, 3, pp. 14–15, 98; R. Russell, *Learning and Living in Lindsey: 1830–1890: a history of adult education in north Lincolnshire*, Hull, 1994, p. 1; Furth.Vis. Ret.

60 *Hist. Sch.* 3, pp. 97–8.

61 Rawding, *Binbrook*, p. 66; T. W. Laquer, *Religion and Respectability: Sunday schools and working class culture 1780–1850*, New Haven and London, 1976, pp. 243–4; *Rel. & Rur. Soc.*, pp. 279, 301–11; J. Cox, *The English Churches in a Secular Society: Lambeth, 1870–1930*, Oxford, 1982, p. 93; Ch. in Lincs., p. 269.

62 R. C. Russell, *A History of Elementary Schools and Adult Education in Nettleton and Caistor*, Part One, *1870 to 1875*, [Nettleton, 1960], p. 82; *GJ*, 19 May 1860.

63 Furth. Vis. Ret.; *Barrow Monthly Monitor*, no. 120, July 1888.

64 Rel. Wor., p. ccxi; *Cath. Dir.*, 1851, pp. 53–4.

65 *1851 Census Ret.*, pp. 2, 108, 226; *LRSM*, 29 August 1845, 3 and 10 August 1849, 1 February 1861.

66 *LRSM*, 14 August 1840; *1851 Census Ret.*, pp. 188, 203, 225, 264–5; *Eng. Cath. Com,,* p. 423; M. Middlebrook, *The Catholic Church in Boston*, Boston, 1977, pp. 19–20; Grimsby Central Library, I. C. Drakes, 'A few hasty jottings from my recollections of the earlier days of the Grimsby mission; M. Gerrish, 'Special Industrial Migration in Nineteenth-Century Britain: a case study of the port of Grimsby 1841–1861', University of Hull, Ph.D. thesis, 1992, pp. 39, 59, 70, 73–6, 90, 114, 123.

67 *1851 Census Rets.*, p. 203; *Eng. Cath. Com.*, pp. 337–41; *LRSM.,* 10 and 24 November 1848, 11 October 1850.

68 *Cath. Dir.*, 1851, p. 54; *Spalding*, pp. 128–9.

69 *Spalding*, p. 129; *LRSM*, 11 November 1842, 17 December 1869, 9 June 1882, 3 December 1886.

70 Middlebrook, *Catholic Church in Boston*, p. 23; *GN*, 2 April 1887, 26 May 1888 and 12 April 1889; M. Heimann, *Catholic Devotion in Victorian England*, Oxford, 1995, p. 38; *Vict. Linc.*, p. 34.

71 *Cath. Dir.*, 1851, p. 98, 1875, p. 98; *LRSM*, 18 May 1849; Heimann, *Catholic Devotion*, pp. 72, 79, 126–7; *Eng. Cath. Com.*, p. 385; *LRSM*, 28 January 1848.

72 *Spalding*, p. 129; *19th C. Brigg,* pp. 50–51; J. Sharp, *Reapers of the Harvest: the Redemptorists in Great Britain and Ireland 1843–1898*, Dublin, 1989, pp. 5, 224.

CHAPTER VII

NONCONFORMITY AND THE LOCAL COMMUNITY

THE PATTERN OF CHAPEL LIFE

The influence of nonconformity in the lives of Lincolnshire parishes extended beyond Sunday and week-night worship so that, with the Sunday schools, there was a wide range of activities at local chapels. Many of these functions had a strong social element, with an emphasis on raising funds, and became part of the regular round of events in communities where chapels had been built. They ranged from weekly meetings to annual special events such as Sunday school and chapel anniversaries. Interspersed with less routine occasions like the opening of new buildings, these services and meetings not only provided a social dimension to the lives of the people associated with chapels, but became an important part of the general social calendar of parish communities. Individuals and families were given the opportunity to shape lifestyles for themselves that were based on participation in chapel-based activities, although their levels of engagement were also frequently conditioned by the eclecticism that many Lincolnshire people exhibited in their religious attitudes. This meant that they often took part in those elements of chapel life that met their need for association on a social level without necessarily entering into the full range of activities, religious or otherwise, that were offered. There were few fundamental differences in the form and content of the activities associated with the various nonconformist chapels, although different social groups tended to associate with the chapels that they found to be most socially congenial. The ties of family and kinship that often bound together an inner core of members became more important as falling village populations meant that greater demands began to be made on those who supported and maintained chapels on a regular basis.

The cycle of activities associated with the Primitive Methodists at Great Gonerby provides an example of the place chapels came to occupy in the parish communities in which they were established. The foundation stone of the village's new chapel was laid in 1857 when a tea for 170 people was held in the Wesleyan chapel that had been lent for the occasion. In the evening there was a public meeting addressed by six speakers. Special

meetings and services were held in February of the next year to raise money
for the new chapel and attracted large numbers, including 160 at another
public tea. Speakers included the local Wesleyan and Methodist New
Connexion ministers. When the new chapel was actually opened the
occasion was marked by more special services and meetings, with a strong
social element, all of which also served to raise money. There were two
public teas and a lecture on 'the idolatrous worship, customs and
ceremonies prevalent in the East Indies, illustrated by numerous diagrams'.
The new chapel was maintained and sustained by annual special services
and meetings. These raised further funds and, as well as demonstrating the
achievements of the Primitives, they provided entertainment and recreation
for a wide section of the village community.[1]

The annual anniversary of the opening of the chapel was celebrated with
special sermons and a tea meeting. In 1865 many were unable to find a
place in the building for an evening lecture on Martin Luther, while in 1866
between three and four hundred people attended the chapel anniversary tea,
followed by a lecture on 'The Young Man's Hindrances to True
Greatness'. The number of people attracted to the chapel increased and in
1863, even before the lecture on Luther had filled the building, it had been
'enlarged and improved, and a new schoolroom added'. The cost of the
work in 1863 was met by special services and events. A tea and lecture on
'True Heroes' marked their completion. In 1864 the annual chapel
anniversary raised £15 10s 7d towards paying off the remaining debt of
£120, together with collections of £17 10s at sermons and public meetings,
but these efforts were not enough to meet the demand for accommodation
in the chapel. There were said to be insufficient sittings for those who
wished to worship there by 1873, and a new chapel was opened. Although
£220 had already been raised towards its cost a debt of £330 remained and a
new round of fund raising became necessary.[2]

CHAPEL BUILDING

The accommodation that was provided by chapel buildings, with the school
rooms and meeting halls that were often addded to them, were seen as
essential to the maintenance of an effective presence in local communities.
The need to meet the cost of building and maintaining them provided a
stimulus and imparted a sense of purpose to their congregations. The
existence of other nonconformist chapels in a place led to a degree of
implicit competition between them. The involvement of substantial
sections of local people in their support spread the costs of maintaining
chapels, while sympathizers were drawn across parish boundaries on
important occasions in the chapel year. Yet, when added to ongoing
expenditure, including the payment of ministers, chapel premises made
heavy demands on some congregations even before rural depopulation and

agricultural depression began to undermine their economic bases. The effort that was required to service the debts that had been incurred in building and rebuilding chapels also created tensions by laying emphasis on local needs at the expense of wider denominational commitments. The Donington Primitive Methodist circuit usually had a deficit from 1860 onwards. Such debts were to become an oppressive burden that made chapel life less positively attractive. Cornelius Stovin of Binbrook wrote in 1874 of the 'nightmare' that he prayed would be lifted so that the Free Methodists, of which he was a leading local member, could 'become tenfold more hopeful and confident in our work of saving souls'. The burden of new chapels after the Wesleyan Reform divisions was particularly onerous. Ten had been built by the Reformers on the Louth circuit between 1855 and 1870, with another at Sotby in 1894, at a total cost of £10,604. Their debts were said to be leading the circuit into bankruptcy and just short of £3,239 was owed in the 1890s.[3]

Chapel debts were incurred in a spirit of expansive optimism and there was no apparent relationship between their size and the strength of the local societies that carried them. The chapel at Gosberton Clough had the largest debt in the Donington Primitive Methodist circuit in 1868 at £290, but only eight members to support it. Chapel leaders like Stovin did not forget the need for religious revival, although even among churches that were as strongly orientated towards conversionary revivalism as the Primitive Methodists these imperatives came to be subsumed by more mundane financial preoccupations. In December 1860 when a Mrs Sanderson was asked to come 'to assist in holding a few revival services' on the Spalding and Holbeach branch of Donington circuit, she was requested to 'make collections for lighting and heating' at Holbeach. In Wesleyan Methodism also the link between the religious content of special occasions and their purpose as fund-raising events became blurred. When the famous preacher William Morley Punshon appeared at Horncastle, the service at which he preached was held in connection with a bazaar. The considerable sum of £444 was raised from the vast crowd that was attracted by the occasion. Charles Richardson's soubriquet, 'The Lincolnshire Thrasher', added an air of entertaining novelty to his work as a Wesleyan revivalist. Even though his engagements began to assume something of an established pattern, it was a cachet that was attractive to the Wesleyan congregations of the large towns that he visited, while conferring an authenticating rusticity to his preaching in country chapels. Richardson's reputation meant that his successes were monetary as well as spiritual and on his last visit to the Wesleyan Missionary Society meetings at Louth in April 1864 £300 was raised.[4]

Chapel building by Methodists continued up to the end of the 19th century, but this was often based on locally specific circumstances that existed for a relatively short time and that went against the longer-term trends that impinged inexorably on rural nonconformity. The leadership given by the Pinder family to the Wesleyan Methodists in the south Lincolnshire village of Morton was an example of the continuing importance of committed families in small village nonconformist communities. A new chapel to seat 200 people was opened in 1892 at a cost of £400. Its debt of £150 was cleared within six years. A society was started at Bulby on the Bourne circuit in 1885 and there was a local membership of five in 1890 and 1891, but it could not be sustained and the preaching house was closed in 1892. As their numbers decreased the burden borne by committted chapel members grew greater, and the work of preachers was increasingly orientated towards strengthening and supporting the convictions of those who were already members rather than adding to their numbers.[5]

When Cornelius Stovin preached at Tealby in 1874 he reported that although the congregation was 'very thin' there was a 'powerful time' at the evening service. The 'few disciples present were aroused and sinners convinced' although 'they would not yield'. If 'the Gospel chariot' began to move, Stovin believed, the circuit would 'rise'. Even when he took part in the anniversary of the town chapel at Grimsby he was preoccupied by its debt. Yet it was the suburbs of the large towns that provided an environment in which chapels could flourish. The Welhome Congregational church in Grimsby, begun as a mission building towards the end of the century, and in a more suburban setting than the town's Free Methodist chapel, was provided with extensive subsidiary halls and meeting rooms to house the range of activities associated with it. These imparted an air of buoyancy that was attractive to middle-class suburbanites moving to what were essentially new and expanding communities. In villages with declining populations the cost of maintaining far more modest buildings induced a less positively welcoming introversion among an inner core of members.[6]

SUNDAY SCHOOLS

Sunday schools played a significant part in local chapel life, not just because of the social activities associated with them, important though they were, but also because of the contribution that they, like the church day-schools, made to the diffusion of general religious understanding in the county. Their position changed in the course of the 19th century as their importance as providers of a more general education, including the inculcation of social discipline, was replaced by one in which they came to be seen by the religious denominations to which they belonged as a source of potential converts and members. Their early aims were less specifically denominationally orientated. There was no mention of Methodism as such, beyond its title, in the aims of the Grimsby Wesleyan Sunday school committee as set out in 1823. Its purpose was said to be to raise 'the fallen sons of Adam, from a state of moral degradation, to the knowledge of Salvation by Faith, and to a participation of Gospel Grace'.[7]

The sort of cooperation between Wesleyans and Anglicans that was a feature of adult worship in some places still continued over Sunday schools in the middle of the 19th century. The 200 Sunday scholars in Bardney attended church and chapel on alternate Sundays in 1851. It was a situation in which both church and chapel were strong, but in Laceby, which was also large enough to support two Sunday schools, interdenominational arrangements were given up. It was harder for nonconformists to establish Sunday schools in smaller villages where there was the tighter control that favoured the interests of the Church of England. The school at Walesby was a joint venture between the Wesleyans and Primitive Methodists, although after a new incumbent arrived in 1853 it gradually came under his control.[8]

In 1851, 391 of the 830 Sunday schools in Lincolnshire were nonconformist, slightly fewer than those belonging to the Church of England, although they were on average larger. It was said that 31,527

Fig. 46   Conisholme. The provision of chapels and their schoolrooms involved considerable effort on the part of local Methodists, and these efforts were duplicated by the congregations of each of its branches. At Conisholme the Wesleyan chapel and the United Methodist Free Churches' schoolroom of 1871 (left) were built side by side.

children attended Sunday schools provided by nonconformists, just over 55 per cent of all Sunday scholars in Lincolnshire, who comprised nearly 20 per cent of children in the county. It was possible for Sunday schools to achieve high levels of participation at a local level and in 1857 the workers on the Spalding Town Mission found that only 347 of the 2,525 children in the town that they judged to be capable of benefitting from Sunday school were not attending one. The rest were undergoing instruction more or less regularly. There were a number of places with a Wesleyan presence but no Sunday school, and even more among the Primitives, while the distribution of Baptist Sunday schools was related to the more localized presence of their churches in the county. Nonetheless the Wesleyans were by far the largest nonconformist provider of Sunday schools in 1851 with 247 schools and just over 20,000 pupils, followed by the Primitive Methodists with 60 Sunday schools and 3,573 scholars. The Baptists were not far behind with 2,740 scholars in their 36 schools.[9]

There is some suggestion that writing as well as reading was taught in Primitive Methodist Sunday schools. Quills and writing paper were also bought for the Wesleyan Sunday school at Lincoln between 1823 and 1825. Wesleyan schools generally appear to have taught only reading by the 1820s, although it was still found necessary to incorporate a rule forbidding teaching 'the art of Writing, or any other merely Secular Branch of Knowledge' into the Grimsby Wesleyan Sunday school rules in the 1840s. The pupils at Cleethorpes Sunday school spent about twenty minutes in a reading lesson and another twenty on spelling, after their day's work had been opened with singing and prayer, in the late 1820s. Reading was a suitable Sabbath day employment that enabled pupils to read their Bibles, although the libraries associated with larger schools such as that at Grimsby provided a range of material that extended beyond the Scriptures. *The Pirates of the Isle of Cuba* and *The Duke of Marlborough* were among the books that could be borrowed from it in 1825, together with more spiritually orientated fare such as *The Pilgrim's Progress* and copies of the *Methodist Magazine*.[10]

The Methodist library established at Cleethorpes in 1830 was founded to counteract 'pernicious and infidel publications'. Anxiety about literature of this type was a product of the period in which the early Sunday school libraries were established. A broader concern with personal conduct extended into what became the more general, if implicit, role of Sunday schools as purveyors of a culture of religiously informed self-discipline that patterned the lives of the people identified with chapels. A Methodist Sunday school had been established at Binbrook in 1819 'for the benefit of the many poor children' of the parish, and the full day of religious education and worship that the Sunday schools provided was credited with improving standards of public behaviour. That at Lincoln was said to have kept 'hundreds of poor children' from 'annoying the streets and commtting acts of flagrant immorality on the Lord's day'. The general standards of conduct expected outside the school from scholars at Grimsby Wesleyan Sunday school were firmly embedded in its rules and maintained through its discipline. In 1842 the superintendent of the Waltham Wesleyan Sunday school was empowered to 'inflict such reproof or punishment' as was deemed necessary on any scholar 'coming Dirty, or found Guilty of Lying, Swearing, Stealing, Sabbath-breaking, or Negligence'.[11]

Despite the hegemonic nature of their rules on personal conduct, the transactions of Sunday school life were more subtle and less of a one-way process than might at first be implied from the attempt to impose patterns of behaviour, such as those laid down for the refractory youth of Waltham. The 'Bad Boys' classes and similar arrangements for girls at Horncastle Wesleyan Sunday school in 1817, together with the 'Disgraced Class' that had been established there by 1840, were symptomatic of the strong disciplinary ethos of the Sunday schools, but it was a discipline that people like William Wright, a joiner, who had been born at Butterwick in 1806, were prepared to accept voluntarily for the benefits that they obtained from their teaching. It was said that Wright owed his entire secular education to the Wesleyan Sunday school. Like him, consciously and less consciously, the people in Lincolnshire were able to use nonconformist Sunday schools to provide a religious and social experience that met a wide range of their needs.[12]

The schools were accessible and even responsive, because in many places the backgrounds of the people who taught in them were often very close to those of their pupils. The large numbers of teachers involved meant that there was need to recruit widely in the local community. It was necessary to reach deep into the town congregation at Bourne General Baptist church to provide 38 teachers for its 240 scholars in 1863, while 13 teachers were involved in Sunday school work in the same year in the fenland village of Pinchbeck. The work also provided an outlet for the energies and talents of women in a world dominated by male office holders. Even among the Primitive Methodists, where there were still full-time women preachers in the middle of the century, men were more commonly the superintendents of Sunday schools. Although a Miss Walker played a prominent part in the opening services for the Primitive chapel at Cleethorpes in 1848, the Sunday school that was started in it was superintended by two of the leading local male worthies. Long-serving officers like them did, however, bring stability and continuity to the schools, linking their work with chapel and circuit affairs through the overlapping offices that they often held. Thomas Wesley Bryant who lived in Stickney between 1851 and 1877 was a class leader, society, chapel, and

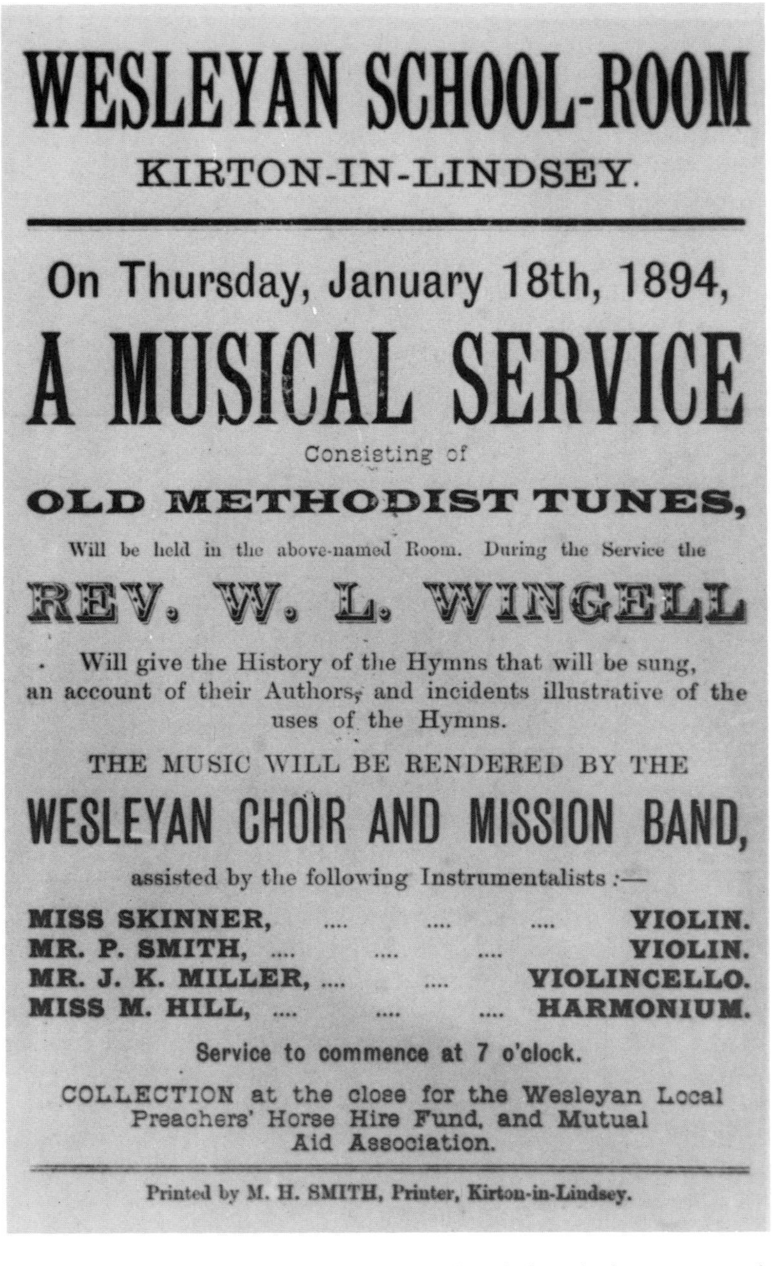

Fig. 47   Kirton in Lindsey Wesleyan poster. Although described as a service, the entertainment that was also provided by fund-raising functions of this type was an important element in local chapel life.

circuit steward, trustee for several chapels on the circuit, a local preacher and Superintendent of the local Sunday School.[13]

The virtues and values inculcated in Sunday schools were displayed at their anniversaries, another of the fixed points in the calendar of local communities where worship was combined with entertainment in a generally recreational ambience. The nature of these changed with the development of Sunday schools. The 'very creditable appearance and order' and the 'steadiness and attention' of the children in their public examination not only 'gave considerable satisfaction', but induced many of the inhabitants to subscribe to the funds of the Market Rasen Wesleyan Methodist Sunday school in 1813. An element of public performance had been introduced into the anniversary parade of the Nettleham Wesleyan Sunday scholars by 1835, when they 'walked in procession round the village and its vicinity, accompanied with music and singing' while the teachers solicited contributions for the coming year. Later in the century the demonstration of the pedagogical element of the work of Sunday schools had been transformed into a more generally upliftingly entertaining presentation of the ability of the Sunday school to prepare its pupils for public performance. At the Sunday school anniversary of the Commercial Road Primitive Methodist chapel in Grantham the children, situated in a temporary gallery erected for them, gave recitations and 'dialogues' at the three Sunday services in the chapel, specially decorated for the occasion. On the Monday the proceeds from a tea meeting addressed by four speakers, and at which there were more recitations, were added to the £5 10s 6d collected on the Sunday for school funds.[14]

As adult membership levels began to decline both in absolute terms and in relation to the size of the population of Lincolnshire, Sunday schools came to be seen increasingly as a source of recruitment for full church members. The establishment of separate central Sunday school committees in the different nonconformist bodies, including a Primitive Methodist Sunday School Union in 1874, marked a new perception of the role of the schools in nonconformist church life. The General Baptists also turned increasingly to their Sunday schools for converts in the 1880s. They were, according to a Primitive Methodist report of 1893, no longer 'Merely Seminaries for teaching, but saving agencies'.[15]

Yet the larger proportions of young people leaving the villages from the 1870s meant that they were a weakening base on which to build the future of local chapel life. Adult Wesleyan membership at Belchford declined from 56 to 40 in the last decade of the 19th century, while the young people who had been attracted into junior membership disapppeared from the local records altogether. A Sunday school continued for a number of years, but it was associated with a diminishing body of adult church members. Town Sunday schools continued to attract large numbers. There were 508

Fig. 48   Boston Centenary Wesleyan Methodist chapel, built 1839. This interior view, centred on pulpit and organ, reflects the importance of preaching and music in a building that was, in effect, an auditorium as well as a place of worship.

Fig. 49   Boston Centenary Wesleyan Methodist church hall interior.
The provision of halls and other associated premises enabled local
nonconformist churches to provide a range of meetings and social activities.

in 1890 at Grimsby's George Street town centre chapel, although it was
nearly equalled in size by that at South Parade, one of the chapels that
served the developing areas of the town. It had 478 scholars. The Sunday
school at Lincoln's Wesley chapel was said to have reached its 'peak years'
in the late 1870s before 'the rapid movement of people from the centre to
the suburbs'. Yet, despite their continuing numerical strength compared
with their demographically threatened rural counterparts, these urban
Sunday schools were ultimately unable to provide the basis for church
growth that was expected by denominational leaders, although they
continued to be one of the chapel-based organizations to which people
were attracted.[16]

SOCIAL LIFE AND SELF IMPROVEMENT

The range of activities associated with chapels was dependent on the size of
their membership and congregations. At Horncastle the Wesleyan
Methodists had a benefit society, established in 1838, provided a venue for
temperance activities, had a Young Men's Mutual Improvement
Association, and a Young Men's Institute. The emphasis on male-based
organizations showed a degree of anxiety to attract younger men into the
life of the chapel where older male office holders were dominant. The role
of women was reflected in the way their activities tended to be seen as

supportive of the official business of chapel life. This was seen at Binbrook in 1872 when Mrs Benn 'delivered up' to the Free Methodist chapel treasurer the money from the sewing meetings that she had organized. While some of the organizations affiliated to chapels had a local base, others were connected to national organizations. They helped to broaden the horizons of their members and focus on more than local concerns. The need to raise money for denominational purposes and, in particular, for missionary work also put congregations in touch with a wider world. The information dispensed by missionary societies added an educational element to the wider sense of purpose engendered by the meetings held in their support. The people at Benniworth Free Methodist chapel were said to 'enjoy exceedingly' reports of Livingstone's journeys related at the Sunday school anniversary in August 1872. According to Corneluis Stovin who also took part in the meeting the 'sphere of our geographical vision' had been 'considerably enlarged'.[17]

Temperance

Temperance provided a platform on which nonconformists, especially the various branches of Methodism, could unite, despite official ambivalence among the Wesleyan Methodists. This was as much a product of Wesleyan distrust of bodies that ran across denominational structures, seen in the concern expressed by Conference about temperance organizations in the period leading up to the Reform divisions, as of the principles espoused by the movement. These feelings were hardly assuaged by the radical stance of many early teetotal leaders. The Primitives officially supported the temperance movement from the 1830s although it was not until the 1870s that it had any official recognition from the Wesleyans. The Revd E. Jope was the first Wesleyan Superintendent minister to speak on the temperance platform in Horncastle chapel. This was in December 1899.[18]

Temperance activities were informative in their content as well as reformative in their aims and linked the branches that were based on chapels through their organization into a wider network of activity and interest. Official coolness did not prevent many chapels being caught up in temperance activities at a local level, and the cycle of meetings and festivals, with the children's organizations that were also part of them, added a further element to the social calendar of Lincolnshire towns and villages. They were little different in their form and content to the events arranged by the chapel congregations themselves and there was considerable overlap between the people involved. There was a public tea meeting and recitations by children from the Band of Hope at what was described as the Great Gonerby temperance society's second anniverary held in the village's Primitive Methodist chapel in 1870. It was said that the 'services were performed in a most gratifying manner upon purely

Christian principles' when the temperance hall was opened at Tetney in 1852. In what was in essence the equivalent of revival conversion, eighteen people were moved by the occasion to sign the temperance pledge to abstain from alcoholic drink.[19]

The temperance movement was one of a range of organizations and interests connected with nonconformist chapels through which they established a place in the public lives of local communities. However, as the number of people who were associated with nonconformity through these activities fell, only a committed inner core of members was left to maintain rural chapel life. The nonconformist churches and chapels that served the leafier parts of Grimsby and Lincoln and whose congregations came from the villas that had appeared on the outskirts of towns such as Gainsborough, Boston, Bourne, Horncastle, or Sleaford were less exposed to demographic change; but the extent to which the specifically religious content of their activities had been subordinated to other collective activities, more relevant to the maintenance of chapel life than to its growth through mission, meant that they were vulnerable to the competition of other agencies and institutions that offered new and more socially attractive opportunities for service and recreation.[20]

Bishop King had been worried by the apparent strength of religious dissent and his apprehension was shared by clergymen in many country parishes as they saw themselves becoming increasingly marginalized in parish life. Where the structures of parish life had been open enough to accommodate nonconformist chapels, the Church of England had not been able to match the attractive inclusiveness of the organizations with which they were surrounded. Yet, although its clergy worked within radically changed parameters as they came to occupy a new role in parish communities, the Church of England ultimately proved to be relatively less threatened because of its inherent historic institutional strength.

Family ties were still sufficiently strong and the rites of passage still valued enough to stimulate occasional attendance at both church and chapel. In many rural parishes there was still also sufficient pride in the fabric of their ancient church buildings for their people to retain some vestigial sense of the religious associations of the old parish community. By the 20th century a faithful remnant remained to support the regular worship of both churches and chapels. For them the teachings that they imbibed and their experience of worship gave sufficient meaning to their lives to ensure a more coherent and committed level of adherence than had been common among the larger groups of people whose associations with church and chapel had been shaped in communities where the place of religion had been more generally important, but also more diffused.[21]

Notes to Chapter VII

1   *GJ*, 17 October 1857, 27 February, 6 March 1858, 11 May 1861.

2   *GJ*, 30 May 1863, 2 April 1864, 29 April 1865, 7 April 1866, 19 April 1873, 18 October 1873, 22 November 1873.

3   SGS, Prim. Meth.1; *Journals*, p. 141; LA, Meth B/Louth/66/1.

4   SGS Prim. Meth.1, Prim. Meth. 2, 6 December 1860; *Rel. & Rur. Soc.*, pp. 213–14; *Peas. Prea.*, p. 350.

5   G. Burrows, *Forward with Christ: the story of the Bourne Methodist circuit (1801–1995)*, [no place], 1998, pp. 36–7.

6   *Journals*, pp. 142, 153–4.

7   *Hist. Sch.* 2, pp. 35, 50–51.

8   *1851 Census Ret.*, pp. 100–101; *Hist. Sch.* 2, pp. 50–51; K. D. M. Snell, 'The Sunday-School Movement in England and Wales: child labour, denominational control and working class culture', *P&P*, 164 (August 1999), p. 164.

9   Tab. Sch., pp. lxxvi, clxxvii; *Rel. & Rur. Soc.*, pp. 193, 228; *SFP*, 19 May 1857.

10 *PMM*, 6 (March 1825), pp. 94–5, XVI (new ser.) (1893), p. 182; *Clee. Meth.*, p. 73; *Hist. Sch.* 2, pp. 53, 64, 77–81, 83–4.

11 *Clee. Meth.*, pp. 72–3, 75; *Hist. Sch.* 2, pp. 40–41, 72.

12 *Hornc. Meth.*, p. 62; *WMM*, VI (6th ser.) (March 1882), pp. 169–70.

13 MNCGB, 1863, pp. 14, 17; *Clee. Meth.*, p. 126.

14 *Hist. Sch.*, 2, pp. 41, 43; *GJ*, 27 May 1865.

15 S. J. D. Green, *Religion in the Age of Decline: organisation and experience in industrial Yorkshire, 1870–1920*, Cambridge, 1996, p. 212; P. B. Cliff, *The Rise and Development of the Sunday School Movement in England 1780–1980,* Redhill, pp. 74, 179; *Orig. & Hist.*, II, p. 530; *GBYB*, 1885, p. 75.

16 J. N. Clarke, *Belchford: the history of a Lincolnshire Wolds village*, [Belchford], 1987, p. 87; Lester, *Grims. Meth.*, pp. 72, 81; W. E. Selby, *One Hundred Years 1836–1936: the story of Wesley chapel Lincoln*, Lincoln, [1936], pp. 43, 46.

17 *Hornc. Meth.*, pp. 156, 160–62; *Journals*, pp. 77, 82.

18 B. Harrison, *Drink and the Victorians: the temperance question in England 1815–72,* London, 1971, pp. 108–9; *Orig. & Hist.*, I, pp. 470–71; R. W. Moss, 'Wesleyan Methodism – the Last Fifty Years' in *New Hist. Meth.*, London, 1909, p. 465; *Hornc. Meth.*, p. 161.

19 *GJ*, 31 December 1870; R. C. Russell, *The Water Drinkers in Lindsey: 1837–1860: the earlier temperance movement*, Barton-upon-Humber, 1987, pp. 15–16.

20 Green, *Religion in the Age of Decline,* pp. 386–8.

21 G. Neville, 'Churches and Religious Life', in *Twentieth Century Lincolnshire*, ed. D. R. Mills, Lincoln, 1989, pp. 286–7.

ABBREVIATIONS AND BIBLIOGRAPHY

Note: Abbreviations beginning with numbers are listed as if they were spelled out in full.

ABBREVIATION	FULL TITLE
AASR	*Associated Architectural Societies Reports and Papers*
Archd. Vis.	J. Varley, 'An Archdiaconal Visitation of Stow, 1752', *LAAS*, new ser. 3, 2 (1945)
Art. of Enq.	LA, Articles of Enquiry to Churchwardens and Sidesmen, 1858
Art. of Vis.	LA, Cragg 2/9, *Articles of Visitation and Enquiry Concerning Matters Ecclesiastical Exhibited to the Ministers, Churchwardens and Sides-men of Every Parish within the Diocese of Lincoln. In the First Episcopal Visitation of the Right Reverend Father in God Robert, by Divine Permission, Lord Bishop of Lincoln*, London, 1662
Ast. & Don. Ch. Book	LA 12 BAPT/ Asterby and Donington on Bain Baptist Church Book, 1698–1868
Atlas	S. Bennett and N. Bennett, *An Historical Atlas of Lincolnshire*, Hull, 1993
Bapt. Min.	*Minutes of the General Assembly of the Baptist Churches in England with Kindred Records*, I, *1654–1728*, ed W. T. Whitley, London [1909]
BH	*The Baptist Handbook*
Binbrook	C. Rawding (ed.), *Binbrook in the 19th Century*, Binbrook, 1980
Biog. Sket.	G. Herod, *Biographical Sketches of Some of Those Preachers Whose Labours contributed to the Origination and Early Extension of the Primitive Methodist Connexion*, London [n.d.]
Bish., Cler. & Peop.	F. Knight, 'Bishop, Clergy and People: John Kaye and the Diocese of Lincoln, 1827–1853, Unpublished Ph.D. thesis, University of Cambridge, 1990
BL	The British Library, London
BLLSH	*The Boston, Lincoln, Louth and Spalding Herald*

BM	*The Baptist Magazine*
Bost. Ch. Book	LA 24 BAPT/1/ Boston General Baptist Church Minute Book, 1715–1791
Booth	H. Begbie, *Life of William Booth the Founder of the Salvation Army*, I, London, 1920
Bourne Ch. Book	Bourne Baptist Church, Book of Church Affairs, 1702–1891
BQ	*The Baptist Quarterly*
Brief Acc.	[J. Besse], *A Brief Account of Many of the Prosecutions of People Called Quakers in the Exchequer, Ecclesiastical and Other Courts for Demands Recoverable by the Acts made in the 7th and 8th Years of the Reign of King William the Third, for the More Easy Recovery of Tithes, Church-Rates &c.*, London, 1736
BSLH	*The Boston, Stamford and Lincoln Herald*
Build. 18th C. Ch.	B. F. L. Clarke, *The Building of the Eighteenth-Century Church*, London, 1963
Bull. JRULM	*Bulletin of the John Rylands University Library of Manchester*
Burtts	M. B. Burtt, *The Burtts: a Lincolnshire Quaker Family*, Hull, 1937
Calamy	*Calamy Revised: being a revision of Edward Calamy's Account of ministers and others ejected and silenced 1660–1662*, ed. A. G. Matthews, Oxford, 1934
Cath. Dir.	*The Catholic Directory and Annual Register*
Ch. Briefs	W. A. Bewes, *Church Briefs, or Royal Warrants for Collections for Charitable Objects*, London, 1896
Ch. in Age of Neglig.	P. Virgin, *The Church in an Age of Negligence: ecclesiastical structure and problems of church reform 1700–1840*, Cambridge, 1989
Ch. Miss. Soc.	C. Hole, *The Early History of the Church Missionary Society for Africa and the East to the End of AD 1814*, London, 1896
Ch. Miss. Soc. Proc.	*Proceedings of the Church Missionary Society for Africa and the East*, I, London, 1801–1805; IV, London, 1813–1815

Ch. of Eng.	J. Walsh, C. Haydon and S. Taylor (eds.), *The Church of England from* c. *1689*–c. *1833: from Toleration to Tractarianism*, Cambridge, 1993
Ch. in Lincs.	[T. W. Mossman], 'The Church in Lincolnshire', *The Union Review*, III (1865)
Ch. in Eng.	J. Morrill, 'The Church in England, 1642–1649', in J. B. Morrill (ed.), *Reactions to the English Civil War*, London, 1982
Ch. P.	LA, Churchwardens Presentments
Ch. Work Stats.	LA, Lincoln Diocesan Trust/ Statistics of Church Work and Finance/ 1900–1901
Ches. Coll. Arch.	Cheshunt College Foundation Archives, Westminster College, Cambridge, Lady Huntingdon's Papers
Clee. Meth.	F. Baker, *The Story of Cleethorpes and the Contribution of Methodism through Two Hundred Years*, Cleethorpes, 1953
CM	*Congregational Magazine*
Compt. Cen.	*The Compton Census of 1676: a critical edition*, ed. A. Whiteman, London, 1986
Con. Ch. Book	Regent's Park College, Oxford, Angus Library, 1/3/16 Coningsby Baptist Church Book
Cong. in Lincs.	J. T. Barker, *Congregationalism in Lincolnshire*, London, 1860, DWL copy with annotations by C. E. Surman
CRS	Catholic Record Society
CSPD	*Calendars of State Papers Domestic*
CW	*Christian Words: or the organ of the Wesleyan Reform Union*
CYB	*The Congregational Year Book*
DEB	*The Blackwell Dictionary of Evangelical Biography*, I, Oxford, 1995
Dec. of Indulg.	F. Bate, *The Declaration of Indulgence: a study of the rise of organised dissent*, London, 1908
Dir. Lincs.	W. White, *A History, Gazetteer and Directory of Lincolnshire*, Sheffield, 1856, repr. 1969
Diss. Certs.	J. Varley, 'Dissenters' Certificates in the Lincoln Diocesan Records', *LH*, 4 (1949)

Diss.	M. R. Watts, *The Dissenters*, I, *From the Reformation to the French Revolution*, Oxford, 1978; II, *The Expansion of Evangelical Nonconformity* , Oxford, 1995
DNB	*Dictionary of National Biography*
DSN	*Drakard's Stamford News and General Advertiser*
DWL	Dr Williams's Library, London
Earl. Vict. Meth.	*Early Victorian Methodism: the correspondence of Jabez Bunting 1830–1858*, ed. W. R. Ward, Oxford, 1976
Eccles. & Relig. Life	J. E. Swaby, 'Ecclesiastical and Religious Life in Lincolnshire 1640–1660, Unpublished Ph.D. thesis, University of Leicester, 1982
EHR	*English Historical Review*
1851 Census Ret.	*Lincolnshire Returns of the Census of Religious Worship 1851*, ed. R. W. Ambler, LRS, 72, Lincoln, 1979
1851 Tab. Ret.	Office of Population Censuses and Surveys, London, Tabulated Returns of the 1851 Census of Religious Worship for Lincolnshire
18th C. Ch.	*18th Century Churches in Lincolnshire*, The Lincolnshire Churches Trust, Third Annual Report [Lincoln], 1955
18th C. Chap.	W. Leary, 'Eighteenth Century Chapels', *JLMHS*, 12 (Spring 1969)
18th C. Eng Bapt.	R. Brown, *English Baptists of the Eighteenth Century*, London, 1986
EM	*Evangelical Magazine*
EMBA Deeds	Didcot, Baptist Union Corporation, East Midland Baptist Association Trusteeship Files and Deeds
Eng. Cath. Com.	J. Bossy, *The English Catholic Community, 1570–1850,* London, 1975
Eng. Gen. Bapt.	A. Taylor, *A History of the English General Baptists,* I, *The English General Baptists of the Seventeenth Century*, London, 1818; II, *The New Connexion of General Baptists*, London, 1818
Ep. Ch. Book	LA TONGE 1, The Epworth Baptist Church Book

Ep. Cir. Trusts	LA Meth B/ Epworth and Crowle/ 32/ 1 Epworth Circuit Trusts and Trustees 1814–1839
Ep. Par. Life	A. F. Messiter, *Notes on Epworth Parish Life in the Eighteenth Century*, London, 1912
Episc. Vis.	Episcopal Visitation
Episc. & Archd. Vis.	Episcopal & Archdiaconal Visitation
Estab. Ch.	D. W. Lovegrove, *Established Church, Sectarian People. Itinerancy and the Transformation of English Dissent, 1780–1830*, Cambridge, 1988
Evans List	DWL MS 38.4 The John Evans List of Dissenting Congregations 1715–1729
Examples	Mrs Gutch and M. Peacock, *Examples of Printed Folk-Lore Concerning Lincolnshire*, 1908, repr. Liechtenstein 1967
Extr. 2	*Extracts from State Papers Relating to Friends*, 2nd ser., 1659–1664, London, 1911
Extr. 3	*Extracts from State Papers Relating to Friends*, 3rd ser., 1664 to 1669, London, 1912
FH	Friends House, London
FL	Friends Library, London,
Free. After Eject.	*Freedom After Ejection: a review (1690–1692) of Presbyterian and Congregational Nonconformity in England and Wales,* ed. A. Gordon, Manchester, 1917
Furth. Vis. Ret.	LA V/ ix/ 2 Further Visitation Returns
Gains. Min.	*The First Minute Book of the Society of Friends, 1669–1719*, ed. H. W. Brace, 3 vols., LRS, 38, 40 and 44, Hereford, 1948, 1949 and 1951
Gains. MSS Min.	LA SOC FR 12/16 Gainsborough Monthly Meeting Minute Book, 1719–1783
Georg. Linc.	Sir Francis Hill, *Georgian Lincoln*, Cambridge, 1966
GBM	*General Baptist Magazine and Missionary Observer*
GBR	*General Baptist Repository and Missionary Observer*
GBYB	*General Baptist Year Book*
GJ	*Grantham Journal, Melton Mowbray, Bourne and Rutland Advertiser*
GN	*The Gainsborough News*

Gran. Wes. Meth.	T. Cocking, *The History of Wesleyan Methodism in Grantham and its Vicinity*, London, 1836
Grims. & Hornc. Rec.	SHARO 326/1/1 Grimsby and Horncastle Methodist Circuit Records, 1719–1782
Grims. Meth.	G. Lester, *Grimsby Methodism (1743–1889) and the Wesleys in Lincolnshire*, London, 1890
Hist. & Antiq.	P. Thompson, *The History and Antiquities of Boston*, Boston, 1856
Hist. Eng. Bapt. 1	T. Crosby, *The History of the English Baptists from the Reformation to the Beginning of the Reign of King George I*, III, *Containing their History from the End of the Reign of King Charles II to the End of the Glorious Reign of King William III of Immortal Memory*, London, 1740
Hist. Eng. Bapt. 2	J. Ivemey, *History of the English Baptists*, II, *Containing Biographical Sketches of Above Three Hundred Ministers, and Historical Accounts, Alphabetically Arranged, of One Hundred and Thirty Churches in the Different Counties of England from about the Year 1610 till 1700*, London, 1814 IV, *Comprising the Principal Events of the History of Protestant Dissenters during the Reign of George III*, London, 1830
Hist. Louth	J. E. Swaby, *A History of Louth*, London, 1951
Hist. Meth. Ch.	R. Davies and G. Rupp (eds.), *A History of the Methodist Church in Great Britain*, I, London 1965; R. Davies, A. R. George and G. Rupp (eds.) *A History of the Methodist Church in Great Britain* II, London, 1978
Hist. PM	J. Petty, *The History of the Primitive Methodist Connexion, from its Origin to the Conference of 1860, the First Jubilee Year of the Connexion*, revised and enlarged by J. Macpherson, London, 1880
Hist. Sch. 1	R. C. Russell, *A History of Schools and Education in Lindsey, Lincolnshire, 1800–1902*, Part One, *The Foundation and Maintenance of Schools for the Poor*, [Lincoln], 1965
Hist. Sch. 2	R. C. Russell, *A History of Schools and Education in Lindsey, Lincolnshire, 1800–1902*, Part Two, *Sunday Schools in Lindsey. The 'miserable compromise' of the Sunday school,* [Lincoln], 1965

Hist. Sch. 3	R. C. Russell, *A History of Schools and Education in Lindsey, Lincolnshire, 1800–1902*, Part Three, *The Church of England and the Provision of Elementary Education*, [Lincoln], 1966
Hist. Sch. 4	R. C. Russell, *A History of Schools and Education in Lindsey, Lincolnshire, 1800–1902*, Part Four, *Methodism and the Provision of Day Schools*, [Lincoln], 1967
HL	House of Lords Record Office, London
HMC	Historical Manuscripts Commission
Hornc. Meth.	J. N. Clarke and C. L. Anderson, *Methodism in the Countryside. Horncastle Circuit, 1786–1986*, [Horncastle, 1986]
Hunt. Coll.	BL Add Mss 24484, Hunter Collection, 'Britannica Puritanica, or Outline of the History of the Various Congregations of Presbyterians and Independents which arose out of the schism of the Church of England of 1662'
J. Eccles. Hist.	*Journal of Ecclesiastical History*
JFHS	*Journal of the Friends Historical Society*
JLMHS	*Journal of the Lincolnshire Methodist History Society*
Journals	*Journals of a Methodist Farmer 1871–1875*, ed. J. Stovin, London, 1982
JURHS	*Journal of the United Reformed Church Historical Society*
Kaye Corr.	LA Cor B5, Correspondence of John Kaye, Bishop of Lincoln, 1827–1853
Kest.	J. Varley, *The Parts of Kesteven; studies in law and local government*, [Sleaford] 1974
King	O. Chadwick, *Edward King, Bishop of Lincoln, 1885–1910*, Lincoln, 1968
LA	Lincolnshire Archives, Lincoln
LAAS	*Lincolnshire Architectural and Archaeological Society Reports and Papers*
Later Per.	R. M. Jones, *The Later Periods of Quakerism*, 2 vols, London, 1921
Lay Peop.	W. M. Jacob, *Lay People and Religion in the Early Eighteenth Century*, Cambridge, 1996

Letters	D. R. J. Neave, 'Letters of Edward Steere', *LHA*, 2 (1967)
LH	*Lincolnshire Historian*
LHA	*Lincolnshire History and Archaeology*
Life & Writ.	*The Life and Writings of John Whitehead an Early and Eminent Minister of the Gospel in the Society of Friends*, London, 1852
Linc. G. B. Ch.	LA BAPT, Typescript, W.S. Linton, 'The History of the General Baptist Church in Lincoln, now known as the Thomas Cooper Memorial Baptist Church', 1911
Linc. Meth.	A. Watmough, *A History of Methodism in the Neighbourhood and City of Lincoln*, Lincoln, 1829
Linc. Meth. Reg.	PRO, RG4, 1644, Non Parochial Registers, Lincoln Wesleyan Methodist Baptismal Register, 1810–1839
Linc. Min. St. Ch.	LA, 1 BAPT/29, Mint Street, Lincoln, Baptist Church Book, 1870–1909
Lincs. Cler.	E. and R. Russell, 'Lincolnshire Clergy and Schools: 1814', *LH*, 2 (1962)
Lincs. Fac.	R. E. G. Cole, 'Some Lincolnshire Faculties, AD 1663–1693', *AASR*, 30, 1 (1909)
Lincs. Meth.	W. Leary, *Lincolnshire Methodism*, Buckingham, 1988
Lincs. Pol.	R. G. Olney, *Lincolnshire Politics 1832–1885*, Oxford, 1973
Lives	*The Lives of the Early Methodist Preachers. Chiefly Written by Themselves*, ed. T. Jackson, I & VI, London, 1871
Louth Free Meth.	P. W. Robinson, 'Louth and the Rise of Free Methodism', *JLMHS*, 3, 1 (Autumn 1977)
LRS	Lincoln Record Society
LRSM	*Lincoln, Rutland and Stamford Mercury*
Meet. Hou.	D. M. Butler, ' Meeting Houses Built and Meetings Settled; answers to the Yearly Meeting Queries, 1688–1791', *JFHS*, 51, 3 (1967)
Memoir	I[srael] W[orsley], 'Memoir Relating to the Estate at Kirkstead, in Lincolnshire, Lately Recovered to Dissenters', *MR*, VIII (February 1813)

Memoirs	A. Taylor, *Memoirs of the Rev. Dan Taylor, Late Pastor of the General Baptist Church, Whitechapel, London*, London, 1820
Meth. Arch.	John Rylands University Library of Manchester, Methodist Archives
Meth. Sec.	D. Gowland, *Methodist Secessions. The origins of Free Methodism in Three Lancashire Towns: Manchester, Rochdale, Liverpool*, Manchester, 1979
Min.	*Minutes of the Proceedings in Quarter Sessions held for the Parts of Kesteven in the County of Lincoln, 1674–1695*, ed. S. A. Peyton, 2 vols., LRS 25 and 26, Lincoln, 1931
MM	*Methodist Magazine*
MNCGB	*Minutes of the Association of the New Connexion of General Baptists*
MNCMin.	*Minutes of the Annual Conference of the Methodist New Connexion*
MR	*Monthly Repository of Theology and General Literature*
Names	J. Cosin, *The Names of the Roman Catholics, Nonjurors and Others, who Refus'd to take the Oaths to His Late Majesty King George*, London, 1745, repr. 1862
NC MSS	DWL, New College Manuscripts
New Hist. Meth.	W. J. Townsend, H. B. Workman, and G. Eayrs, *A New History of Methodism*, I, London, 1909
9 Charges	*Nine Charges Delivered to the Clergy of the Diocese of Lincoln, with Some Other Works by John Kaye, D.D., Late Lord Bishop of Lincoln*, ed W. F. J. Kaye, London, 1854
19th C. Brigg	F. Henthorn, *A History of 19th Century Brigg*, Stamford, 1987
19th C. Ch.	F. Knight, *The Nineteenth-Century Church and English Society*, Cambridge, 1995
19th C. Eng. Bapt.	J. H. Y. Briggs, *The English Baptists of the Nineteenth Century*, London, 1994
Orig. & Hist.	H. B. Kendall, *The Origin and History of the Primitive Methodist Church*, 2 vols., London. [*c.*1905]

Orig. Rec.	*Original Records of Early Nonconformity under Persecution and Indulgence*, ed. G. L. Turner, II, London, 1911
Oxtoby	G. Shaw, *The Life of John Oxtoby ('Praying Johnny')*, Hull, 1894
P&P	*Past and Present*
Parl. P.	Parliamentary Papers
Peas. Prea.	J. E. Coulson, *The Peasant Preacher. Memorials of Mr. Charles Richardson, a Wesleyan Evangelist, Commonly Known as the 'Lincolnshire Thrasher'*, London, 1865
Pevsner 1	N. Pevsner and J. Harris, *Lincolnshire*, 1st. edit. Harmondsworth, 1964
Pevsner 2	N. Pevsner and J. Harris, *Lincolnshire*, 2nd ed., rev. by J. Antram, London, 1989
PMM	*Primitive Methodist Magazine*
PMMin.	*Minutary Records; being rules regulations and reports, made and published by the Primitive Methodist Connexion*
Prim. Meth. Conn.	J. S. Werner, *The Primitive Methodist Connexion: its background and early history*, Wisconsin, 1984
PRO	Public Record Office, London
Prot. Cong.	DWL, Protestant Congregations in England and Wales, 1774–1776
Purit. to Unit.	J. C. Warren, 'From Puritanism to Unitarianism at Lincoln', *TUHS*, II (1919–22)
Qu. in Lincs.	S. Davies, *Quakerism in Lincolnshire: an informal history*, Lincoln, 1989
Qu. Soc. Hist.	A. Lloyd, *Quaker Social History 1669–1738*, London, 1950
Quart. Min.	LA SOC FR 1&3, Society of Friends, Lincolnshire Quarterly Minutes , 1668–1699. Quarterly Meeting Sufferings, 1654–1719
Reas. Enthus.	H. D. Rack, *Reasonable Enthusiast: John Wesley and the rise of Methodism*, London, 1989
Rec. Ch. of Christ	*Records of the Churches of Christ gathered at Fenstanton, Warboys and Hexham, 1644–1720*, ed. E. B. Underhill, London, 1854

Recollect.	G. Barratt, *Recollections of Methodism and Methodists in the City of Lincoln*, Lincoln, 1866
Records	*Records of the English Province of the Society of Jesus*
Reg. Book	G. F. Engelbach, 'The Register Book of the Catholic Chapel, Market Rasen, Lincolnshire, 1797–1840', *Miscellanea*, CRS 22, 1921
Rel. & Rur. Soc.	J. Obelkevich, *Religion and Rural Society: south Lindsey 1825–1875*, Oxford, 1976
Rel. Cen.	S. A. Peyton, 'The Religious Census of 1676' *EHR*, 48 (1933)
Rel. Wor.	Parl. P., 1852–52, LXXXIX (1690), Population of Great Britain, 1851, Religious Worship (England and Wales)
Report	*Report from the Clergy of a District in the Diocese of Lincoln*, London, 1800
Rest. Ch.	J. Spurr, *The Restoration Church of England, 1646–1689*, London, 1991
Return	LA, Parts of Kesteven, Clerk of the Peace's Papers, A Return of the Number of Places not of the Church of England, June 1829
Rise of Indep.	G. F. Nuttall, 'The Rise of Independency in Lincolnshire: Thomas Wilson and the students', *JURHS*, 4, 1 (October 1987)
Rob. Sand.	C. E. Davies, 'Robert Sanderson, Restoration Bishop; his administration of the diocese of Lincoln 1660–1663', 2 vols., Unpublished University of Oxford B. Litt. thesis, 1969
Rub., Ord. & Dir.	Parl. P., 1867–68, XXVIII, [4016], Second Report of the Commissioners Appointed to Inquire into the Rubrics, Orders, and Directions for Regulating the Course and Conduct of Public Worship, &c.
SCH	*Studies in Church History*
2nd Per.	W. C. Braithwaite, *The Second Period of Quakerism*, 2nd. ed., prep. by H. J. Cadbury, Cambridge, 1961
17th & 18th C. Lincs.	C. Brears, *Lincolnshire in the Seventeenth and Eighteenth Centuries*, London, 1940
17th C. Lincs.	C. Holmes, *Seventeenth-Century Lincolnshire*, Lincoln, 1980

SFP	*Spalding Free Press and Eastern Counties Advertiser*
SG	*Sleaford Gazette and South Lincolnshire Advertiser*
SGS Meth. 1	Spalding Gentlemen's Society, Methodist Archives, Box 1, Spalding Circuit, Baptismal Register, 1823–1837
SGS Meth 10	Spalding Gentlemen's Society, Methodist Archives, Box 10, Spalding Circuit Membership Book, 1823–1838
SGS Prim. Meth. 1	Spalding Gentlemen's Society, Methodist Archives, Primitive Methodist Church, Donington Circuit Records, Account Book, 1853–1878
SGS Prim. Meth. 2	Spalding Gentlemen's Society, Methodist Archives, Primitive Methodist Church, Donington Circuit Records, Spalding and Holbeach Quarterly Meeting Minute Book, 1860–1862
SHARO	South Humberside Area Record Office, Grimsby
Sketches	[R. Yerburgh], *Sketches Illustrative of the Topography and History of Old and New Sleaford*, Sleaford, 1825
Soc. Comp.	R. W. Ambler, 'The Social Composition of Church Leadership: nonconformist trustees in Lincolnshire, 1800–1870', *Bull. JRULM*, 75, 1 (Spring 1993)
Soc. Struct. 18th C.	M. Avery, 'The Social Structure of Methodism in North Lincolnshire in the Late Eighteenth Century', Unpublished University of Hull Certificate in Regional and Local History Dissertation, 1986
Sp. Ch. Book	LA 14 BAPT 1/ Spalding Baptist Church Minute Book, 1792–1837
Spalding	N. Leverett and M. J. Elsdon, *Aspects of Spalding 1790–1930*, Spalding, 1986
Spec.	*Speculum Dioceseos Lincolniensis sub Episcopis Gul. Wake et Edm. Gibson, AD 1705–1723*, ed. R. E. G. Cole, LRS 4, Lincoln, 1913
Spec. 3	LA, SPE 3, Speculum Dioceseos Lincolniensis sub Episcopis Johanne Thomas AD 1744–1761
Spec. 4	LA, SPE 4, Speculum, 1788–1792
Spirit. Pilg.	E. Welch, *Spiritual Pilgrim: a reassessment of the life of the Countess of Huntingdon*, Cardiff, 1995

Stats.	J. Taylor, *Statistics of the New Connexion of General Baptists from its Formation in 1770, to 1843*, ed. J. Goadby, Ashby de la Zouch, [1844]
Stow Ch. Res.	*Stow Church Restored, 1846–1866*, ed. M. Spurrell, LRS 75, Lincoln, 1984
Stow Visitat.	*A Stow Visitation: being notes on the churches in the archdeaconry of Stow, 1845, by the Venerable W. B. Stonehouse*, ed. N. S. Harding, Lincoln, 1940
Suff.	J. Besse, *A Collection of the Sufferings of the People Called Quakers, for the Testimony of Good Conscience, from the Time of their being First Distinguished by that Name in the year 1659, to the Time of the Act Commonly Called the Act of Toleration, Granted to Protestant Dissenters in the First Year of the Reign of King William the Third and Queen Mary, in the year 1689*, I, London, 1753
Tab. Sch.	Parl. P., XC, 1852–53 [1692], Census of Great Britain, Tables Relating to Schools, &c.
TCHS	*Transactions of the Congregational Historical Society*
300 Years	G. C. Bolam, *Three Hundred Years, 1662–1962: the story of the churches forming the North Midlands Presbyterian and Unitarian Association*, Nottingham. 1962
Thomp. List	DWL MS 38, 5–6 Josiah Thompson's List of Dissenting Congregations in England and Wales, 1715–1773
Top. Acc.	E. Oldfield, *A Topographical and Historical Account of Wainfleet and the Wapentakes of Candleshoe, in the County of Lincoln*, London, 1829
Torr. Diar.	*The Torrington Diaries containing the Tours through England and Wales of the Hon. John Byng (later Fifth Viscount Torrington) between the years 1781 and 1794*, ed. C. B. Anderson, II, London 1934
Tour. Ch. Guide	*Tourists' Church Guide*
Trans. Roy. Hist. Soc.	*Transactions of the Royal Historical Society*
Tud. & Stu. Linc.	J. W. F. Hill, *Tudor and Stuart Lincoln*, Cambridge, 1956
TUHS	*Transactions of the Unitarian Historical Society*

200 Years   W. O. B. Allen, and E. McClure, *Two Hundred Years: the history of the Society for Promoting Christian Knowledge*, London, 1898

UMFC Min.   *Minutes of the Annual Assembly of the Representatives of the United Methodist Free Churches*

Vict. Linc.   Sir Francis Hill, *Victorian Lincoln*, Cambridge, 1974

Vindic.   J. Benson, *A Vindication of the People Called Methodists in Answer to a 'Report from the Clergy of a District in the Diocese of Lincoln' in a letter to Thomas Thompson, esq. Banker, in Hull*, London, 1800

Wake   N. Sykes, *William Wake. Archbishop of Canterbury 1657–1737*, I, Cambridge, 1957

Wes. Assoc. Min.   *Minutes of the Association of the Representatives of the Wesleyan Association*

Wes. J. 6   *The Journal of the Rev. John Wesley*, ed. N. Curnock, VI, London, 1915

Wes. J. 7   *The Journal of the Rev. John Wesley*, ed. N. Curnock, VII, London, 1916

Wes. J. 8   *The Journal of the Rev. John Wesley*, ed. N. Curnock, VIII, London, 1916

Wes. Min.   *Minutes of the Methodist Conference, from the First, held in London, by the late Rev. John Wesley, A.M. in the Year 1744*

Wesley 18   *The Works of John Wesley, 18, Journals, Diaries and Letters*, I (1735–38), ed. W. R. Ward and R. P. Heitzenrater, Nashville, 1998

Wesley 19   *The Works of John Wesley, 19, Journals, Diaries and Letters*, II (1738–43), ed. W. R. Ward and R. P. Heitzenrater, Nashville, 1990

Wesley 20   *The Works of John Wesley, 20, Journals, Diaries and Letters*, III (1743–54), ed. W. R. Ward and R. P. Heitzenrater, Nashville, 1991

Wesley 21   *The Works of John Wesley, 21, Journals, Diaries and Letters*, IV (1755–65), ed. W. R. Ward and R. P. Heitzenrater, Nashville, 1992

Wesley 22   *The Works of John Wesley, 22, Journals, Diaries and Letters*, V (1765–75), ed. W. R. Ward and R. P. Heitzenrater, Nashville, 1993

Wesley 23	*The Works of John Wesley*, 23, *Journals and Diaries*, VI (1776–86), ed. W. R. Ward and R. P. Heitzenrater, Nashville, 1995
Wilb. MSS	Bodleian Library, Oxford, Wilb MSS, Correspondence of Samuel Wilberforce with Sir Charles Anderson
Wilson MSS	DWL Wilson MSS
Words.	J. H. Overton and E. Wordsworth, *Christopher Wordsworth, Bishop of Lincoln, 1807–1885*, London, 1888
Works	*The Works of John Kaye, Bishop of Lincoln*, VII, *Charges, Speeches and Letters*, London, 1888
WMM	*Wesleyan Methodist Magazine*
WRUM	*Wesleyan Reform Union Magazine*

INDEX

Counties are given for places outside Lincolnshire. References in italics refer to the page numbers of illustrations.

Matins, 203; ordinands, number of, 52, 181; ordinations, 5, 6, 52, 181; pluralism, 54–5, 69, 179; ritual, Ritualism, 204, 206; schools, 208–15, *209*; *see also* clergy, communicants, confirmation, confraternities, patronage

churching *see* Thanksgiving after Childbirth

churchwardens, and role in parish affairs, 197; presentments, 8, 9–13, 21, 27, 47–8, 78

churchyard, 2, 185, 188–91

civil registration *see* Parliament, Acts of

Civil Wars, 5–6, 9

Clark, George, rector of East Barkwith, 131

Claxby by Normanby, 78, 79, 80, 186

Claxby Pluckacre, 80

Claypole, 158, 191

Claypon, Joseph, of Boston, banker, 111, 112

Cleatham, parish of Manton, 119

Clee, 67, *189*, 203

Cleethorpes, 131, 146, *159*, 230, 231

clergy, authority, 188, 195; in public office, 54; income, 51, 180–81, 215–16; houses, 179; relations with parishioners, 54; residence, 51–4, 55, 56, 136, 179, 181; role, 51, 181–2; social position, 54, *55*; status, 194

Cliff, the Lincolnshire, 3

Clixby, 38, *39*, 41, 78

Clowes, William, Primitive Methodist leader, 152, 153, 154

Coates family of Gainsborough and Norwich, 19

Coates by Stow, 53

Coates, Great, 51

Coates, Matthew, mercer of Gainsborough, 19

Cock, John, of Doddington, 5

Cockerington, 77; *see also* Alvingham

Codd, Mary, of Upton, 37

Codd, Rebekah, of Upton, 37

Coggan, Robert, 72

Coleby, 91, 207

Colenso, John William, bishop of Natal, 213

Collier, Sarah, of Brigg, 94

Colsterworth *see* Woolsthorpe

Commandments, Ten, 63, 68

Common Fund, 16, 19

Common Prayer, Book of, 5, 7, 14, 16, 49, 70, 187

Commonwealth, 5–6

communicants, numbers of, 49–50

Communion, Holy, 7, 11, 16, 48–51, 64, 65, 66, 69, 102, 118, 130, 143, 169; collections, 66, 72, 201, 202–4

community, concept of, 3

Compline, 220

Compton Census (1676), *15*, 21, *22*, 30, *39*

Compton family, of Girsby, 40, 41

confirmation, 67–8, 193–4, 201, 203, 204; preparation for, 193, 194

confraternities, church societies, guilds, 207, 208, 220; *see also* Horncastle

Congregation of the Most Holy Redeemer, 220

Congregational, Congregationalists, Congregationalism, 16, *17*, 18–19, 87–88, 91, 113–14, 185; Church Aid and Home Missionary Society, 113; congregations, 19; Lincolnshire Union, 86; ministers, 16

Coningsby, 101, 102, 103, 104, 106, 119, 151; Baptist church, *17*, 21, *22*, 24, 25, 100, 101, 102; Wesleyan Methodist circuit, 164

Conisholme, *229*

Consolidated Act, *see* Parliament, Acts of

Constable family, of Everingham, Yorkshire, 80, 81

Conventicle Acts, *see* Parliament, Acts of

Cooke, Brother, of Coningsby Baptist church, 102

Cooper, Thomas of Gainsborough, 152

Corbett, Mr, 209

Corby, 78; vicar of, 211

Cornwall, 129

Corrie, Daniel, Evangelical clergyman, 77

Corrie, George, Evangelical clergyman, 77

Small, William, of Boston, surgeon, 162

Smellie, William, of Grimsby, Countess of Huntingdon's preacher and Independent minister, 110

Smith, Isabel, of Spalding Baptist church, 102

Smith, John, of Sixhills, 30

Smith, Sir Edward, 60

Smith, William, of Elsham, 35

Smith, William, wife of, of Spalding Baptist church, 103

Smyth, Edward, rector of Beelsby, 16

Smyth, Sampson, Roman Catholic benefactor, 80

Societas Evangelica, 107, 110

societies, religious, 69–70, 130–31, 141

Society for the Propagation of the Gospel (SPG), 207

Society for Promoting Christian Knowledge (SPCK), 69–70, 71, 74

Society for the Reformation of Manners, 43, 69

Somerby, 16

Somersby, 202

Somercotes, North, 73, 143, 210

Somercotes, South, 73

South Marsh, Baptist church (Burgh and Monksthorpe), 24, 27, 100

South, Richard, 37

Southcott, family of Blyborough, 77

Southwell, diocese of, 3

Southwell, John, of Sibsey, 37

Spalding, and district, 18, 19, 29, 34, 65, 67, 71, 112, 113, 117, 118, 122, 152, 163, 202, 217, 220; Baptist church, 20, 22, 24, 25, 28, 89, 102, 103, 104, 105, 107, 119, 120, 121, 122; Board of Guardians, 166; Common, 121; Improvement Commissioners, 166; prison, 33; Quaker Monthly Meeting, 31; Roman Catholic church of the Immaculate Conception and St Norbert, 218; School Board, 166; Town Mission, 230; United Methodist Free Churches circuit, 133, 169; Wesleyan Methodist circuit, 144, 148, 165, 166

Spalding and Holbeach Branch Primitive Methodist branch or circuit, 227

Spelkes, William, of Wrangle, 72

Spilsby, and district, 34, 53, 71, 77, 131, 132, 177, 199

Spridlington, 184

Springthorpe, 200

Spurgeon, Charles Haddon, Particular Baptist preacher, 124

Spurr, Thomas, of Louth, 78

Squire, John, of Coningsby Baptist church, 103

Squire, Joshua, of Metheringham, 11

St Albans, duke of, 209

St Andrew's Day (30 November), 67

St Bartholomew's Day (24 August), 14

St Hugh of Lincoln, Jesuit District or Residence, 38, 80

St Thomas's Day (21 December), 67

Staffordshire, 129, 152

Stainby, 198

Stainfield, near Wragby, 41, 50

Stainton, Market, 73

Stamford, and district, 14, 18, 70, 71, 107, 109, 113, 118, 132, 140, 151, 177, 210, 216, 217, 218, 220; mayor of, 109; St John's, 16; St Mary's parish, 66; United Methodists Free Churches circuit, 133

Stamp, John, Primitive Methodist minister and teetotal advocate, 170

Stanhope, family, of Revesby, 178

Starke, Alice, 9

Starke, George, 9

Stationers, Company of, 71

Steere, Edward, curate of Skegness, 191, 206

Stephenson, Hester, of Elsham, 37

Stickney, 202, 231; Free School, 72

Stoke, North, 75

Stoke, South (Stoke Rochford), 27, 75

Stonehouse, W. B., vicar of Owston Ferry and archdeacon of Stow, 176, 199

Stovin, Cornelius, of Binbrook, 227, 228, 236

Stovin, George, J.P. of Epworth, 131

Stow, 199; archdeaconry of, 2, 7, 9, 12, 47, 54, 68, 75

Stukeley, William, antiquary and physician, 72

Sturton by Stow, 154